teacher education for
DEMOCRACY AND SOCIAL JUSTICE

teacher education for
DEMOCRACY AND SOCIAL JUSTICE

EDITED BY

nicholas m. michelli and david lee keiser

ROUTLEDGE
NEW YORK AND LONDON

Published in 2005 by
Routledge
Taylor & Francis Group
270 Madison Avenue
New York, NY 10016
www.routledge-ny.com

Published in Great Britain by
Routledge
Taylor & Francis Group
2 Park Square
Milton Park, Abingdon
Oxon OX14 4RN
www.routledge.co.uk

10 9 8 7 6 5 4 3 2 1

Library of Congress Cataloging-in-Publication Data

Teacher education for democracy and social justice / Nicholas M. Michelli and
David Lee Keiser, editors.
    p. cm.
    Includes bibliographical references and index.
    ISBN 0-415-95032-5 (hardback : alk. paper) — ISBN 0-415-95033-3 (pbk. : alk. paper)
    1. Teachers—Training of—United States. 2. Social justice—Study and teaching—United
States. 3. Critical pedagogy—United States. I. Michelli, Nicholas M., 1942. II. Keiser,
David Lee.

LB1715.T414 2005
370'.71'1—dc22

2004016008

Editors' Dedication

To three women who have had an impact on our lives in profound
and important ways:

To our mothers, Mrs. Elissa Pezzuti Keiser and Mrs. Susan H. Michelli,
who led by selfless example and who taught us that fairness
and justice outrank righteousness.

And to Dr. Tina Jacobowitz, a compassionate educator and tireless
advocate for democracy and social justice. For Nick, a loving life partner
and for both of us, a friend, a colleague, and an inspiration
for her courage and leadership.

Contents

Acknowledgments

We are thankful for the work of our contributors, who not only produced chapters in a timely and professional manner, but who responded to our call with the passion and perseverance needed for working for democracy and social justice. We appreciate the work of all educators—P–12, university, and those not based in schools or universities—who strive to provide access to education for all students.

We acknowledge the support of our colleagues in the National Network for Educational Renewal, educators who seek out school partnership work because they know the importance of school/university collaboration and understand the moral dimensions of education. With mounting pressures on public schools to improve test scores, and on universities to generate external grants and to produce more and more narrowly defined scholarship, we must recognize those educators who selflessly collaborate and contribute to educational renewal at all levels. They are exemplars of what it means to teach and work for democracy and social justice through their scholarship.

Although it is impossible to acknowledge by name those countless students, teachers, and colleagues who continue to inspire our work, our current colleagues at the City University of New York and Montclair State University are particularly inspirational, and we thank them for their models of democratic and socially just teacher education programs.

Lastly, we thank all our friends and family members that remind us of the need to be socially just and democratic not only in our work, but in our personal lives as well. Keeping the focus on justice and on the potential of our current social and political democracy during difficult times is challenging, but our students and our country demand that we continue to teach and learn not only for high test scores, but for equity, community participation, and a more peaceful future.

Foreword

John I. Goodlad

Authors of books are requested by the marketing division of the publisher to identify the anticipated groups of potential readers. The title of this one targets teacher educators. But there is something in what follows for everyone who resonates with the quote from Peter Cookson in Chapter Four: "Free and universal public education is part of the social contract that citizens make with one another to protect children and ensure that successive generations of citizens have a deep and abiding commitment to democracy. There is no escape clause in the social contract."

I chose the word "resonates" carefully. I might have used "believes" or "assumes" and thus selected and narrowed the audience. Michelli and Keiser's book should be read also by that disappointingly large audience of people who have not thought about or do not believe in this contract. This nation very much needs sustained conversation among those who agree and disagree with Cookson's statement and its implications: policymakers, school administrators, teachers, and the general public, as well as in the meeting places and classes of teacher educators. Elements of this conversation might well occur on airplane flights, as Richard Clark describes his with "Chester" in the Afterword of this publication.

Let the conversation begin here between the reader and the written words of the authors. The human conversation is much larger than the spoken exchange among family members, neighbors, friends, and people who meet in the marketplace. The arts speak in many languages to influence the way people think and behave. Books are such powerful teachers that even those teaching the great lessons of caring for one another and our habitat to ensure the immortality of humankind often are fought over.

Clearly, this is not the outcome, however spirited, one would hope to be the result of people with differing views reading a book on democracy and social justice. Nonetheless, on engaging this one in silent conversation, I felt within me stirrings akin to those Alfred North Whitehead must have been feeling in writing, "When one considers in its length and breadth the importance of a nation's young, the broken lives, the defeated hopes, the national failures, which result from the frivolous inertia with which it [education] is treated, it is difficult to restrain within oneself a savage rage."[1] And Whitehead was writing nearly 90 years ago, before the Grinch stole local control and conversation from our schools.

Conversation

For more than a dozen years, colleagues and I have been having intentional, disciplined, scheduled conversations with representatives of three educational cultures seeking to integrate their respective roles in the collaborative renewal that necessarily characterizes wisely conducted teacher education programs. They come from colleges of education, schools of the arts and sciences, and the partner "teaching" schools joined with the universities of which their colleges and schools are a part. These three cultures constitute each setting of a much larger collaboration: the National Network for Educational Renewal (NNER), currently embracing 23 such settings in 20 states comprising 40 colleges and universities and some 1,000 partner schools. There is now in each setting a cadre of leaders who share considerable understanding of the public purpose of schooling in a democracy and the implications of this understanding for ongoing work. There is reference in pages that follow to the NNER and its commitment to a guiding agenda: Agenda for Education in a Democracy.[2]

The programs designed to prepare teams for this leadership role include the reading and discussion, sometimes with the authors, of a good many books and papers. At first, participants were puzzled by sessions billed as conversations when the guest authors sometimes took up much of their allotted time with presentations. This concern took us into consideration of how one has silent conversation with a book, film, dance, painting, or speaker. We came to understand that there are layers of meaning in both the media of conversation and conversation itself, something that Marshall McLuhan so effectively taught us years ago.[3]

This understanding is critical to our conduct of democracy at all levels and in all of its component elements—from seeking to understand a child, to caring for the aged, to giving as well as taking, to addressing the injustices in educational policy, to learning what it means to be human, to understanding the ecosystem of which we all are a part, and to civic engagement. Conversation and democracy go hand in hand.

However, many of our daily exchanges do not penetrate the inner layers of consequential conversation. Worldwide, people address one another at a level that is "safe," whatever the political context: casual greetings, mention of the weather, queries regarding personal well-being. Move beyond and the context quickly comes into play. Totalitarian regimes limit and control the information sources that fuel conversation, forcing debate about consequential matters underground. Little wonder that citizens passing one another in the streets avoid eye contact so as to protect themselves from unwanted engagement in talk that might arouse suspicion.[4] Wendell Berry's cautionary essay on the extent to which some people are willing to give up freedoms in the face of fear—even the freedom to express their opinions—reached an audience of many thousands of sensitive readers worldwide within months of its publication.[5]

To introduce the layered complexity of conversation, we chose for initial reading and the first discussion session of the leadership program referred to above a piece *about* Michael Oakeshott in the *American Scholar*.[6] Here, we gave a nod to the democratic concept of equity in seeking to use a reading that we assumed nobody in the group had previously read and discussed with others. And, also as assumed, the piece served in all of the groups we brought together to bring out for everyone the layered nature of *uncensored* or, shall we say, *democratic* conversation. In a group focused on the arts in teaching and teacher education, some participants chose dance as the medium for expressing their reactions to their reading.

The most obvious and common layer in conversation is that of sharing with another something of mutual interest. We were not far into the Oakeshott piece, however, before his habit of pulling from a shelf a book that his visitor might read taught us that a conversation can be satisfyingly extended without the presence of the other person. Then, we became increasingly aware that Oakeshott, as scholar and teacher, was taking us to another layer of conversation—the human conversation for which lifelong education must prepare us or then we linger at some lesser stage of self-transcendence and social participation. From here, it was but a step to conversation about the injustice—the sheer immorality—of sustaining caste systems, be they economic, hereditary, religious, sexual, or whatever that bar large sectors of humankind from gaining access to this education.

"The human conversation" is a metaphor for all human associations, be they of family, friends, neighbors, the citizenry, ecclesiastical, or secular. "The dispositions of fairness, equality, caring, relatedness, and the like ... are learned."[7] If schools are to do much of the necessary teaching, they require the context of a civil society. They cannot directly build this society, but they can, given the charge, articulate the mission and educate the young for the future society:

> Civil society is a societal dwelling place that is neither a capital building nor a shopping mall. It shares with the private sector the gift of liberty; it is voluntary and is constituted by freely associating individuals and groups. But unlike the private sector, it aims at common ground and consensual, integrative, and collaborative action. Civil society is thus public without being coercive, voluntary without being private.[8]

This Book

But what has the foregoing to do with this book? The answer is "a great deal." This is a book for conversation; indeed, it is about conversation. But it is about conversation in the multilayered sense that I tried to convey in describing use of the Oakeshott piece in our leadership programs. There is a layer in the human conversation that calls out for action.

If we are to have the civil society that is at the very core of The American Dream, we must have common ground and the consensual, integrative, and collaborative action that Barber calls for. In Chapter Two, Nicholas Michelli provides a summary analysis of the common ground that he and his coauthors, colleagues in the National Network for Educational Renewal, and like-minded colleagues beyond have been talking about for a considerable period of time. More than that, they have been taking actions to which their conversations have led them, only a fraction of which are described in several chapters.

The many references to other conversations and actions stemming from them make clear that what these colleagues in common cause are engaged in is not some boutique project likely to disappear when grant money runs out. Indeed, the theme of the critical relationship between education and democracy has been seen by officers of several major philanthropic foundations as of such significance that they have helped to sustain the conversations and related actions over a period of nearly two decades—this at a time when state and federal school "reform" has been driven by a quite different drumbeat. Asher and Eidman's chapter describes foundation recognition of the central mission of education in sustaining democracy and social justice and the implications of long-term school renewal for sustaining this mission.

A deep understanding and commitment to this democratic mission underlies the collaborative, integrative actions required to advance it over time. Michelli introduces it early on. Interestingly, however, although the mission is scarcely articulated in some of the later chapters, the reader is almost always aware of the role of this layer in conversing with the manuscript. Clearly, the authors think, write, and act in the moral ethos of democratic mission. The practices they describe in the later chapters are not in the mold of the all-too-familiar linear model of politically driven school reform. Rather, they deal with the complexity of the ecosystem of school and classroom where the several cultures of schooling are rarely in productive harmony.

The contrast is striking. The mandates of the No Child Left Behind Act bear no relationship to the lofty language of the goals the Act enunciates. Put bluntly, they are not grounded in the rhetorical moral ethos of their justification. At the implementation end of the mandates' trajectory, the impact is more like that of missile strikes than the dropping of care packages. Disturbing analyses of the long-term consequences are not yet reaching the general public. But some of the immediate consequences are being carried home by the children. And the later chapters of this book highlight the struggle of educators to fulfill their commitments and responsibility to educate the young for satisfying, responsible citizenship.

The profound difference between the work described in chapters of this book and that called for in many school reform treatises and mandates is in the integration of practices and the concepts, principles, or theories presumed to be guiding them—between the outer layer of conversation, so to speak, and actions. The integration of theory and practice in work described subsequently in these pages is clear and compelling. There is a yawning gulf, however, between the execution of the No Child Left Behind Act and its goals (with which the writers here appear to be in considerable agreement). The same can be said about many initiatives of politically driven school reform over recent years.

One of the most impressive layers of the conversation embedded in this book is subtle. Earlier, I cited the sentence from Whitehead in which he expresses the emotional difficulty he had in contemplating the neglect in educating the nation's young. In what follows here, the reader gets only a hint of the exasperation the authors have with the follies of No Child Left Behind (NCLB).

It would be an overstatement, I think, to say that any of them expresses anger. Wisely, the writers who address NCLB directly inquire critically into the Act's provisions but do not take up time and space with emotionally charged attack. Plenty of that already is in print elsewhere. The authors of the later chapters make clear the difficulties they face in working around what implementation of the Act has wrought in regard to narrowing curricula and pedagogy in classrooms. Nonetheless, NCLB is ever-present, a little like the unseen but felt presence of the ghosts in houses supposedly haunted. The mood throughout comes through to me as remarkably upbeat, given circumstances that today are for many educators so depressing. The spirit is one of "these things I believe and guided by these beliefs I shall act."

Toward the end of Chapter Two, Nicholas Michelli briefly describes the National Network for Educational Renewal, the mission of the Agenda for Education in a Democracy, and the Leadership for Educational Renewal program first offered by the Institute for Educational Inquiry in 1992 and still ongoing. He refers to the reading of "important works on democratic practice, school change, stewardship, and access to knowledge" that undergird this program and helped prepare leaders for the settings of the National Network. It is my expectation that *Teacher Education for Democracy and Social Justice* will become a rich resource for continuing this multilayered conversation—from democratic belief to democratic action—that is the hallmark of educational renewal.

Notes

1. Alfred North Whitehead, *The Aims of Education* (New York: Macmillan, 1916), 22.
2. For a short but comprehensive description of the Agenda and the work ongoing in the National Network for Educational Renewal, see John I. Goodlad, Corinne Mantle-Bromley, and Stephen J. Goodlad, *Education for Everyone: Agenda for Education in a Democracy* (San Francisco: Jossey-Bass, 2004).
3. See, for example, among Marshall McLuhan's writings, *Understanding Media: The Extensions of Man* (New York: McGraw-Hill, 1964); and, with Quentin Fiore, *The Medium Is the Message: An Inventory of Effects* (New York: Bantam Books, 1967).
4. Robert M. Cornett in his little book, *Is It Time for a Grandparent's Manifesto?* (Georgetown, KY: Six Sons Press, 2002), writes about the *recent* experiences of a friend who was shocked by the continued prevalence of this behavior on the part of people on the streets of Russian cities who had lived with fear for so long.
5. Wendell Berry, *In the Presence of Fear* (Great Barrington, MA: The Orion Society, 2001).
6. Josiah Lee Auspitz, "Michael Oakeshott, 1901–1990," *American Scholar* 60 (Summer 1991): 351–370.
7. John I. Goodlad, *In Praise of Education* (New York: Teachers College Press, 1997), 51.
8. Benjamin R. Barber, "Searching for Civil Society," *National Civic Review* 84 (Spring 1995): 114.

Introduction

Teacher Education for Democracy and Social Justice

Nicholas M. Michelli and David Lee Keiser

> What if we seriously were to commit ourselves to educating children and youth to become enlightened and engaged democratic citizens? With all the social and psychological forces compelling them (and us) toward a life of comfortable idiocy, this would be an extraordinary aim. Were we to be successful, it would be an extraordinary achievement. What would that work entail? How would it look and feel?[1]

As Walter Parker and others remind us, committing to educate students (and teachers, the "us" to whom he refers) for democratic participation during the early part of the Twenty-First Century is no small challenge. What this work would entail and what it might "look and feel" like serves as the focus of this book. As thousands of teachers and teacher educators know, current conceptions of the purposes of public schooling focus extensively on quantitative measures of student achievement rather than the development of "enlightened and engaged democratic citizens." We not only worry about the pedagogical implications and ramifications of measures such as high-stakes testing, but about the social and political ones as well. What does it say about our civic commitment to public schools and their students that issues of democracy, social justice, and critical thinking have largely disappeared from school curricula, which is now increasingly determined by test preparation? How best can teachers and teacher educators not only cope with the narrowing of the curriculum, but also provide alternatives for students? We are fortunate to have rich historical evidence to support our "extraordinary aim." If we look at the history of public education in the United States we find at least four enduring purposes:

1. Preparing students to be active, involved participants in democracy.
2. Preparing students to have access to knowledge and critical thinking within the disciplines.
3. Preparing students to lead rich and rewarding personal lives, and to be responsible and responsive community members.
4. Preparing students to assume their highest possible place in the economy.

Many educators believe that these four historic purposes of public education, especially those related to the promotion of democracy and social justice, need to be sustained, and we continue to work toward their attainment even when those purposes are being reshaped and challenged by national and state policies. This book is intended to provide a deeper understanding of the meaning of education for democracy and social justice and to connect educators with a common vision for teacher education.

At the beginning of the Twenty-First Century, we see education moving away from these four purposes. Instead of being a vehicle for the education of a democratic citizenry that fosters community participation, and prepares students for rich and rewarding personal lives and high levels of understanding, it has become increasingly more technical and instrumental, with a primary focus on the economic outcomes of education, and undergirded by a resolute belief in meritocracy. Unsurprisingly, this narrowing of purpose has expanded an already troubling emphasis on high-stakes testing, with tests increasingly linked with student curriculum guides developed by the same publishers who produce the tests, and required both by state and national legislation, which may evaluate aspects of the second purpose of education—access to knowledge—but not the others. Conversely, the tests themselves, including their norming, development, and execution, as well as the resultant student sorting and stratification by race and class they often achieve, complicate the attainment of democratic and socially just public education. As a rule, test scores correlate positively with income levels, and given how low-income students are often denied access to a highly qualified teaching force, it is unlikely that results from high-stakes tests will benefit all students. Those in favor of high-stakes testing often argue the opposite, however, that the universality of the tests makes them equitable and that they actually ensure equal opportunity for all students to meet high standards.

To the extent that tests and standards actually represent the best interests of poor and minority students and families, and seek to level rather than stratify, they are not by themselves problematic. However, educators are placed under extraordinary pressure to focus on the curriculum that will be tested, usually reading and mathematics, and which will ostensibly measure the success of the teachers, their supervisors, and the students. Forget for a moment the improbability that it is possible to quantify the variegated roles, responsibilities, and outcomes of these three groups the chilling effect of this high-stakes push is a narrowing of the curriculum, undertaken at great peril to choice, democratic life, social justice, and the development of well-rounded individuals. Often areas such as social studies, aesthetic education, foreign languages, and even the sciences are dangerously minimized and seen as superfluous to test preparation.

Education crucial to developing critical, informed citizens is increasingly seen as superfluous, complicating, and even threatening by some policymakers and pressure groups who increasingly see any curriculum not tied to basic literacy or numeracy as disposable and inappropriate. Educators committed to just and democratic public education must marshal initiatives and evidence that counteract the conclusion that such qualitative goals are somehow inconsistent with, or detrimental to academic success. We do not believe the only way to ensure public schools' accountability is by market competition, privatization, and the threat of punitive measures. The message from the United States Department of Education has consisted of admonishments to achieve and imperatives to action, but without a holistic and credible perspective on the needs of students throughout the country.

How can educators who believe strongly in education that is transformative and the basis for democratic life, for advancing social justice, and for the full development of young people, continue our work? We do not believe that high-stakes testing, federal regulations in No Child Left Behind, and the emphasis on the most easily measured standards make the broader and richer goals of education impossible to achieve. We do, however directly question the ideological direction of public schooling in the United States, and disagree with the focus on the market as the answer to school challenges. We do not intend this book, primarily, as an ideological critique of current policy, although a critique is necessarily part of what we present. The primary purpose is to examine just how these important goals—education for democracy and social justice—can be achieved from the perspective of those who work in teacher education, P–12 schools, state and national networks, and arts organizations. We consider our contribution a small bell within a needed clarion call for education for democracy and social justice. This work must go on despite any political challenges or disfavor. These contributors have not given up, and believe that we can pursue our democratic goals within the current context.

Teacher education is, we believe, an important vehicle for bringing about change, but it must be an approach to teacher education framed by moral dimensions and connected to P–12 education. What are the characteristics of this approach to teacher education? In specifying them, we draw heavily from the work of John Goodlad and his associates in the Seattle-based Institute for Educational Inquiry and our colleagues in The National Network for Educational Renewal. These characteristics, derived from Goodlad's postulates,[2] demonstrate the kind of teacher education program that must be present to effectively address the issues of democracy and social justice that form the basis for this book. Though neither exhaustive nor exclusionary, the characteristics are these:

- Teacher education programs and programs in public schools must be renewed simultaneously.
- Teacher education must be carried out by faculty in education, the arts and sciences, and the public schools as equal partners in the preparation of future educators and the renewal of current educators.
- Structures and policies to allow deep collaboration must be present, and appropriate connections with the communities must be nurtured.
- Programs for preparing teachers and public school educators must have a clear, unambiguous shared vision that addresses the four enduring purposes of public education. The vision must be the basis for all important decisions, and the program must be assessed based on the vision.
- We must be clear about the meaning of terms we use and the challenges we face.
- We need to organize and join advocates for teaching for democracy and social justice at the federal, state, and local levels to support and defend public schools, teachers, and excellent teacher education programs.

Simultaneous renewal refers to programs that prepare teachers and the public schools they serve which are developed, sustained, and renewed in tandem. We argue that changes affecting teacher education must emanate from, and be endorsed by, both higher education and the schools in which student teachers are placed. Unlike school reform, educational renewal refers to vision and imagination, along with change. As Wilson and Davidson point out later in this volume, renewal and reform are very different concepts. The concept of reform is static, top-down, and finite, while the concept of renewal is dynamic, systemic, and ongoing.

Simultaneous change and renewal require very close connections between schools and programs that prepare teachers. This connected approach to renewal is important to reintroduce concepts such as education for democracy and social justice into the schools, as the meanings of, and means to, achieve these concepts need to be agreed upon.

These ideals are not without detractors, and we explore some of their perspectives later in this volume. We argue that forging deep commitments shared by programs preparing teachers and the schools they serve is one important way of enhancing the likelihood of sustainability and success.

Related to the concept of simultaneous renewal is our contention that teacher education is not and cannot be the responsibility of education faculty alone. Often education faculty retain administrative and instructional "control" of programs for teacher education, while in fact the success of such programs depends largely on the participation of faculty in arts and science and, most directly, teachers in schools. The deep disciplinary knowledge expected of teachers should come from their arts and sciences experiences. Arts and sciences faculty need to understand the particular needs of future teachers and the curriculum of the public schools as they work to renew that curriculum. In many states the major assessment of future teachers focuses on the knowledge gained in arts and science courses, and so full participation and responsibility by arts and sciences faculty is essential. In New York State, for example, three tests are required. Two of them, a test of liberal arts and science and a content specialty examination, are dependent on preparation by arts and science faculty. Public school faculty provide the field experiences essential to successful programs, and they, too, need to share in the values and goals of the program. Colleagues outside education should play a clear, equitable role in building programs that work.

Structures and policies that both support and allow this extraordinary partnership can result in well-developed school/university partnerships for faculty in education, arts and science, and public schools that are meaningful to each "culture" and that reward collaboration for the education of educators. Framing such partnerships must be an unambiguous shared vision that bridges the collaboration. For our purposes, we believe that the vision must address the issues of the role of public education in a democracy, designed to promote social justice, and the implications of such a vision for the education of educators and the education of their students. That vision must guide all decisions, including the selection of teacher candidates, the construction of curriculum, the structuring of field experiences in appropriate settings, and the assessment of the success of programs.

The following chapters are in three sections following the Foreword and this introductory chapter; a section providing conceptual grounding for the work, a section of programmatic examples largely in schools, and a section on implementation strategies. We close with a section on moving forward and provide a variety of perspectives from which to argue for democracy and social justice in teacher education. We draw from colleagues in education, the arts, and across school disciplines. We offer elements of a vision for teaching and teacher education for democracy and social justice, and do so with a wide range of contributions.

Conceptual Grounding

Raising questions about the meanings of such education—the civic, civil, academic meanings, as well as the implications of aesthetic education and civil rights for public education—Michelli's initial chapter, Education for Democracy: What Can It Be? explores and examines the question of the limitations of the concept of citizenship, as well as the issue of democratic education from the perspectives of Dewey through Gutmann. He examines barriers to education for democracy in current policy and beliefs, as well as hopeful signs in the work of national higher education associations, a foundation, and the National Network for Educational Renewal. He concludes by stressing the importance of sponsoring evaluation and research on this important work.

In his introductory chapter on teacher education for social justice, which he conceives as a conceptual understanding, an imaginative possibility, and a programmatic imperative, Keiser conceptualizes teacher education for social justice from perspectives of imagination, distribution, and, following Cochran-Smith, as both a learning problem and a political problem. He places responsibility for the narrowing of the curriculum as well as the privatization of education squarely on market-driven forces in search of profit rather than process, and who see test scores as the sole means to measure and reward success. After short descriptions of two university-based teacher education programs for social justice, and a concluding set of recommendations dependent on the ability to critique current policy, he argues for a resurgence of focus on affective components of education.

In her chapter on federal education policy, Earley provides us with a careful analyzes of two critical pieces of federal legislation, the Higher Education Act, especially Title II, and No Child Left Behind, neither of which, she argues, embraces a broad view of education that includes issues of democracy and social justice. Both pieces of legislation promote an instrumental view of education, which focuses more on the private purposes of education, and promotes competition designed to improve pass rates on examinations and promote social mobility. She concludes with suggestions and advice for educators as to how they might have an impact on bringing about changes in the direction of federal legislation.

Programmatic Examples

Social studies would seem to be the most receptive place for discussions about, and pedagogy for, social justice, but Rubin and Justice point out that although "a concern for social justice has long been at the forefront of K–12 social studies education," this standing has not come "without much debate." In the context of a thick description of their own practices in educating both elementary and secondary teachers to teach with a social justice perspective, they conclude that within "meaty" and "contentious" debates, there exists an inherent struggle between conformity and agency, and that this "contested terrain" is key ground in the struggle to maintain a curricular and theoretical focus on social justice. Within a public university's social studies education program, they delineate the successes and challenges of preparing teachers to teach all students ethically and justly.

Maulucci and Calabrese Barton use the lens of science pedagogy to question the lack of "joy" in test-driven science. They make a strong case with rich descriptions of a critical science classroom where a teacher makes full use of pedagogical freedom within what Paulo Freire referred to as "limit-situations." The authors define and describe the power of feeling a "freedom to teach" as it applies within a constructivist, hands-on science class. They ground their sense of teaching science with a social justice perspective in three literature bases: multicultural teaching, caring politics, and critical approaches to teaching science. And they conclude that science is a most opportune site for teaching for social justice, given its propensity to investigate, generate new knowledge, and nurture student agency.

Holzer provides specific insights into the role of aesthetic education in the promotion of democracy and social justice. Her work is based on the approach to aesthetic education employed by *The Lincoln Center Institute*. *The Institute*, through its Teacher Education Collaborative's 10-year history in working with teacher education programs, has developed very specific methodologies to promote aesthetics as a means of transforming student perceptions. By examining works of art, college-based teacher educators, future teachers, in-service teachers, and P–12 students learn how to promote both arts and imagination. In this way, educators and students can learn to overcome "passivity and carelessness" and see the possibilities that must be present in democratic, socially just societies.

Keiser's second chapter, in which he describes three examples of inquiry for social justice at a diverse high school, offers anecdotal and field-based data that support our vision for teacher education. Within the framework of professional development schools, he argues, there are possibilities for increased collaboration in the service of teacher education for social justice. In various settings such as a preservice teacher education course, an undergraduate course, and a high school small learning community for social justice, he cites examples of high school and college students engaging in projects which exemplify educational renewal and democratic practices.

Strategies for Implementation

Lucas makes the explicit connection between service learning and social justice and the implications for teacher education. After her overview of the nature and meaning of service learning, she describes the evolution of a perspective on service learning within an individual faculty member within the context of a program committed to social justice. Even more important, the program's students reveal the changes they have undergone as a result of carefully planned service learning experiences. Lucas notes that before developing a commitment to enhancing social justice, one must become sensitive to social injustice. The students she describes become articulate social critics and see the implications of their experiences for their teaching. Perhaps even more importantly they become more sensitive to the role societal inequities play in the education and care of the children with whom they work.

Wilson and Davidson's narrative about the establishment and continual development of the Colorado Partnership for Educational Renewal reminds us of the purpose and the power of collaboration and cooperation within school/university partnerships, and how the time and the care devoted to building consensus bears great fruit in the form of sustainable, far-reaching alliances positioned to best help students and teachers maintain social justice perspectives. Using the four-part mission of the Agenda for Education in a Democracy—namely education for school stewardship, access to knowledge, nurturing pedagogy, and democratic practice—as a foundation, they cite a long-standing, well-known partnership as evidence that teacher education can thrive when its underlying mission is not steeped exclusively in quantitative measures of student achievement. They do not sugarcoat the difficulty of creating and sustaining partnerships, especially when political climates change, but rather focus on the snowballing effect of the power of a partnership recognized for its inclusiveness, scope and clear vision, and resilience when navigating the sticky terrain of social justice.

Martin reviews the history of critical thinking in both teacher education programs and P–12 education. He connects this analysis to examining alternative ways of teaching for critical thinking and for evaluating both teacher education programs and published critical thinking programs. Martin also reflects on the implications of critical thinking for any effort to infuse democracy and social justice into education, including the abilities to make intelligent decisions that transfer to daily life, to consider alternative viewpoints in forming positions, and to see different aspects of an issue. Martin grounds his recommendations on the work of both cognitive psychologists and philosophers, including Feuerstein and Dewey.

In her chapter with Eidman, Asher explores the particular role of foundation funding for educational renewal. She delineates an evolution of a school-university partnership and the trajectory of programs and products that emanate from grants and concomitant collaborations. While we hope that schools and teacher preparation programs would not need to raise external funds to create collaborative programs that serve democracy, we know that tight funding is perennial. Developing relationships with funding organizations such as foundations is crucial to sustaining our vision for teacher education, particularly when political realities and timings work in resistance to teaching for democracy and social justice. We link our vision, and the importance of this volume, to the precarious social and political realities at the time of this writing.

Clearly, the century has not begun auspiciously. A contested election for a president, terrorist attacks both within our own borders and across the globe, multiple wars in the Middle East and Central Asia, and uncertainties about the economy at home create an environment where children must learn how to negotiate the world anew from within our fragile democracy. The context is a dangerous one, but the goal of renewing public education and the education of educators for democracy and social justice is too important to abandon, no matter how daunting the challenges.

Notes

1. Walter C. Parker, *Teaching Democracy* (New York: Teachers College Press, 2003), 54.
2. John Goodlad, *Educational Renewal* (San Francisco: Jossey-Bass, 1994).

CHAPTER 1

Education for Democracy: What Can It Be?

NICHOLAS M. MICHELLI

There is a democratic education problem in the United States. The young are not learning properly to care for the body politic and the body politic is not adequately caring for the young.[1]

The title for this chapter has a number of embedded meanings. In one sense, we must approach education for democracy in the context of what it can mean, and we find that there are many possible meanings. In another sense, the title suggests what education for democracy can become. In this chapter, we explore both of these attributes of education for democracy. However, the position we put forth is that we are at great risk if we do not attend carefully to preparing the young for life in a democracy and for its concomitant characteristic, a society built on social justice.

Meanings and Possibilities

We make an assertion in our Introduction that one of the primary purposes of public education in the United States of America is to prepare students to be participating citizens in our social and political democracy. What was your reaction to the assertion? For many educators it passes unnoticed. They have seen it before, whether in school mission statements, in textbooks on education, as part of conceptual frameworks for accreditation, perhaps in something they have read by John Dewey or John Goodlad. It is an assumption that many take for granted, and do nothing about. In this chapter we explore the assumption, and the consequences of doing nothing about it. In fact, our focus is on what it would mean to do something to put into practice our expectations for the role of education in supporting and extending democracy.

First, we should recognize that education for democracy does have many different meanings. For some it means carrying out our civic responsibilities as citizens, that is, to register and vote in elections, perhaps to sit on juries when called, and whatever else one might imagine a citizen, narrowly defined, would be expected to do. It should be noted that while students may be citizens in their schools, and in their classrooms, they may not be United States citizens. This is particularly true in urban colleges and universities, including the author's home university, The City University of New York (CUNY), where a good many students in teacher education programs are not citizens in the technical and legal sense, and that is true as well for students in the P–12 schools we serve. It was only recently that the New York State Board of Regents dropped the requirement for citizenship or being in the process of gaining citizenship to be eligible for initial certification as an educator. New York education regulations now permit individuals with permanent residence status through the United States Citizenship and Immigration Services to qualify for a certificate to teach.[2]

A narrow definition of citizenship is inadequate to cover what teaching for democratic life might be. That isn't to say that the civic responsibilities and civic engagement we have mentioned are unimportant, or shouldn't be included in the curriculum; indeed, they are most often seen as the purview of social studies teachers. The fact that students may not be "citizens" in the legal sense can create some difficulties for the pursuit of democratic education in that students, and their teachers, misunderstand the broader meaning of democracy. At one City University of New York college where an overall revision of the general education program has led to specifically including teaching for democracy as a goal, students were very concerned when they read that preparing to be citizens in a democracy was explicit in the new requirements. Some said, "Do you mean that I now have to be a citizen of the United States to attend this college?" My discussions with Provost Marcia Keizs, charged with leading the revision of general education, made clear the sensitivity of the issue. One alternative that emerged was that since we are talking about a broader definition of education for democracy, the general education goal might be preparing students for critical participation in democratic life. Some, including James Banks, continue to argue that citizenship is the right word because of its broader meaning within an institution or community. Our view is that if citizenship as a legal concept is problematic for students, then both a discussion of the meaning of citizenship beyond the legal term and the use of alternative language is important and appropriate. We will discuss the role of general education, and overall undergraduate education for democracy, in the context of the American Association of State Colleges and Universities' American Democracy Project later in this chapter. Of course, we do believe that the ultimate goal of citizenship in the nation for those students who seek that status should be encouraged, and some universities, including CUNY, actively support progress of students toward citizenship, but it is not the only or perhaps even the most important purpose of education for democracy.

One of the broader ways to think about education for democracy is to consider the "civil" responsibilities of individuals.[3] What does it mean to be civil as a participant in a democratic society? How does one deal with disagreements and resolve them? How might we treat other persons we encounter, especially when their beliefs and views are different from our own? What are the implications for flexibility and empathy in dealing with other perspectives? How do we examine and engender respect for others in the way we deal with differing positions? If these are qualities of a democratic life, and we would contend that they are, then the responsibility goes beyond the social studies teacher, and becomes the responsibility of all teachers. Learning to be respectful does not mean accepting all positions put forth as equally valid; we deal with this distinction in the context of our discussion of learning to argue well.

A third way of thinking about preparation for democracy is by thinking of the meaning of civil rights and liberties in our society. Some of these rights were expressed in the Bill of Rights of the Constitution, some aspects of freedom are expressed as civil rights and liberties, either memorialized in the Constitution or not.[4] Examining the evolution of civil rights in our society, including the abolition of slavery, the right of women to vote, and the end of legally enforced segregation are civil rights that are now explicit in the Constitution or on the interpretations of the Constitution. Emerging civil rights, such as the rights of gay, lesbian, and transgendered individuals, are embedded in some state laws, and such individuals are considered "protected classes" in some venues for affirmative action/ equal opportunity purposes, but they are not universally recognized and not yet in the Constitution or subsequent federal legislation. Similarly the issue of education as a "civil right" has emerged in the court cases that have supported equal funding for urban education in a number of states, including New Jersey and New York.[5] Future teachers must understand that democracy is an evolving concept, and nowhere is that clearer than in the continued legal definition of the civil liberties of members of a democratic society. Of course, any consideration of civil rights moves into the territory of social justice as well, and into the issue of beliefs and dispositions that candidates to become teachers have or will develop.

Fourth, and closely related to our discussion of civil rights, is the centrality of liberty to democracy, which is often overlooked in our effort to focus on the mechanics of democracy. One of the early observers of American democracy, Alexis de Tocqueville wrote: "It cannot be repeated too often that nothing is more fertile in prodigies than the art of being free; but there is nothing more arduous than the apprenticeship of liberty."[6] Learning to be free may be as difficult, or perhaps harder than gaining freedom. Tocqueville did not suggest the role of public education in the apprenticeship of liberty, but we do. Future teachers need to be able to explain the fundamental rights embedded in our society to their students. How do we do that for future teachers, or for our students in P–12 public schools? The issue of privacy, for example, has seldom been more at the forefront than at the beginning of the Twenty-First Century, especially in the context of concerns about terrorism. A consideration of personal liberty is and should be a basis for the development of confidence and self-concept for students. This is an area where social studies education can take the lead, but all teachers again need to understand their obligations and to know the personal rights inherent in democracy. We think teaching about rights explores one of the essential meanings of teaching for democracy.

Next, no consideration of the relationship between education and democracy is complete without examining the importance of the arts in a democratic society. Freedom of speech has one of its most important expressions in the production of art. Imagination is central to solving complex problems involved in democratic living and the arts play a central role in its development. Maxine Greene, one of our leading philosophers of education, has observed that

> We are interested in education here, not in schooling. We are interested in openings, in unexplored possibilities, not in the predictable or the quantifiable, not in what is thought of as social control. For us, education signifies an initiation into new ways of seeing, hearing, feeling, moving. It signifies the nature of a special kind of reflectiveness and expressiveness, a reaching out for meanings, a learning to learn....We do not regard aesthetic education as in any sense a fringe undertaking, a species of "frill." We see it as integral to the development of persons—to the cognitive, perceptual, emotional, and imaginative development. We see it as part of the

human effort (so often forgotten today) to seek a greater coherence in the world. We see it as an effort to move individuals (working together, searching together) to seek a grounding for themselves, so that they may break through the "cotton wool" of dailyness and passivity and boredom and come awake to the colored sounding, problematic world.[7]

In the sense that Greene sees aesthetic education as "integral to the development of persons—to their cognitive, perceptual, emotional, and imaginative development," we argue that aesthetic education is essential for the full development of participants in a democracy. Participants, through aesthetic education, avoid "passivity and boredom and come awake to the colored, sounding, problematic world." Preparing students for democracy means preparing them to see the problematic and to act on it. We need them to be active, not passive; engaged, not bored, and aesthetic education is one of the key vehicles to achieving these ends. Of course, we are in a time when learning to be aesthetically literate is often minimized in our approaches to education, especially as the focus is increasingly on outcomes measured by high-stakes standardized tests. In many instances we find future teachers have themselves been denied exposure to aesthetic education in their own P–12 studies as a result either of cost-cutting strategies or a focus on those subjects measured by standardized tests. Ignoring aesthetic education is another way to minimize our hopes for fully functioning democratic citizens. How does one overcome such deficits, or enhance aesthetic understandings, when students often come with little experience in aesthetic education because of periodic cycles of cutting the arts in public schools, especially urban and rural schools? The City University of New York is fortunate to be located in one of the great cultural centers of the world.

We approach this obligation to prepare future teachers for aesthetic education in two ways. First, and most fully developed, we work with the Lincoln Center Institute for Arts Education, a relationship explored further in Madeleine Holzer's chapter in this book. Second, we have developed "cultural passports" for future teachers that allow them to have access to dozens of museums across the city as well as access to opera and drama. These programs are always connected to academic learning and to thinking about how future teachers can use the arts and aesthetic education in the context of providing a fuller education for their future students. And, this is essential not for teachers of art, but for all future teachers.

Another aspect of learning to live in a democracy we will consider is in the art of arguing well for one's beliefs, and learning to be flexible when better arguments emerge. This is, we would suggest, an intellectual attribute of living in a democracy that certainly permeates the other meanings we have explored, but also stands by itself. One prominent pedagogical example that focuses on this area is critical thinking, especially as advanced by philosophers like Dewey and Matthew Lipman.[8] This approach specifically engages students in making good judgments and exploring their validity with others. We will explore critical thinking and its connection to democracy later in this chapter and more fully in David Martin's chapter in this volume. We conceive of learning to make good judgments in the context of thinking critically as an important aspect of what teaching for democracy can be. We want students to be engaged civically and act civilly, but we want them to do so in the context of good, well thought-out judgments.

Our contention is that all of these elements come together in defining what teaching for democracy can be—teaching for the civic responsibility of students, teaching for the civil responsibility of students, teaching for the understanding of what it means to be free and to engage in the "apprenticeship of liberty," becoming aesthetically literate, and learning to make excellent judgments and to argue well for one's beliefs. But focusing on democracy in this way, as we shall see, is incomplete unless we also consider what it means to be civically engaged and how we can promote such engagement.

This is a perspective of education for democracy that can permeate all parts of the act of teaching. Of course, to achieve education for democracy as a central part of public education in the United States, two things must happen. First, public education must embrace this as a purpose in practice, and not only in rhetoric. Second, and simultaneously, we must examine our teacher education programs to be certain that teachers are indeed prepared to teach for these purposes.

This is not easy work; in fact we make it clear that thinking of public education's role in furthering democracy is a contested concept, and one that is not held by all educators or policy makers. My most dramatic experience that brought this point home occurred when I made a presentation to a group of policy makers, primarily legislators and governor's aides, on preparing excellent teachers. The claim was made then, as it is now, that we have an obligation to prepare students for life in a democratic society, and therefore must prepare teachers for this important work. At the end of the presentation, a legislator from a New England state rose to his feet and said, "You mean you want teachers to teach about democracy? Why, that's un-American!" I'm not entirely sure what he meant, although I have reflected on it often over the years. I believe he meant that schools have one purpose—the transmission of knowledge, or perhaps even information.

I think that in his mind anything we do that takes from the time spent in delivering knowledge in the traditional sense detracts from the purposes of American schools, and that exchange was before the current focus on high-stakes testing. Today, the same arguments are heard. In an article titled "Faulty Engineering," Chester E. Finn Jr. argues against civic education. He writes:

> Civic education may sound like a good idea in theory, but in practice public schools could even do harm in this realm. Some educators harbor worrisome values: moral relativism, atheism, doubts about the superiority of democracy, undue deference to the "pluribus" at the expense of the "unum," discomfort with patriotism, cynicism toward established cultural conventions and civic institutions. Transmitting those values to children will gradually erode the foundations of a free society. Perhaps society would be better off if its schools stuck to the three R's and did a solid job in domains where they enjoy both competence and wide public support.[9]

And so Finn would rather not have schools deal with civic education because of his fears of the values that might be transmitted, a view held by many with a conservative perspective on the public purposes of education. We argue that we want students to question government and each other and see those qualities as essential for democracy and social justice.

Even when they are not made explicit, criticisms are de facto in practice when the only thing that counts in measuring the quality of education or the success of the teacher is the single score generated by a standardized examination for a group of students. And so we must think seriously about what we mean by education for democracy and what it can be. If we adopt the position that it is a critical purpose of schools in democratic nations, then we can expect to encounter some serious disagreements with that perspective. To respond to the current instrumental definitions of education it is incumbent upon teacher educators to think carefully about how we will assess our programs and students. One approach is to demonstrate that programs designed to develop facility with education for democracy and social justice do at least as well in traditional measures of success—academic success—as programs that do not incorporate this moral perspective.

Where does the responsibility for being certain that public schools fulfill their mission of preparing students for democratic life reside? Is it within the curriculum of the public schools or in the preparation of teachers? Our argument, of course, is that it must be both, although our focus here is primarily on the preparation of teachers. John Goodlad first introduced the concept of the "simultaneous renewal of schools and the education of educators" in *Teachers for Our Nation's Schools* and developed it further in *Educational Renewal.*[10] Prior to that it was impossible to find the connection between teacher education and public school change in the literature on educational change. The connection, when one thinks about it, is obvious. If we believe that most educational change that is successful and enduring is change in teachers, not just change in materials used in teaching or the curriculum, then attention to the human dimension of change is critically important. The history of innovation in education is replete with examples of failed change that did not take into account the importance of sustained professional development and support for teachers (BSCS Biology, PSSC Physics, MACOS, New Math to name just a few from a past decade). Goodlad's insight that the changes must take place simultaneously in P–12 schools and in teacher education programs makes perfect sense in the light of that history. We cannot put into place major educational changes for which there are no teachers prepared to implement them, and it makes no sense to prepare teachers for programs and schools that do not exist!

Of course, this argues for the critical importance of close alliances between public schools and the places where teachers are prepared. For that reason, although the title of this book and its primary focus is "Teacher Education for Democracy and Social Justice" it goes without saying that we must also have P–12 schools for democracy and social justice. Furthermore, teacher education should not be narrowly construed to mean preservice teacher education. Professional development is teacher education as well. However, while we will focus here on the teacher education side of the equation for preparing teachers who indeed can teach for democracy and social justice, many of our examples take place in schools where the practices are carried out. Furthermore, our conception of teacher education is not that it takes place in colleges removed from public schools. Rather, it is instead a mutual responsibility of colleges and public school systems, just as excellent P–12 education in public schools should reflect that mutual responsibility as well. We examine the role of a national network in supporting school partnerships in this chapter, and the role of a statewide partnership in promoting democracy and social justice in Wilson and Davidson's chapter later in this volume.

In the balance of this chapter we will explore the meaning of education for democracy through views of some major political, educational, psychological, and philosophical theorists. We turn to expanding on some of the specific examples we have already raised, and we conclude by exploring the forces that now inhibit or promote a view of public education as preparing young people for life in a democracy.

Why Democracy and Education?

At the beginning of the Republic, the founding fathers understood the connection between education and democracy. Jefferson wrote, "Those who hope to live in a state that is both ignorant and free, ask for what never was and never will be."[11] One of Jefferson's great rivals in the seminal days of the founding of the nation was John Adams, although there were many points of agreement between the two, including agreement on the importance of education in a democracy. Adams was the primary architect of a section of the Constitution of Massachusetts, which said:

> Wisdom and Knowledge, as virtue, diffused generally among the body of the people being necessary for the preservation of their rights and liberties; and as these depend on spreading the opportunities and advantages of education in various parts of the country, and among the different orders of the people, it shall be the duty of legislators and magistrates in all future periods of this commonwealth to cherish the interests of literature and the sciences, and all the seminaries of them, especially the university at Cambridge, public schools, and grammar schools in the towns; to encourage private societies and public institutions, rewards and immunities, for the promotion of agriculture, arts, sciences, commerce trades, manufactures, and a natural history of the country; to countenance and inculcate the principles of humanity and general benevolence, public and private charity, industry and frugality, honesty and punctuality in their dealings, sincerity, good humor, and all social affections, and generous sentiments among the people.[12]

No founding father was clearer in his deep commitment to education, including public education, and to connecting it to the preservation of the rights and liberties expected in a democracy.

Among philosophers John Dewey is most often cited for his arguments regarding the connections between education and democracy. In *Democracy and Education*, for example, he argues that, "The devotion of democracy to education is a familiar fact. The superficial explanation is that a government resting upon popular suffrage cannot be successful unless those who elect and who obey their governors are educated."[13] Dewey believed that this was not a good enough case for the connection between education and democracy and proceeds to argue that

> A democracy is more than a form of government; it is primarily a mode of associated living of conjoint communicated experience. The extension in space of the number of individuals who participate

in an interest so that each has to refer his own action to that of others, and to consider the action of others to give point and direction to his own, is equivalent to the breaking down of those barriers of class, race, and national territory which kept men from perceiving the full import of their activity.[14]

In his school at the University of Chicago, and in his subsequent writing, Dewey attempted to model schools that fostered associated living. And so it is through education that Dewey expected future citizens to become able to make the judgments they had to make, and to learn to consider the impact of their action upon others, regardless of class, race, or national origin. Amy Gutmann embraces Dewey's expectations but adds an important caveat to one of Dewey's most widely quoted positions, that "what the best and wisest parent wants for his own child, that must the community want for all of its children." In arguing that this is not enough, she introduces two important dimensions into the meaning of democratic education. Gutmann writes:

A democratic society must not be constrained to legislate what the wisest parents want for their child, yet it must be constrained not to legislate policies that render democracy repressive or discriminatory. A democratic theory of education recognizes the importance of empowering citizens to make educational policy with those principles—of nonrepression and nondiscrimination—that preserve the intellectual and social foundations of democratic deliberations. A society that empowers citizens to make educational policy, moderated by these two principled constraints, realizes the democratic ideal of education.[15]

These principles of nondiscrimination and nonrepression should be embedded in how we use education to prepare young people for participation in our democracy. The implications for teacher education are significant. How do we prepare teachers who themselves hold to these values, or can we? Are commitments to nondiscrimination and nonrepression intellectual skills, or are they dispositions? If they are dispositions, can they in fact be developed adequately when they are not already in evidence in our future teachers, or do we need to use them as a basis for admission to teacher education programs? Political scientist Benjamin Barber argues that

Democracy is not a natural form of association; it is an extraordinarily rare contrivance of cultivated imagination. Empower the merely ignorant and endow the uneducated with a right to make collective decisions and what results is not democracy but, at best, mob rule: the government of private prejudice and the tyranny of opinion—all those perversions that liberty's enemies like to pretend (and its friends fear) constitute democracy. For true democracy to flourish, however, there must be citizens. Citizens are women and men educated for excellence—by which term I mean the knowledge and competence to govern in common their own lives. The democratic faith is rooted in the belief that all humans are capable of such excellence and have not just the right but also the capacity to become citizens. Democratic education mediates the ancient quarrel between the rule of opinion and the rule of excellence by informing opinion and, through universal education in excellence, creating an aristocracy for everyone.[16]

Barber goes on to make the case for experiential learning, especially service learning, as one of the key vehicles for learning to live and participate in a democracy. Service learning, as proposed by Barber, Thomas Erlich through the American Democracy Project described in this chapter, and examined by Tamara Lucas and David Keiser in this volume can support both education for democracy and for social justice.

Many others could be cited for their contributions to our thinking about democracy and its connection to education. Gary Fenstermacher, for example, reminds us that "[w]e must attend to our manner as human beings as well as our method as pedagogues. It is the manner in which we communicate our disciplines that conveys our beliefs and understandings of democratic community. The promotion of our discipline, our content, is the occasion for the display of manner. It is the occasion to communicate to learners the best of what it means to be human, using what John Goodlad calls 'nurturing pedagogies.'"[17] We have not, in this chapter, explored Robert Putnam's important work on building social capital, but it is included in Wilson and Davidson's chapter.

Barber reminds us of how rare democracy is—an "extraordinarily rare contrivance." It is also fragile in that it depends on an educated and engaged citizenry, and, we argue, a population that behaves toward each other in civil and democratic ways. Not only do we believe that democracy is rare, we believe that the commitment to its deeper meaning has to be re-created with each new generation, and that public education is the vehicle for that re-creation. It is our argument that it falls to public education, and therefore to teachers, future and current, to support democratic practice, and we turn now to the question of what can we do to support democracy through our work as educators.

What Can Education for Democracy Be in the Classroom?

We begin with the easiest example, the one that connects education for democracy and social justice most directly with the most widely perceived function of schools: providing access to knowledge. No one questions that providing access to knowledge is one of the critical purposes of education, but the issue becomes more complicated when we ask seemingly obvious questions like: access to which knowledge? Or, when we ask, access to knowledge for which purposes? It becomes still more complicated when we ask, should the same knowledge be provided for all students? These are difficult questions because they go to the core of the public purposes of education in the United States in the Twenty-First Century.

The question of "which knowledge" can be preceded by the question of "what is knowledge?" Perhaps all considerations of knowledge must be preceded by that epistemological question. If we assume that knowledge is in flux and created by thinking individuals, then not only is the question of which knowledge more difficult, but so is the question of how students learn knowledge. This is the issue raised by constructivists, who believe that individuals must process knowledge in order to construct meaning, and so transmitted knowledge—facts—is of limited value. It is only in thinking about the knowledge and using it to solve problems that it becomes meaningful, with obvious implications for the pedagogy of providing access to knowledge.

The question of the purposes of providing access to knowledge also is complicated. If the purpose is the preparation of an individual for a specific job then chances are that we are talking about knowledge that is to be transmitted, with relatively little "processing." Learning how to operate a piece of machinery, learning how to fill out a required form, or learning when to ask clients if they want French fries with their order are examples of preparation for work where little variation can be tolerated. More complex jobs, designing software programs, planning advertising campaigns, and, it is hoped, learning to teach a lesson, require problem solving and cannot depend on the transmission of a particular, defined set of knowledge.

We move quickly into issues of democracy and social justice when we raise the third question of whether or not access to the same knowledge should be provided for all students. It brings us face to face with what we mean when we say, "all children can learn." There is substantial evidence that teachers in urban settings mean something different from that of teachers in suburban schools.[18] The evidence is that teachers in urban schools are much more likely to mean knowledge that is in fact transmitted to students. The fact that the jobs that require a higher-order kind of knowledge are the ones that pay better in this society cannot be overlooked.

Could it be that systematically children in poor socioeconomic settings receive an education that is likely to sustain their lower socioeconomic status and provide low-level workers for the economy? In part, that is what the courts have found in sustaining the case for equitable funding for urban schools.

For us, if you answer the question of access to which knowledge and access for what purposes with the conclusion that our goal is to prepare an educated populace capable of participating effectively in a social and political democracy, then we believe that the same expectations must be appropriate for all children. Specifically, we argue that we need to provide access to knowledge and critical thinking within the disciplines if we are in fact to prepare individuals for democratic life and participation.

It is through learning knowledge in a way that depends on critical thinking that students, and their teachers, will learn how to make good judgments, how to argue well for their positions, and how to be flexible and willing to alter their positions in the face of evidence. These are the essential ingredients of democratic life, and the things we can expect from a focus on critical thinking. While there are a number of conceptions of critical thinking, some from the perspective of cognitive science and some from the perspective of philosophy (see Martin's chapter in this book), following one such conception can illustrate the point. The philosophical perspective on critical thinking, associated with Matthew Lipman, reflecting the work of John Dewey,[19] holds that critical thinking is thinking that leads to good judgment because it is dependent on criteria, sensitive to context, and characterized by self-correction in a community of inquiry.[20] Everyone makes judgments every day, although we may call them by different names (decisions, choices, and selections, for example). Some are more important than others are, and some are directly related to life in a democracy and how we act toward others based on judgments we make. We should add here that judgments are also central to purely academic learning. For example, the critique of a play in an English class is a judgment, just as is a hypothesis put forth in a science class. Both can be considered different forms of judgments, different, as we shall see, because each is dependent on different criteria, requiring different exploration in a community of inquiry, and each contextualized by the disciplines in which each occurs.

Notice the distinction made between a judgment and a good judgment. Lipman argues that we make good judgments only when we can be clear about the criteria we used in making the judgment, the circumstances of the judgment, and the process of self-correction. Knowing the criteria (and that the appropriate set of criteria was used) allows one to argue more strongly for a position. The question of "why did you support one candidate or another" can be answered by identifying the criteria used in making the judgment. The context is important because different sets of criteria are appropriate for different circumstances. For example, the criteria used to judge the quality of an essay in English are not the same criteria used to judge a hypothesis in science. In fact, when students learn that the differences in expectations their teachers hold for them are not a matter of idiosyncrasy, but rather a matter of standards, or appropriate criteria within a discipline, the expectations are clearer and learning more likely to occur. Certainly the depth of knowledge required of teachers to teach for critical thinking is significant. Teachers must understand the appropriate arguments to validate knowledge within the disciplines they teach, not simply the current array of validated knowledge.

The concept of self-correction in a community of inquiry is particularly powerful for our purposes. It holds that the evolution of good judgment requires that one's position must be explored by and with others.[21] This principle gets played out on different scales, but with the same concept in play across disciplines and venues. Scientists, for example, are expected to publish their research for review by other experts in the field—a large-scale community of inquiry. Only after the "judgments" or conclusions are vetted in this way do they begin to become established scientific explanations. On a very different scale, students exploring a work of art in a classroom can't get away by saying "I liked it." The question is why? Which criteria—personal or derived from the artistic venue—were used in making the judgment? In social studies classrooms, students are seldom allowed to get away with opinions, but often it is "facts" that are sought by teachers to sustain explanations. If we are engaged in critical thinking, facts are not enough. Students would have to go to the next level to draw on criteria that support their conclusion, and in effect explain why the "facts" used are relevant and reflect currently held positions by experts in the field—historians, for example, in social studies classrooms.

This sort of classroom practice requires a very concrete commitment by teacher education programs. Future teachers need to learn how to conduct discussions within the context of communities of inquiry, and they must learn to develop situations in which students learn to be willing to test their ideas with their classmates. They must provide opportunities for their students to give reasons for their positions and require that they treat different positions with respect if they can be shown to meet the criteria for good judgments. Perhaps most important, teachers need to learn how to encourage students to demonstrate flexibility in positions as new evidence, supported by criteria and tested in a community of inquiry, comes forward. The only way to do this is, of course, for teachers themselves to know their disciplines well enough to help students identify criteria, examine positions, and draw conclusions that are appropriately valid.

We can and should turn this argument for good judgment to our teacher education programs as well. On one level, we make significant judgments when we admit students to our programs. What are the criteria we use in making such a judgment? Do they include consideration of the dispositions of the teacher education candidate toward preparing his or her students for democracy? Furthermore, the judgments teachers make in classrooms can be made more explicit by the use of critical thinking. How do we make those decisions about pedagogy, about out of school assignments, or about grades? In a sense, the emergence of rubrics in the evaluation of students provides criteria for making appropriate judgments. The power of a program with a clear conceptual framework around both critical thinking and teaching for democracy that is shared not only within the university faculty but with public school faculty as well cannot be underestimated.[22]

The application of this to democracy and democratic practice should be fairly obvious. When Jefferson argued that one cannot have a society that is "ignorant and free," he didn't directly cite the ability to argue for one's position. But argument and exchange based on interaction are essential qualities of democratic behavior. The ability to engage in such dialogue, to be flexible, to respond to alternate points of view can be embedded in virtually all teaching, and by doing so classroom teachers prepare future citizens, in the broadest sense, for life in a democracy.

Again, preparing teachers for classrooms that value academic learning along with encouraging students to develop positions—to make judgments—begs for schools that concur with the position that education should be designed to encourage debate, discussion, and the rational consideration of important issues.

But it is important to point out that this is not enough. Learning to think well about making judgments in the classroom does not in any way assure that students will in fact participate in the democratic process and bring their intellectual ability to bear as they consider the positions of candidates for office or argue for equity where it is not present. This issue of participation in democratic process was so important in ancient Greece. Consider Pericles' position in 431 B.C.E.:

> Our Constitution favors the many instead of the few; this is why it is called a democracy.... Our people have, besides politics, their private affairs to attend to, and our ordinary citizens, though occupied with the pursuits of industry, are still fair judges of public matters; for, unlike any other nation [we regard] him who takes no

part in these duties not as unambitious but as useless, and instead of evoking discussion as a stumbling block, we think it an indispensable preliminary to any action at all.[23]

Walter Parker explores this issue in *Democratic Education* by contrasting the terms "idiocy" and "citizenship." He argues that the term "idiotic" in its origins in ancient Greece came from the root "idios" meaning private, separate, or self-centered. An idiot was one who focused on his or her private needs rather than the public needs. The public interests are expressed in the term "polites" from which the term political is derived.[24] And, as Roger Soder notes:

> In a democracy, all people—not just a mandarin class, but all people—have to be able to think critically; they must be able to engage in free and open inquiry. In a democracy we have to reject the kind of thinking in Tennyson's *Charge of the Light Brigade*, "theirs is not the reason why, theirs is but to do or die…." In the place of this kind of thinking, we must side with John Dewey, who talked about democracy in terms of the free play of facts and ideas, secured by effective guarantees of free inquiry, free assembly, and free communication.[25]

Amy Gutmann argues for the critical role of political participation as an important goal of education, writing,

> Even the ability to think critically about politics is an incomplete virtue from a democratic perspective. If primary schooling leaves students with a capacity for political criticism, but no capacity for political participation or sense of social commitment, either because it fails to cultivate their sense of political efficacy, or because of success in teaching them deference to authority, then it will have failed to cultivate a virtue essential to democracy.[26]

It is this need to cultivate participation in democracy and social justice that must be explicit in our work, and requires that we work in schools that embrace the values we have described and with others to cultivate this commitment.

Barriers and Hopeful Signs

Is the glass half full, or half empty? Clearly, there are significant barriers to engaging in this work at the beginning of the Twenty-First Century, many of them reflected in the approach to education undertaken through federal policy.

Fortunately, the context includes some hopeful signs. Two major national higher education associations, a national foundation, a national network connecting more than 40 colleges, universities, and hundreds of public schools are taking the need for attention to democratic practice with a core of social justice seriously. Also, higher education and P–12 teachers who believe that their work goes beyond the most easily measurable outcomes should not overlook the current press for assessment. Because they are part of the context, we will examine these developments here, although they could be viewed as programs as well.

Barriers

After around the clock work in conference committees, the first legislative act of the Bush administration, HR 1, became The No Child Left Behind Act of 2001. As he signed the bill into law, President Bush declared the beginning of "a new era, a new time in public education in our country. … As of this hour, America's schools will be on a new path of reform and a new path of results." How does this piece of legislation, described as "landmark" in the changes it proposed for the federal role in education and passed by extraordinary margins (381–41 in the House and 87–10 in the Senate), impact on the evolution of schools for democracy and social justice? I will leave it to Penny Earley to explore this fully in her chapter, but there are several qualities of NCLB that are pretty clear in their impact on this work. One of these is the emphasis on outcomes defined in terms of student performance on standardized tests, outcomes deemed consistent with the goal of "scientifically based research," a mantra repeated more than a hundred times in the law. Every state is required to develop (or approve) and administer annual standardized tests in mathematics and reading for all students in grades three through eight. These tests are then linked for the requirement of Adequate Yearly Progress (AYP) to assure that all students are at proficient or higher levels within 12 years. The scores, further, must be disaggregated by such factors as socioeconomic status and race to assure that the gaps between groups are narrowed. Requirements that students in failing schools be allowed to transfer to successful schools and that outside of school tutoring be provided to children below the standards put, as yet, unfunded burdens on schools and educators. Also, the law requires that all teachers be "highly qualified" in that they meet state certification programs or are enrolled in alternative certification programs.

Who could argue with the apparent goals: assure highly qualified teachers, close achievement gaps, provide new opportunities for students in failing schools, and use data to assess progress? The problem is that the measures of success are narrowly defined and focus on content knowledge.

Similarly, the definition of teacher quality is limited in that it focuses on knowledge of the content to be taught as measured by state certification tests. While requiring that states avoid temporary licenses, states can redefine certification through alternate certification programs that sometimes have the effect of lowering state standards.[27] And, some are concerned that the practices of reassigning students from failing schools to successful schools will lead to overcrowding in successful schools and conceivably to a decline in achievement there. In practice, the sum of these requirements places enormous pressure on teachers, on school building leaders, and on district leaders to focus on what is measured by the tests.

To the extent that some argue that teaching for democracy and social justice detracts from the knowledge to be measured by these tests, the choice is on meeting the prescribed outcomes at the expense of other learning. This conclusion creates very difficult circumstances for those of us who believe that both outcomes—learning to live in a socially just democracy and learning content knowledge well—are important, and we would argue, not mutually exclusive goals. However, the survival instinct of many educators has and will continue to force them to focus narrowly on what is explicitly measured by the tests. To the extent that this happens, the focus on and momentum for teachers and schools with a broader view of education for social and political democracy is lost.

Hopeful Signs

The American Democracy Project and the Arts of Democracy. Two of the best examples of the recognition of the need for a focus on democracy in education that have emerged are the American Democracy Project of the American Association of State Colleges and Universities (AASCU) and the New York Times, and the Arts of Democracy Project of the American Association of Colleges and Universities (AAC&U). AASCU is an association of 400 state colleges and universities that represent the American public colleges and universities that produce the largest numbers of teachers for schools in the United States. The project is based on the premise that "[t]oday's college graduates are less engaged in community affairs and public life than those of any preceding generation." The American Democracy Project argues that colleges and universities can play a critical role in confronting this problem by working to "produce graduates who understand and are committed to engaging in meaningful actions as citizens in a democracy."[28] The project uses *Civic Responsibility and Higher Education* as a "text."[29] Education for democratic citizenship is, in the context of this work, based on a broad set of substantive values, ideals, and standards, some of which are connected to the academic enterprise itself such as intellectual integrity, concern for truth, mutual respect, public discussion of contested ideas, and some of which are derived from the core values of American democracy, including tolerance, concern for both the rights and welfare of individuals and the community, a commitment to civil and rational discourse.

Annually, AASCU sponsors meetings of presidents and provosts committed to the project. Questions that are asked are designed to expand those discussions into a campuswide conversation about education for democratic citizenship. The American Democracy Project (ADP) encourages chief academic officers to convene a group of at least 20 faculty members for a year-long conversation, with the first half of the year focusing on the theory and practice of civic engagement, and the second half focusing on building those goals and practices into campus planning. The guide includes questions and guidance such as:

- What questions or concerns do you think students, faculty, and staff on your campus may have about the kind of education endorsed by Educating Citizens and the American Democracy Project? For example, some people worry that these goals detract from a focus on academic learning. Others are concerned about the danger of indoctrinating students, or they think students have already formed their civic identities before coming to college.
- What should a civically responsible graduate of your campus look like? What examples of recent graduates come to mind and what kinds of college experiences did they have that seem to have contributed to their civic education? Did they have an important mentor on the campus? Were they part of a student club or group that got them involved in community problems? Did they take an influential course that provided opportunities to delve into the complexities of social questions related to a discipline?
- Are the goals of the ADP built into the general education requirements at your institution? How? How might students be encouraged to enroll in general education courses that focus on moral and civic issues? To what extent are the goals of the American Democracy Project reflected in the "de facto" core curriculum (i.e., the small group of courses that most students take)? How could these courses be modified or supplemented so as to ensure that moral and civic learning is integrated with academic learning?

Of course, we would ask these same questions of all teacher education programs. But, ultimately, we would be better off if we were able to build on a commitment of the kind represented by the American Democracy

Project through the general education programs for all students. Certainly, it is critical that programs located at AASCU campuses participating in the American Democracy Project learn of the work on their campuses and build upon it. When the program was introduced to all City University of New York provosts at one of their regular meetings, this one held at the New York Times headquarters, deans and directors of teacher education programs from across the system were invited to join the meeting. A small group of provosts and deans of education at the University, now meet regularly to extend the work and assure that programs to prepare teachers build upon it. Plans are now under way to provide daily copies of *The New York Times* to future teachers as part of a pilot program to enhance civic literacy and critical thinking at CUNY institutions.

As posted on their website, "AAC&U's more than 900 institutional members are liberal arts colleges, two-year colleges, research and doctoral-granting universities, master's-degree colleges and universities, professional universities, and systems offices. They are independent and public, large and small, rural and urban, residential and commuter. Through their membership in AAC&U, they express their belief in the importance of a liberal education for all of their students."

AAC&U's Arts of Democracy Project, supported by the Fund for the Improvement of Postsecondary Education, is designed to work with colleges and universities to develop societal, civic, and global knowledge in their graduates by linking liberal education and democracy in the context of our interdependent but unequal world. The project's objectives are:

1. to generate new knowledge about global studies,
2. to spur greater civic engagement and social responsibility,
3. to promote in faculty and students a deeper knowledge of, debate about, and practice of democracy, and
4. to cultivate intercultural competencies with the faculty as well as the students.

At Brooklyn College of the City University of New York, one of the systems largest producers of teachers, both the Arts in Democracy and the American Democracy Project are actively pursued. Brooklyn College describes the Arts in Democracy Project as follows:

Brooklyn College seeks to become a "community of diversity" as opposed to a diverse community. Located in ethnically diverse Brooklyn, the student body of Brooklyn College comes from the world. In the past the development and implementation of democracy, democratic training, and citizenship in the curriculum, although widespread, was not in the forefront. In fact, it is precisely the presence of that larger world in which we are enmeshed that compels us now to take democracy more seriously, and move synergistically and comprehensively in our approach. Through curriculum and faculty development, democratic pedagogies, reaching out into the community through a combination of discipline-based internships, service learning and field work, creating both physical and virtual centers to focus our energies and help to pull our various initiatives into coherent and powerful whole. Our goal is to help faculty to articulate and students to appreciate the profound importance of democracy in the present moment.[30]

The AASCU Project, now adopted by more than 170 colleges and universities, and the AAC&U Project have attracted criticism from those who believe that anything that diverts from the transmission of knowledge to students weakens the college education.

For example, at Brooklyn College Provost Roberta Matthews has led the introduction of an adaptation of both projects. The work at Brooklyn includes courses such as Literature and Cultural Diversity, the American Urban Experience, and Peoples of the United States designed to provide a perspective on cultural diversity within the United States and its implications for democracy. One faculty member has argued very publicly that such a program "doesn't have anything to do with democracy but serves a political agenda of diversity and multiculturalism." Further he "accuses Brooklyn College of lowering standards by choosing cultural relativism rather than exposing students to content from Western civilization."[31] As is the case with many arguments against efforts to infuse preparation for life in a democratic and diverse society, the false assumption is made that there is a dichotomy between such efforts and high academic standards.

The Carnegie Corporation of New York's Civic Mission of Schools. One of our major national foundations, joining with the Center for Information and Research on Civic Learning and Engagement has published a report, *The Civic Mission of Schools,* focusing on the critical mission of schools in civic education and the role of teacher education programs in promoting such programs. Its perspective mirrors many of the arguments we make in this volume.

Arguing that the schools are the only institutions with the capacity and mandate to reach virtually every young person in the country, the Carnegie report sees schools as systematically and directly responding for imparting citizen norms. Schools are best equipped to address the cognitive aspects of good citizenship. The schools are communities where young people can learn to interact, argue, and work together with others.[32] The report defines competent and responsible citizens as being informed and thoughtful participants in their communities, acting politically, and having moral and civic virtues. Citizens are concerned with the rights and welfare of others, are socially responsible, willing to listen to alternative perspectives, confident in their capacity to make a difference, and ready to contribute personally to civic and political action.

The report sees schools as systematically and directly responding for imparting citizen norms. It argues that schools are best equipped to address the cognitive aspects of good citizenship. The schools are viewed as communities where young people can learn to interact, argue, and work together with others.[33]

Barriers to implementing education for democracy considered in the report include teachers' fear of criticism or litigation if they address controversial or political issues. It cites the impact of high-stakes testing and the absence of civic education as a goal of education that is measured and therefore validated as important. Finally, they report that schools tend to have standardized structures that limit experimentation with alternative approaches in civic education such as structuring schools as communities where students have rights and obligations.[34]

One of the many recommendations of the report is strengthening the civic education dimensions of preservice and in-service teacher education. They argue, "Schools of education must help teachers and administrators understand the democratic and civic mission of schools and the first principles of our framing documents."[35] It is encouraging that a major foundation would issue an important report encouraging a focus on education for democracy and social justice in programs that prepare teachers and in our public schools. The corporation is launching a grant opportunity for states that wish to enhance attention to democracy in the public schools.

The National Network for Educational Renewal (NNER). One of the major national networks to support teacher education (the others include the Holmes Partnership and the Renaissance Group) has a particular mission related to education for a democracy. In 1986, three years after *A Nation at Risk* was published, John Goodlad initiated the National Network for Educational Renewal bringing together 10 school/university projects. The endeavor worked diligently on school renewal, and in the late 1980s and early 1990s, a series of books was published through the NNER's sponsoring agency, the Center for Educational Renewal at the University of Washington. These included *Teachers for Our Nation's Schools, The Moral Dimensions of Teaching, and Places Where Teachers Are Taught.*[36] Out of this work came an Agenda for Education in a Democracy with a focus on a four-part mission:

- Enculturating the young into our democracy (preparing critical participants in our democracy)
- Providing access to knowledge for all students
- Practicing a nurturing and culturally responsive pedagogy
- Responsible stewardship of schools.

Each of these four dimensions of the conceptual framework of the agenda are characterized as having a "moral" dimensions and implications for how teacher education programs are organized and delivered. We have already explored in some depth the first two dimensions, preparing our future teachers to teach students who will be critical participants in a democracy[37] and the importance of providing access to knowledge for all. Practicing nurturing and culturally responsive pedagogy is an outgrowth of these first two dimensions in that it is necessarily the vehicle for delivering the kind of education for democratic action and access to knowledge we seek.

When the agenda began, culturally responsive pedagogy was not part of the conception. But as part of the evolution of the work, such pedagogy is increasingly important, as we understand how to respond to cultural differences as our society becomes even more diverse. Many settings in the NNER use the work of Ana Maria Villegas and Tamara Lucas to inform this effort.[38] The concept of "stewardship of best practice" calls for all teachers to assume responsibility for the educational context in which children live. It is, in a sense, the essence of professionalism in that teachers are called upon to tolerate nothing less than excellent practices in their own teaching and in the teaching of their colleagues.

The agenda is in turn supported by a statement of conditions or "postulates" deemed necessary for success.[39] To assure that the NNER was true to this new moral agenda, the NNER was disbanded and reconstituted in 1992 with a focus on the mission and postulates. Out of several hundred applicants, eight school/university partnerships were chosen and began work on the agenda. Since then the network has grown to more than 40 colleges and universities in 21 settings in 17 states, representing more than 1,000 partner schools. Universities and colleges and their public school partners joining the network make a commitment to the mission. The teacher education programs at the institutions commit to working closely with arts and science colleagues as equal partners as well as with public school partners to simultaneously renew their teacher education programs and the public schools.

One particularly positive strategy for change within the NNER has been the Leadership for Educational Renewal program, initiated by the independent nonprofit affiliate of the Center for Educational Renewal (CER), the Institute for Educational Inquiry, in 1992. Under this program, replicated across the network, faculty in education, in the arts and science, and in the public schools read important works on democratic practice, school change, stewardship, and access to knowledge and become leaders in their own settings. The support of major foundations for initiating this work is explored in Carla Asher's chapter in this book. Institutions participating in this work—focused on education for democracy—range from small liberal arts colleges such as Columbia College in South Carolina and Maryville College in Missouri, to the University of Washington, the University of South Carolina, the City University of New York, and the University of Connecticut. A second series of books on the work of the NNER has been published and can be consulted by colleges struggling with these issues. These include *Centers of Pedagogy: New Structures for Educational Renewal,* detailing the structures for collaboration across three cultures, *Leadership for Educational Renewal* describing the professional development program of the Network, *The Last Best Hope: A Democracy Reader,* and *Developing Democratic Character in the Young.*[40]

For members of the NNER, having institutions with the same goals has been an extraordinary support for change. Deans and faculty members in education and arts and sciences and administrators and teachers in public schools can call colleagues across the country to find ideas and support for difficult change. The chapter by Wilson and Davidson in this volume examines just such a case. The network meets annually to review progress and challenges. And so, the largest network linking teacher education programs has as its core theme the development of teachers who can prepare students for effective democratic participation in schools that share that mission. Finding like-mined colleagues is a critically important strategy in this work.

Social and Emotional Learning. One field of study that is just beginning to be recognized for its potential in advancing the goals of developing effective participants in a socially just democracy is social and emotional education. The field, with disciplinary roots in psychology, social work, curriculum development has developed a role in P–12 schools related to risk prevention, health/mental health promotion, and character education. Of course, just as is the case with the concepts of democracy and social justice, social and emotional education has many possible meanings. One use of the work, if appropriately focused, includes integrating social, emotional, ethical and cognitive teaching to promote students' ability to achieve academically, to solve problems nonviolently, and to foster the capacity to be an effective participant in a democracy. It is this application that has the most promise from our view.

The area of emotional health—emotional IQ—is associated with the ground-breaking work of Dan Goleman,[41] but many others working in the field are making specific connections to teacher education for democratic practice and social justice. Most notably, the City University of New York, in collaboration with faculty coordinator Janet Patti of Hunter College and Jonathan Cohen, CEO of the Center for Social and Emotional Education, has developed a certificate sequence specifically designed to enable current and future teachers to enhance their teaching to account for the social and emotional health of P–12 students. Patti's work includes the preparation of school leaders with attention to emotional intelligence and Cohen's work has been used in schools and universities across the country with P–12 educators.[42] The growing interest in social and emotional learning is partly related to the school violence that has been prominent in the news in recent years, but it has potential as well to develop self-efficacy and concept in students to enhance their perception of their ability to succeed. The consideration of social and emotional education as a vehicle for learning how to interact with peers in a constructive way is a clear extension of our belief that teaching for democratic participation includes the interpersonal qualities one brings to daily life.

The certificate will be offered through CUNY's School of Professional Studies at the graduate level, and the work will be integrated into teacher education programs across the CUNY system. Discussion has begun with the New York Board of Regents to develop a state certificate extension for teachers to engage in social and emotional education.

Assessing Outcomes. If we are to promote education for democracy and social justice in these times, one strategy is to join with those who focus on outcomes and demonstrate that the kinds of teacher education programs and schools we propose do in fact have a positive effect on student learning as measured by standardized tests. There is significant research already that leads us in this direction. For example, the work of Harold Wenglinsky shows that when teachers learn to teach in a multicultural environment and use critical thinking in their instruction, the mathematics scores of students in their classes increase.[43] In New York City, we have begun a major study to test some of these beliefs, called the Pathways to Teaching study. Using a team of researchers from the Rockefeller School at SUNY Albany and at Stanford University, we have begun to systematically collect data on the dozens of pathways that teachers can use to enter the New York City teaching force.

We will, as part of the study, identify the conceptual framework that guides each program—is it focused on teaching for democracy, on direct instruction, on culturally responsive teaching, or some other framework? Then we will examine the integrity with which the conceptual framework and program is implemented. Finally, we will compare pathways on data that include student outcomes on standardized tests. We will learn which pathways and which elements of pathways make the greatest difference. We will learn whether or not pathways with a moral agenda are more or less successful than more narrowly defined pathways in their effect on student learning. What if we learn that in fact they are as successful as other pathways in promoting student learning? If so, then we will have no excuses for choosing to ignore the goal of promoting participants for a socially just democracy.[44]

Conclusions

These are difficult times for those who believe that a central purpose of public education is the promotion of democratic practices in the young so that they learn what it means to live in a democratic society characterized by social justice and live their lives to promote the twin goals of democracy and social justice. If we believe that this is important we must engage in work among faculties of education, and in collaboration with faculties in arts and science and in schools, to be clear about what we believe in. We must explore the meaning of democracy and define it broadly. We must examine the dispositions we expect in students and decide whether we must require that they be present at the time of their admission to teacher education, or that they can in fact be developed. We must consider our curricula and be certain that we attend to the goal of promoting democracy and not simply list it as an outcome we don't seriously pursue. We must find evidence to support the success of our programs and be spokespersons for the kind of education we want for our children, especially in times when resources for education are limited and policy may in fact work against us.

Clearly, there are some positive signs. Networks of colleges, universities, and public schools systems are pursuing this work. Major national organizations are pressing for the inclusion of education for democratic citizenship for all undergraduate students. We need to support these efforts and find like-minded professionals, but ultimately it is what we do in our own programs and in the schools that surround us that will make the most profound difference. We need to make work toward socially just and democratic education the primary work of our professional lives.

Notes

1. Watter C. Parker, Teaching Democracy (New York: Teachers College Press, 2003), p. 14.
2. Regulations of the New York State Commissioner of Education, Part 80–1.3.
3. Our focus is on American democracy. For a historical overview of the development of democracy see Nathan Tarcow, "The Meanings of Democracy," in Democracy, Education and the Schools, ed. Roger Soder (San Francisco: Jossey-Bass, 1996).
4. My colleague John Anderson at the University of Nebraska, Kearney, reminds me that most political scientists think of the Fourteenth Amendment along with the Civil Rights Act of 1965 as establishing civil rights, while civil liberties are created by distinct limitations on government action through the Bill of Rights.
5. See the work of the Center for Fiscal Equity at www.cfequity.org/cfereply9-28-01.pdf.
6. Alexis de Tocqueville, Democracy in America, Vol. I Henry Reeve Text (New York: Vintage Books, 1972), 247–48.
7. Maxine Greene, Blue Guitar (New York: Teachers College Press, 2001), 7.
8. Matthew Lipman, Critical Thinking, What Can it Be? (Upper Montclair, N.J.: Montclair State University-Institute for Critical Thinking, 1988).
9. Chester E. Finn Jr., "Faulty Engineering," Education Next 4, no. 2 (2004): 14.
10. John I. Goodlad, Teachers for Our Nation's Schools (San Francisco: Jossey-Bass, 1990) and Educational Renewal (San Francisco: Jossey-Bass, 1994), 26.
11. This is the most common form of the quotation. See Perspectives: The Newsletter of the Colorado Partnership for Educational Renewal 5, nos. 2–3 (1995). The actual statement from Jefferson is, "If a nation expects to be ignorant and free in a state of civilization it expects something that never was and never will be." Letter to Colonel Charles Yancey, January 6, 1816.
12. John McCullough, John Adams (New York: Simon and Schuster, 2001), 223.
13. John Dewey, Democracy and Education (New York: The Free Press, 1966), 87.
14. Ibid.
15. Amy Gutmann, Democratic Education (Princeton: Princeton University Press, 1987), 14.
16. Benjamin Barber, An Aristocracy for Everyone (New York: Ballentine Books, 1992), 5.
17. Perspectives, 5.
18. See for example, Jean Anyon, "Social Class and School Knowledge," Curriculum Inquiry 11 (1981): 3–42.
19. John Dewey, How We Think (New York: Prometheus Books, 1991).
20. Lipman.
21. See Laurence J. Splitter and Ann M. Sharp, Teaching for Better Thinking: The Classroom Community of Inquiry (Melbourne: The Australian Council for Educational Research, 1995).
22. David S. Martin and Nicholas M. Michelli, "Preparing Teachers of Thinking," in Developing Minds, ed. A. Costa (Alexandria, VA: Association for Supervision and Curriculum Development, 2001), 111–17.
23. Personal communication from Alan Cameron, The Charles Anthon Professor of Classics, Columbia University. Professor Cameron reports that this is an accurate portrayal of Pericles's thinking, but the words are actually from the historian Thucydides, around 431 B.C.E.
24. Palmer, 3. Professor Cameron adds this in a personal communication, idios does mean private or separate, and the original meaning of idiotes is a private person or individual as opposed to the state. Then it means someone who holds no public office or does not take part in public life. Then a person who has no professional knowledge, a layman. From that develops the further meaning of someone with no skills, and finally someone with no skill of any sort, is an ignoramus.
25. Roger Soder, "Teaching the Teachers of the People," in Democracy, Education and the Schools, ed. Roger Soder, (San Francisco: Jossey-Bass, 1996), 246.
26. Gutmann, 92.
27. Nicholas M. Michelli, "Preparing Highly Qualified Teachers: A Contested Concept," in Highly Qualified Teachers (National Evaluation Systems, forthcoming).
28. See the website of the American Association of State Colleges and Universities for a full description of the project. www.aascu.org

29. Thomas Erlich, *Civic Education and Higher Education* (The American Council on Education and Oryx Press, 2000).
30. See the Association of American Colleges and Universities website www.aac&u.org.
31. *The New York Sun*, "Mr. Johnson on the Warpath—Again," December 29, 2003, 19.
32. *The Civic Mission of Schools* (New York: Carnegie Corporation of New York and The Center for Information and Research on Civic Learning and Engagement, 2003), 12.
33. Ibid., 12.
34. Ibid., 14–15.
35. Ibid., 34.
36. John Goodlad, Teachers for Our Nation's Schools (San Francisco: Jossey-Bass, 1990); *Places Where Teachers Are Taught*, ed. John I. Goodlad, Roger Soder, and Kenneth Sirotnik (San Francisco: Jossey-Bass, 1990); John I. Goodlad, Roger Soder, and Ken Sirotnik, eds. *The Moral Dimensions of Teaching* (San Francisco: Jossey-Bass, 1990).
37. Many participants in the agenda have stopped using the original and perfectly good anthropological term "enculturation" because some heard it as "indoctrination." They have instead begun using the idea of preparing the young for critical participation in a democracy.
38. Ana Maria Villegas and Tamara Lucas, *Educating Culturally Responsive Teachers: A Coherent Approach* (Albany: State University of New York Press, 2002).
39. Goodlad, *Educational Renewal*, 67–95.
40. Robert Patterson, Nicholas Michelli, and Arturo Pacheco, *Centers of Pedagogy: New Structures for Educational Renewal* (San Francisco: Jossey-Bass, 1999); Wilma S. Smith and Gary D. Fenstermacher, eds., *Leadership for Educational Renewal* (San Francisco: Jossey-Bass, 1999); Roger Soder, John Goodlad, and Timothy McMannon, eds., *Developing Democratic Character in the Young* (San Francisco: Jossey-Bass, 2001).
41. Daniel Goleman, *Emotional Intelligence: Why It Can Matter More than IQ* (New York: Bantam, 1995).
42. See Janet Patti and James Tobin, *Smart School Leaders: Leading with Emotional Intelligence* (Dubuque: Kendall/Hunt Publishers, 2003); Jonathan Cohen, ed., *Educating Minds and Hearts: Social and Emotional Learning and the Passage into Adolescence* (New York: Teachers College Press, 1999); and Jonathan Cohen, *Safe Classrooms/Intelligent Schools: The Social Emotional Education of Young Children* (New York: Teachers College Press, 2001).
43. Harold Wenglinsky, *Making Teaching Matter: Bringing the Classroom in Discussions of Teacher Quality* (Princeton: Educational Testing Service, 2000).
44. To follow this study and review the instruments, see www.teacherpolicyresearch.org.

CHAPTER 2

Learners not Widgets: Teacher Education for Social Justice during Transformational Times

DAVID LEE KEISER

We do not know how many educators see present demands and prescriptions as obstacles to their own development, or how many find it difficult to breathe. There may be thousands who, in the absence of support systems, have elected to be silent. Thousands of others (sometimes without explanation) are leaving the schools. Surpassing, transcendence, and freedom: Such notions are not being articulated in the conversations now going on.[1]

What Maxine Greene described in 1988 as "present demands and prescriptions" became the No Child Left Behind (NCLB) Act. Teachers and administrators throughout the United States implement various strategies to comply with a new, demanding, and prescriptive education code. Greene's reference to breathing doubtless is metaphoric for teachers who gasp to provide a comprehensive, engaging curriculum, while attending to test preparation and under renewed scrutiny and threat of sanction. But the reference can also be literal for asthmatic children or for schools with toxic materials in and around them.[2] As authors such as Jonathan Kozol have long reminded us, the healthfulness of school buildings and neighborhoods often represent the worst savage inequalities in public schools.[3]

For example, one of the nation's most expensive and visible school construction projects, Belmont Academy High School in Los Angeles, has long been plagued with problems from both hazardous materials and from its location atop three geological fault lines.[4]

In addition to the frustrating reality of a newly constructed high school lying on tenuous fault lines, another Los Angeles high school, Beverly Hills High School, straddles oil wells so toxic as to warrant a class action lawsuit students can join online.[5] This is a school about which they made a television show.[6] What does this say about our society's civic commitment to public high schools? On television schools represent a place of carefree joy and normal teen issues, but in reality some sit on toxic oil wells. Certainly these examples represent situations that many would consider unjust for the students and families involuntarily affected by them.

Using the transcendence to which Greene refers, we need to begin to imagine new possibilities. A TV show cannot portray the challenging, tedious reality of schools and also maintain high ratings. And neither can policy makers, including the U.S. Department of Education, easily present the complexities of education without confusing the public. But rather than embrace and promote the dynamic complexity of teaching and learning, they instead promote simplistic reductions with rhetorical pronouncements and little cohesion. Followed literally, recent initiatives such as NCLB can greatly inhibit teachers from engendering the transformative, or transcendent, education to which Greene alludes. The absence of transcendent conversations that see successful education as more than simply numerical ratings is partially attributable to the push for, and stress about, high-stakes testing. With students and teachers responding to an ultimately punitive system of reform, it is not difficult to understand why some are still "leaving the schools."

During this unparalleled time in American history—post–cold war, in which the United States as the sole superpower is at war in multiple locations—it is necessary to transcend traditional thinking about education in order both to surpass expectations of education, now derived largely from test scores, and to increase pedagogical and occupational choices for students and citizens. But choice for what, and in whose best interest? If parents and students, along with increasingly empowered policy makers, make choices that are good only for themselves individually, public education will continue to develop into a controversial and contested private good; on the other hand, if they can at least consider education as a public good, public education will be more apt to fulfill the mission we outlined in Chapter One.[7]

We see the mission of teacher education for social justice as forging new possibilities in meaningful, dynamic, and healing ways. As schools are charged with the preparation of future citizens, we need to account for students' holistic well-being, as well as their test scores, and need to define school success by affective engagement, democratic participation, and citizenship, as well as by basic reading and math skills.

This chapter explores the theme of social justice in teacher education during times of unprecedented international and civil uncertainty and stated federal concern for public education. After formative definitions of social justice—both literally, as the synthesis of the concepts of social and justice; and practically, from the collective educative vision that sees public schools as integral to enacting democracy, academic and creative success, and community development—this chapter will identify and explore some of the challenges of working within teacher education during an unprecedented federal drive to standardize, target, and perhaps ultimately weaken public education through a narrowing of the curriculum and a privatization of teacher preparation. The chapter will later examine some current enactments of teacher education for social justice and conclude with a suggested set of conditions that might enable teacher education for social justice to reemerge. We maintain that current challenges may be addressed with teaching and teacher preparation that encourages high standards, lifelong learning, reciprocal teaching, dialogue, creativity, and constructive encouragement leading to an expansion rather than a contraction of knowledge. Focusing and holding accountable only achievement on basic skills—high-stakes testing in reading and math only—drives teachers to spend valuable class time preparing for a single, all-important assessment. Inevitably, other equally valuable activities are weakened or eliminated, as teachers and administrators worry about the bottom line of test scores. Challenges facing educators and students are neither particularly new nor acute; since at least the 1983 report "A Nation at Risk," which criticized public education, a particular type or critical attention to public schools has been at center stage. This attention transfers responsibilities for the inherent inequalities of American society, manifested in public scores and test scores, to public school teachers and administrators and university-based teacher educators.[8]

Articulating the Vision: Teacher Education for Social Justice

Often referring to the cultural gap between teachers and their pupils, advocates of the social justice agenda which is an outgrowth of the social reconstructionist tradition of reform in American teacher education see both schooling and teacher education as crucial elements in the making of a more just society.[9]

The theories and wisdom of many scholars within and outside of the field of teacher education inform this text. The inspirational, visionary, and political writings of such scholars of education as Maxine Greene and Marilyn Cochran-Smith, John Dewey and John Goodlad, and Gloria Ladson-Billings and Lisa Delpit make explicit their concerns about equity, race, and culture, as well as creative and critical pedagogy, from perspectives variously referred to as progressive, democratic, liberal, left, and antiracist. While these scholars provide useful fonts of knowledge, and as compelling as their arguments continue to be, they do not have a monopoly on what teacher education for social justice should look like. The argument that high-stakes testing—and the results, penalties, and choices that follow from it—is socially just pervades the policy and literature supporting and defending the No Child Left Behind Act. This book responds to any educational policy that reinforces the myth of absolute meritocracy. For many years, scholars have demonstrated that the possibility of a level playing field is complicated by practices such as the hidden curriculum, tracking, social stratification, and racism and other forms of discrimination.

Three theoretical concepts or ways to think about teacher education for social justice frame this chapter. First, social justice pedagogy must be imaginative; indeed, part of justice is imagining fairness and justice as deserved possibilities. Educators such as Maxine Greene see past current limits, or limit-situations, to imagine what she believes ought to be. Inspirational evidence is found in the poetry of Audre Lorde and Muriel Rukeyser, the mindfulness of Thich Nhat Hanh, and the creative engaging pedagogy of Vivian Paley. Second, the late philosopher John Rawls's theory of distributive justice also helps evaluate the success of education and teacher education for social justice and provides a useful prism through which to view this challenge.[10] Third, Marilyn Cochran-Smith's concept of teacher education for social justice identifies both a learning problem—the need for inquiry along with high standards—and a political problem—the need for education to be both constitutive and reflective of the democratic state.[11] These three theoretical frames—a creative, or imaginative perspective; a just, or distributive perspective; and a problematizing perspective—intersect at the nexus of social justice in teacher education and serve to conceptualize our mission for teacher education.

Defining Social Justice

The collective work of a wide range of social justice advocates frames this chapter. In order to situate the issues within the field of teacher education, however, I offer the following definitions, from the books *Teaching for*

Social Justice and *Learning to Teach for Social Justice* to describe the enormity of the challenge of teaching for social justice and the possibilities inherent in imagining a more just society.

> Learning to teach for social justice is a lifelong undertaking. It involves coming to understand oneself in relation to others; examining how society constructs privilege and inequality and how this affects one's own opportunities as well as those of different people; exploring the experiences of others and appreciating how those inform their worldviews, perspectives, and opportunities; and evaluating how schools and classrooms operate and can be structured to value diverse human experiences and to enable learning for all students.[13]
>
> Teaching for social justice, we must remember, is teaching what we believe ought to be—not merely in terms of moral frameworks, but in material arrangements for people in all spheres of society. Moreover, teaching for social justice is teaching for the sake of arousing the kinds of vivid, reflective, experiential responses that might move students to come together in serious efforts to understand what social justice actually means and what it might demand.[14]

The first definition, written by Linda Darling-Hammond among a collection of narratives from preservice teachers, underscores the enormity of the challenge facing educators for social justice; the "lifelong undertaking" to which she refers is not only difficult but can feel threatening to students and educators from privileged backgrounds. Teacher education for social justice must address the privilege that many teachers and preservice teachers have relative to many students in public schools, both earned and unearned. Meritocracy—the idea that all wealth and income are earned fairly and result from hard work, not privilege or inheritance—is still prevalent, and issues of race and class still impact upon schools and classrooms. Some teacher educators rightly suggest that the social justice agenda has largely focused on the "transformation of White, monolingual English teachers who are the majority of teacher education students," and that practices and pedagogies need to prepare all students.[15]

The second description, written by Maxine Greene, recalls the power of imagination, and the importance of not limiting possibilities by current patterns and relationships. It is hard to overestimate the importance of being able to imagine better and safer times. Although our definition of social justice in teacher education is framed by the four functions of public education as described in the introduction, these functions are clouded at times by the need to conform to NCLB.

With no hint of irony, the Secretary of Education under President Bush, Dr. Roderick Paige, describes the new education code: "For No Child Left Behind to succeed, teachers have to be able to succeed, and that is why the law was written with teachers in mind."[16] The strict requirements, draconian penalties, and potential for deprofessionalization punish rather than reward the profession. Although major professional education associations prior to its passage opposed it, the secretary assures teachers that it was written with them in mind. This seems particularly curious given his recent comparison of the National Education Association, a group representing millions of teachers, to "terrorists." Imagine if the hammer approach taken by this department were applied to other professions. Imagine if doctors were threatened that they would lose their licenses if more of their patients did not heal faster; imagine if public defense attorneys were told their bar memberships would expire without more acquittals. Many experienced teachers now deemed unqualified may question whether the law has them in mind; ask others if test preparation is a good use of instructional time or resources. That the Secretary of Education can state the law responds to the best interests of teachers speaks to a time when "clear skies" describes an environmental policy that increases air pollution and "compassionate conservatism," is the stated philosophy of the Bush administration.

In this context, the slogan "No Child Left Behind" is misleading. I describes and justifies punitive, anti-educator policies driven by high-stakes testing and market ideology. In this context of public education, where the rhetoric behind policies is loaded with double meanings, defining the terms of our argument is essential. And while much of the current imprecision with language comes from the Bush administration, it is important to note that policies such as high-stakes testing, a focus on basic skills, and increased accountability would likely have arisen under a different administration. The policy is a cornerstone of the Bush administration, however, and its success, failure, and ideology can fairly be attributed to its sponsor. An example of why the law is misleading comes from the source of its slogan. Although "No Child Left Behind" and "Leave No Child Behind," a slogan of the progressive Children's Defense Fund, might seem synonymous, in fact the philosophies of the Department of Education under President Bush and the Children's Defense Fund are diametrically opposed. Below find on-line mission statements from the two organizations' websites:

> The *No Child Left Behind Act of 2001 (No Child Left Behind)* is a landmark in education reform designed to improve student achievement and change the culture of America's schools. President

George W. Bush describes this law as the "cornerstone of my administration." ... In amending *ESEA*, the new law represents a sweeping overhaul of federal efforts to support elementary and secondary education in the United States. It is built on four common-sense pillars: accountability for results; an emphasis on doing what works based on scientific research; expanded parental options; and expanded local control and flexibility.[17]

The mission of the Children's Defense Fund (CDF) is to *Leave No Child Behind*® and to ensure every child a Healthy Start, a Head Start, a Fair Start, a Safe Start, and a Moral Start in life and success-ful passage to adulthood with the help of caring families and com-munities. CDF provides a strong, effective voice for all the children of America who cannot vote, lobby, or speak for themselves. We pay particular attention to the needs of poor and minority children and those with disabilities. CDF educates the nation about the needs of children and encourages preventive investment before they get sick or into trouble, drop out of school, or suffer family breakdown.[18]

The last sentence of the CDF statement is especially salient, as the goal of public education ought to include a *priority* to educate the nation's neediest, yet some of the conditions that contribute to the behaviors men-tioned are so far unaddressed in NCLB. To be sure, the organizations are not perfectly analogous, but the contrast is stark: the Bush administration has and continues to try to cut programs—i.e., Head Start, Healthy Start—upon which the mission of the Children's Defense Fund rests. It is this vision for education—one that operates in isolation, rather than as a part of a comprehensive vision—that needs to be questioned. It is easy to argue that the achievement gap is an unjust and perennial challenge, but the real challenge is finding and implementing a comprehensive strategy to address it. Unlike the sweeping generalizations and faith-in-test scores shown by advocates of NCLB, we need to dig more deeply than what hap-pens once students are in schools and classrooms to root out the causes of underachievement. In the words of Ken Zeichner,

> In the end, the achievement gap in U.S. public schooling is largely a reflection of the other gaps that exist in the larger society, and although schooling and teacher education can play a role in lessening these inequalities, they must be viewed as only one aspect of a more comprehensive plan for the equalization of outcomes in the society.[17]

Given the unrealized goal of imagining a society without inequalities, and schools without achievement gaps, the need to argue for a more just distribution of resources is acute. The second way to conceptualize teacher education for social justice emanates from the framework of distributive justice.

Defining Distributive Justice

Although elements of the earlier, dictionary definition of justice broadly relate to education, John Rawls's theory of distributive justice merits further discussion. As cited by two scholars of social justice in schools, Bob Connell and Walter Parker, the definition and purpose of distributive justice begin to take shape. Citing the British sociologist L. T. Hobhouse, writing in 1922, Connell offers that the role of institutions can be good only if they serve a common good.

> Acts and institutions are good not because they suit a majority, but because they make the nearest possible approach to a good shared by every single person whom they affect.[18]

This statement illustrates just how far the United States has to go to achieve distributive justice. We need only to look at the recent series of tax cuts as an example of current challenges; the cuts did, and will continue to benefit the wealthiest citizens, not "every single person whom they affect." Were the latter to be true, not only would the cuts have been distributed more fairly, but they also would not have come at the expense of public service programs and infrastructure. In fact, they have led to concomitant increases in state and local taxes needed to offset losses of federal monies. Thus, the concept of distributive justice, while invisible under the Bush administration, must reemerge within a framework of teacher education for social justice. Programs and policies that reduce students to test-scores, and reduce teachers to technicians, do not at their core represent the good for "every single person whom they affect."

Furthering this commitment to just distribution, Walter Parker cites Rawls directly, using an apt metaphor to graphically explain the concept:

> Rawls uses the example of cutting cake to illustrate reversibility at work. The just citizen who is put in the role of cake cutter would cut it knowing that he or she would ask another person to distribute the pieces, thus placing himself or herself on the receiving end of any indiscretions in the cutting. Knowing that the distribution of pieces of cakes would be blind, it makes no sense to be anything but scrupulously fair in the cutting.[19]

Using a Rawlsian analysis of distributive justice, public education can be seen as a zero-sum game in which all students and educators are considered, or not. Extending this notion, federal policies either consider all students as citizens worth an equal slice of the cake, or not. While few would argue overtly that market-driven educational initiatives and NCLB lie on the zero side, given that public schools are filled with hungry students, the cake needs to be cut by those who see public schools—and the monies they generate—as the right of all students. Given some provisions of NCLB, it is likely that schools will continue to resegregate by race and class.

The idea of vouchers as an educational panacea provides an example of why NCLB is ethically flawed in terms of distributive justice. The idea that those with the least will get even less, as public schools increasingly lose funding, may run contrary to commonly held ideas about equality and justice, but is defended as economically and educationally imperative. But counterarguments from teachers and scholars are routinely dismissed by those who seek to deregulate and privatize education. For example, Frederick Hess, a resident scholar at the *American Enterprise Institute*, argues "the case for being mean," to defend sanctions against those resistant to full compliance with the mandates of the law. Even his seemingly rational arguments reek of anti-educator sentiment and wishful thinking. For example, in *Educational Leadership*, a field journal delivered to thousands of educators each month, he proposes that policy makers actually dismiss the contributions of teachers:

> We will not force painful improvement by convincing those who bear the costs of change that it really is a good idea. *We must leave them no choice in the matter.* [emphasis mine] It's not just a question of making people work harder; it's about forcing managers and leaders to rethink systems and practices....Today, district and school leaders spend their time pleading with their subordinates to cooperate because they can imagine no other ways to drive change. They are mistaken. We can drive change by requiring educators to meet clear performance goals and attaching consequences to success or failure.[20]

Thus, he proposes leaving no child behind by leaving out teachers. It would be hard to imagine a more divisive and misguided assessment of teachers' professionalism, one that takes victim-blaming ideology to new craven depths. Not only does it slap teachers in their collective faces for daring to think they may know what's best for their students, but it also assumes that ongoing professional development and renewal, often in the service of change and accountability, are nothing more than "pleading with subordinates." While Hess is correct in that change can be hard for schools and districts to implement quickly, change in education is neither impossible nor dismissed. For example, several years ago, the best-selling book, *Who Moved My Cheese?* was distributed to teachers in New Jersey as part of their professional development activities, of which they need to complete 100 hours every five years. The seven strands for change, as outlined in the book under the ominous subheading "The Handwriting on the Wall," included "Change Happens," "Anticipate Change," "Monitor Change," "Adapt to Change Quickly," "Change," "Enjoy Change," and "Be Ready to Quickly Change Again and Again."[21] While pithy, these strands speak to the creativity of educators in terms of professional development, and indeed to the acknowledgment that change is inevitable, hardly reflective of a profession unwilling to "rethink systems and practices." The purpose of the book, and the professional development activities it engendered, was to prepare teachers for change by involving them in the process.

Further, busying teachers with testing and credentialing requirements inhibits the very types of useful professional development—i.e., content integration, differentiated instruction—that would more likely lead to socially just teaching. Teacher educators must now do two things simultaneously: they must prepare teachers to be ethical, critical thinkers; and also prepare them for a high-stakes testing environment.

Notwithstanding the history of private, or independent schools, whose presence, cost, and exclusivity testify to the bald influence of wealth upon educational opportunity, we argue that public education is a common and public good. An educated public does not benefit only the individuals educated, but also society, as lowered crime rates, safer streets, improved communication, social harmony, and civic participation contribute to a richer and safer democracy. One key to enacting social justice in teacher education may well be the extent to which community spirit and caring for the other takes root. We argue that it is possible for citizens both to act in their own self-interest and to support equitable distributions of wealth and education, using what educator Diane Goodman calls "interdependent self-interest." Her example of affirmative action identifies some of the benefits:

> White men (or women) may support affirmative action, even though in the short run it reduces the likelihood that they themselves would be hired. They support a practice they feel will lead to the kind of world they want to live in—one with great equity and

the inclusion of important talents and voices that have been discounted. Thus, for all to get educated would seem to be in the public interest, as well as in individuals' interest; it would be more just to distribute education equally and with respect to all affected.[22]

Goodman's optimism belies a public disaffected with perceived-entitlement programs and seemingly receptive to contracting expenditures on education by reversing programs designed to improve access for "important talents and voices that have been discounted." Some questions about education that would help to clarify both current realities and proposed solutions include: Who gets to attend school, and under what circumstances? Who gets to be a teacher at the school? Who gets to teach teachers at the college or university? Which teacher educators does the government hear?

Problematizing Teacher Education for Social Justice

Marilyn Cochran-Smith conceptualizes teacher education for social justice as both a learning problem and a political problem. In terms of a learning problem, she argues that the complexity of learning communities makes inquiry a critical component, arguing,

> Teacher education occurs in the context of inquiry communities wherein everybody is a learner and a researcher; inquiry is an intellectual and political stance rather than a project or time-bounded activity; and, as part of an inquiry stance, teacher research is a way to generate local knowledge of practice that is contextualized, cultural, and critical.[22]

While the staid empiricism of NCLB suggests that highly qualified teachers in all schools who were themselves well prepared will eventually teach all students to meet high standards, the complexity of learning communities is conspicuously absent from the code. NCLB, and the market ideology that supports it, assumes and publicizes that there are simple solutions—test first, and reward or punish later—to extremely complex challenges, and none relate to the importance of inquiry in schools and classrooms.

Many educators consider this demographic shift of the public school population a clarion call for social justice. In the words of Marilyn Cochran-Smith, "The phrase 'the demographic imperative' has been used to draw the conclusion—increasingly inescapable—that the educational community must take action in order to alter the disparities deeply embedded in the American educational system."[23] Notwithstanding that the imperative of the changing demographics of the United States is seen by some less sympathetic as a different kind of problem, the responsibilities of living in a social and political democracy compel teacher educators to maintain focus on concerns about social justice.

While current educational policies paint teachers as apolitical automatons who need to produce higher test scores with standardized curriculum and yearly measures of adequate progress, the inherent political nature of teaching and learning is irrepressible. To discuss the political problems of education, then, is to argue for a more complex view, one that situates teachers and teacher educators as stewards of American democracy. Cochran-Smith writes:

> When teacher education is regarded as a political problem, the critical roles of teaching and teacher education are brought into sharp relief. Democratic societies depend for their existence upon a thoughtful citizenry that believes in democratic ideals and is willing and able to participate in the civic life of the nation....If all free and equal citizens of a society are to have the benefit of a democratic education, all teachers must have the knowledge, skills, and dispositions to teach toward the democratic ideal. In particular, in today's rapidly changing and increasingly diverse society, all teachers need knowledge of the social and cultural contexts that shape education as well as knowledge of the role of culture and language in mediating learning.[24]

With the current narrowing of curriculum, the promotion of test scores as the sole indicator of academic progress and success, and the dismissal of the views of teachers and teacher educators, it is hard to see the "critical roles of teaching and teacher education" in NCLB.

No Child Left Behind: Social Justice or Pedagogical Slavery?

As part of a critique of the push for the market model for public schools, one of the contributors of this volume, Penny Earley, elucidates the contradiction in terms:

> A market policy lens is based on competition, choice, winners and losers, and finding culprits. Yet teachers must assume that all children can learn, so there cannot be winners and losers. Market policies applied to public education are at odds with collaboration and cooperative approaches to teaching and learning.[25]

As logical as this statement is for educators, and as much as it calls into question much of the rationale behind NCLB, educators cannot ignore NCLB or its implications for public schools and teacher education. In using static measures to test dynamic processes of learning, however, the law simplifies and quantifies the country's civic and ethical commitment to the institution of public schooling and the students therein, as well as the dignity and professionalism of teachers. But NCLB proponents wrap themselves around the mantle of social justice as well, defending that to test to hold accountable the inhabitants of public schools is to promote excellence for all. They insist that testing will ensure compliance and eventual success, while threatening financial penalties for not complying with massive, high-stakes testing and bureaucratic ratings.

Early results show some states scrambling to meet requirements, yet others are suing to ease restrictions and even opting out of needed federal dollars, rather than capitulate. As the administration plies its "case for being mean," which has both reactionary and innovative results, both capitulation and resistance surface in response. But even capitulation may have unpredictable results, however, as resistant teachers are "forced" to model for students and parents how to educate for social justice during trying times.

The argument that testing ensures compliance and leads to improvement in the form of choice is both persuasive and pernicious. It is persuasive because U.S. citizens seem to both understand and accept market logic. If a Burger King restaurant is located next to a McDonald's restaurant, customers have the opportunity to choose. As an economic model, this makes sense; and, to those unfamiliar with the complicated nuances of education, it is also persuasive. It is also pernicious, however, because it risks a social Darwinian result, engenders a survival of the fittest mentality, and ensures that schools in which students and families and teachers are unable to raise test scores high enough will be further penalized; those with the least will continue to get the least. Notwithstanding the extent to which this market approach to public schools may make some degree of economic sense, it is civically and ethically unjust and may spell the beginning of the end of public schooling in the United States. Those students and teachers that can't swim or float to the top—due in part to societal inequalities out of their control—will sink more deeply. Because the threat of losing federal dollars weighs more heavily in schools and districts that have the neediest students, and thus the most Title I funds to lose, these programs are, perversely, most at risk.

Another fundamental problem with applying the market model to education is that students are not proverbial widgets or interchangeable, identical parts. The combination of human development, psychology, and micro- and macro-factors in education combine to create a complicated, yet ultimately edifying human endeavor. Teachers and students are subjects, not objects of human history. Teaching is not neutral, and just as one cannot, in the words of Howard Zinn, be "neutral on a moving train," one teaches for or against the status quo.[26] Given the clear history of high-stakes testing resulting in oppression for some and privilege for others, it behooves us to question the logic behind it now.

A dramatic historical comparison may help us to understand the possibility that the logic behind NCLB as a just law will be discredited by history. Many laws and customs that seemed to make sense at the time, were in fact wrong and unjust. For example, the odiousness of slavery is now undisputed, yet during its mendacious duration, it was defended as necessary, inevitable, the "white man's burden." Now, however, the scourge of American slavery is an example of metaphor, history, divisive social issue, or historical injustice, but not of social justice. During slavery, the education of slaves was forbidden, or limited to learning Scripture, or in some cases surreptitious or illegal, but many taught slaves anyway. Was it more socially just to break the law, thereby overriding the racist injustice of slavery? Lynching and miscegenation laws and customs were not only tacitly accepted but also privately and at times publicly condoned by those individuals—police, courts, and Congress—charged with keeping public safety and enforcing justice. In these cases it is not difficult to remember or imagine descriptions and indeed understandings of social justice being enshrouded in divisive rhetoric and handy simplifications.

Now, divisive rhetoric is more readily applied to social and educational challenges. For example, bilingual education was virtually eliminated in California, by a proposition called "English for the Children"; affirmative action, by the "California Civil Rights Initiative"; and now, the privatization of public education is reduced to "No Child Left Behind." In fact, the logic behind high-stakes testing and the penalties that follow it remind us of the logic used to maximize slaves' productivity: make the most productive day's crop the lowest acceptable amount, then expect them to be able to achieve that every day/cultivate that crop/maintain those scores, or else!

In the Nat Turner or Martin Luther King Jr. sense of social justice, where divine law supersedes civil law, education for social justice has long operated under the radar of official acceptance. That is, teachers and teacher educators have long grappled with issues of social justice because of their commitments to the liberatory possibilities of schooling. Now, given the virtual absence of democratic and socially just issues in federal education forums, education for social justice continues, for now, not only somewhat under the radar, but also in direct conflict with the high-stakes testing environment. That is, the policy framework with which teachers now need to comply focuses on "basic subjects," and is not concerned with issues of social justice, democracy, or equity.

Autonomy and Trust within Teaching and Teacher Education

One of the most attractive attributes of the teaching profession is the degree of autonomy afforded teachers; underlying autonomy is trust. Both are essential to effective teaching and learning, and to teacher education.

> What is the significance of trust as a condition of the development of professional accountability? Trust is a relational condition between individuals. It has an outside, where formal systems and client individuals are linked through effective role holders, and an inside, where professional relationships become personalized.[27]

In *The Moral Base of Teacher Professionalism*, Hugh Sockett reminds us of the importance of trust in teacher education. One of the things that distinguishes the profession is the amount of trust and autonomy afforded educators, but unfortunately, under the regulations of NCLB, the feeling of mistrust seems more common. This is true in the larger society as well, as random and summary detainment and surveillance, once the purview of Orwellian nightmares and Cold War aversion, are now more common. Whether through massive fingerprinting or ethnic profiling, the assumption of innocence for some of the most vulnerable citizens of the United States has gone the way of the Twin Towers. Fear and xenophobia have taken a hold on the American psyche, making plain the need for education for social justice teaching in order to renew optimism and minimize fear. Teachers still have significant autonomy in the classroom, but increasingly, teachers' roles are conceptualized as technicians, examiners, or replaceable parts. How can teachers trust a system that now tells them that, irrespective of their successful years' teaching, that they may be unqualified?

Following trust, the autonomy of teaching oxygenizes a profession with modest monetary compensation. The mistrust behind the assumption that teachers do not work hard enough offends many educators, and prerequisites to teachers working efficiently must include trust and respect; that is, parents, administrators, and the public need to trust that teachers are both qualified and committed, and they must respect the difficulty of the job, which, despite policy statements to the contrary, includes content and pedagogical expertise as well as what Lee Shulman calls pedagogical content knowledge: the melding of content and pedagogy and the specific skill set required of teachers to do both well.[28] But no amount of teacher improvement and professionalization will minimize the impact political ideology has on the field of teacher education, and given the climate of education reform in the early Twenty-First Century, it behooves us to understand the underlying ideals and agendas. Marilyn Cochran-Smith offers this caveat:

> Unless underlying ideals, ideologies, and values are debated along with and in relation to "the evidence" about teacher quality and unless we examine the discourse of teacher education policy reform, we will make little progress in understanding the politics of teacher education and the nuances and complexities of the various reform agendas that are currently in competition with one another. We will certainly make little progress in understanding the larger project of teaching and teacher education for social justice.[29]

Educator morale may depend upon perceptions of trust and respect and therefore resonate loudly in teaching and teacher education. By implying that test scores and symbolic/analytical ability are the sole valid indicators of teacher competency, critics of public education undermine the very foundation of pedagogy, the art and science of teaching. And, while groups such as National Education Association, the American Association of Colleges for Teacher Education, and the National Network for Educational Renewal work vigorously to counter such reductions, the fact that millions of educators now need to defend themselves speaks to the current crisis of faith in teachers. Teaching is neither simple nor universal, and those of us in teacher education need to convey the complexity and nonuniversality of the profession.

There is a reason, for example, that many artists cannot teach art, or that many novelists cannot teach writing; professional expertise helps but does not always translate into effective pedagogy. Beyond the admission that teaching is a skill lies the understanding that expertise in the content of one's subject is both essential and developmental, and that this content expertise is not static, but is represented and nurtured by lifelong learning that does not stop when the Department of Education decides the teacher is "highly qualified." The charge of lifelong learning, the need to constantly adapt content and pedagogy, and the ongoing moral responsibilities of teachers do not end with the achievement of "highly qualified teacher" status, but through years of study, teaching experience, and renewal. The popular archetypes of the erudite, all-knowing professor, like John Houseman in the television show *The Paper Chase* or of the expert,

boundless English teacher, like Robin Williams in the film *Dead Poets'*
Society are rare in the vast field of education, and they do not represent
most teachers, but they do represent possibilities. Conversely, other depic-
tions of teachers, such as those in the films *Dangerous Minds* and *Stand by*
Me present individual teachers as saviors rather than stewards. Like other
professions, teaching has its exceptional stars and failures, but most lie in
the middle. While some teachers burn out and lie like deadwood in a
pond, most serve ethically, selflessly, and anonymously for many years.
Just as it would be ludicrous to malign all doctors for the indiscretions of a
few, NCLB irrationally subjects all teachers to punitive regulation for some
schools' underperformance. Further, some of the reasons for the underperformance have little to do with teaching, but with social injustice.

Teacher Education as a Site for Social Justice

Schools continue to mirror the United States's struggle over its evolving
social consciousness. They continue to spawn and engage with battles over
contested issues that reflect constantly changing youth cultures and sociocultural litmus tests.

Two examples of schools at the forefront of social justice work include
the Civil Rights movement and the need to teach about the causes and
results of the 9/11 attacks. That the illegality of segregation was decided in
a school case speaks to the role of schools as sites for resolving social conflict; that 50 years after *Brown*, we still argue whether desegregation
improved or weakened the ability of African Americans to secure equal
opportunities speaks to the challenges still ahead. The challenge of how to
teach about 9/11 remains, as does, by extension, the challenge of how to
teach about cultures and people alien to most Americans. In the wake of
the awful destruction wrought on 9/11 many educators saw, in addition to
tragedy, unique and useful opportunities to learn about Afghanistan,
radical Islam, even Osama Bin Laden. For example, during the fall 2001
semester, a graduate student of mine created for his curriculum project a
proposal for a new advanced placement world history course. The proposal asked students to choose one of several research topics related to
concerns about terrorism, the roots of conflict in the Middle East and
Afghanistan, and the resurgence of global jihad. By the end of his social
studies course, the teacher had a sourcebook of information, produced
by students, which he distributed to the class to help prepare them for the
Advanced Placement exam.

Teacher education programs that embrace our imaginative and distributive definition of social justice would see this both as authentic learning—constructivist, engaged, and timely—and as a needed counter to the

critical impressions of Arabs and Muslims so prevalent in the media. Putting such opportunities into teacher education curricula—namely, to study differences, even during global conflicts ensuing in part from those differences—is one example of teacher education and professional development for social justice. We argue that such opportunities within curricula and assessment are integral, and turn now to two examples that exemplify such integration.

While conceptual understandings—teacher education for social justice as imaginative, distributive, and problematic—are crucial, equally important is the need for examples from the field. Although many teacher education programs claim some connection to diversity and social justice, often in the form of a state-mandated diversity course or other singular measure, fewer actually thread issues of social justice throughout their programs. This section will briefly examine two examples of teacher education programs, as described in books by leading teacher education scholars: Marilyn Cochran-Smith and Ana Maria Villegas and Tamara Lucas. The texts and the programs they describe will be introduced individually, followed by a synthesis of the common elements of each.

Although the examples used are described by visionaries in the field of teacher education, we argue that teacher educators at all levels need to infuse and institutionalize elements of social justice pedagogy. Still, focusing on well-recognized stewards for social justice provides both inspiration and vision for moving the social justice agenda forward. For two decades, Marilyn Cochran-Smith has argued that "the most important goals of teaching and teacher education are social responsibility, social change, and social justice,"[30] and during long tenures at the University of Pennsylvania and Boston College, Cochran-Smith established herself as one of the leading scholars of teacher education, particularly teacher education for diversity, democracy, and social justice. Significantly she has done this within the mainstream educational research community; at the time of this writing, she is president of the American Educational Research Association. In both her curricula and her concomitant riveting scholarship, Cochran-Smith lays out seven pedagogical principles of teaching for social justice: enabling significant work within communities of learners; building on what students bring to school with them—knowledge and interests, cultural and linguistic resources; teaching skills; bridging gaps; working with (not against) individuals, families, and communities; diversifying forms of assessment; and making inequity, power, and activism explicit parts of the curriculum.[31]

It is clear from this list that Cochran-Smith's critical perspective on teacher education for social justice challenges preservice teachers to expand their own lenses and proactively learn from their students. The discomfort and challenge that such expansion elicits recalls the earlier definition by Darling-Hammond: that teaching and learning for social justice will at times be uncomfortable, but that such discomfort is integral to progress. Similarly, Cochran-Smith uses herself as an example, courageously describing her imperfect pedagogy and the ways in which teacher education provides for her a lifelong learning challenge. As part of her descriptive analysis of one of her courses, and more specifically a student of color's questioning of her commitment to diverse perspectives, Cochran-Smith both accepts responsibility and defends how far she has come:

> [M]y lifelong membership in the privileged racial group has helped keep me blind about much of the impact of race...a White female teacher educator with a vision about the importance of making issues of race and diversity explicit parts of the preservice curriculum and in the process, grappling (sometimes blindly) with the tension, contradiction, difficulty, pain, and failure inherent in unlearning racism.[32]

Cochran-Smith suggests that it is not enough to thread readings, discussions, written assignments, and field placements centering on diversity and social justice throughout the teacher education curriculum. Teacher educators also need to start with our own lenses, diverse as we may think they are, in order to continually improve and better respond to our preservice teachers. As a white teacher educator, she is to be commended and followed for this type of ongoing self-critique; and, backed up by two decades of scholarship and academic leadership, she continues to be well-positioned to influence many others.

Cochran-Smith's commitment to, and success within, the field of teacher education is unimpeachable, but it is fair to point out that both the University of Pennsylvania and Boston College are private institutions. While the composition of the student bodies may or may not be significantly different at private colleges and universities from that at similarly prestigious public institutions, often the institutional support provided to students is richer in terms of financial aid, campus resources, and faculty attention. This is not to question the trailblazing and rippling effect Cochran-Smith's work continues to have on the field, including my own work, but rather, to problematize issues of entitlement and insularity that can magnify in a private setting. Similarly, much of the work of John Dewey, Vivian Paley, and, more recently, Linda Darling-Hammond, all influential teachers and scholars for social justice, may be seen in that vein. Would Paley have been able to write *White Teacher* within a public school setting? Would Dewey's Lab School have been possible? These are not cynical questions, but rather, ones that social justice critiques need to ask themselves. By way of comparison, it is useful to reflect upon a program infused with social justice, developed and implemented at a public state university.

At Montclair State University, Ana Maria Villegas and Tamara Lucas have developed an extensive framework for developing culturally responsive teachers which includes a major focus on teaching for social justice:

> We can prepare teachers to be agents of change by encouraging them to develop a personal vision and professional identity that incorporate a commitment to social justice. Once they recognize social injustice and structured inequalities in schools and are conscious of their own values with regard to social justice, prospective teachers can no longer assume an objective stance. They are forced to make a decision either to ignore social injustice (and therefore perpetuate it) or to actively work against it. If they have an ethical commitment to reducing injustice, teachers will be more likely to make the latter decision.[33]

In theory, once teachers decide (if they do) to "actively work against" social injustice, they can become advocates not only for their students, but mentors as well, modeling for them ways to work for social justice. It is hard to overestimate the importance of having a framework so explicit about fighting injustice. Notwithstanding the reality of devilish details, such paradigms serve to illuminate and help imagine possibilities and focus discussions around social justice. And, to the authors' credit, they explicitly address the challenges that such curricular transformation faces; that is, a framework for preparing socially just teachers is but one piece of a complicated, entrenched mosaic. In the final paragraph of their book, *Educating Culturally Responsive Teachers: A Coherent Approach*, Villegas and Lucas offer this cautionary coda:

> We are not so unrealistic as to believe that our schools can single-handedly change the inequities that are embedded throughout society far beyond the schoolhouse door. However, there is much that we can and must do, and the time to start is now. We as educators have an essential role to play—in the classroom, on the campus, in school districts, in the community, and in the political

process. Every small change that we make alters the overall configuration, but these changes have tended to take place in a piecemeal fashion.[34]

Part of the reason for change "in a piecemeal fashion" might reside in the marginality of teacher education, both within academe, and within the public debates surrounding education. To be sure, the "present demands and prescriptions" Greene alluded to in the introduction include a careful reexamination of the value and efficacy of university-based teacher education programs, not necessarily to improve them, but to open them up to market forces.

Further, the wars in Afghanistan and Iraq, combined with the policies and conduct of the executive branch in power during them, have made the policies of the federal government less open to critique and challenge. The importance of the golden rule—that is, to teach others with the same compassion and care one would want for his or her own children—is largely absent from educational policy discussions, let alone political discourse. While the Columbine incident galvanized the Department of Education to support affective and community building grants and projects like small learning communities, the fallout from the 9/11 attacks, combined with the strict regulations of NCLB, has served to narrow the possibilities for teachers and teacher educators by conformity and homogeneity, rather than inclusion and embracing of difference. The clear message is that test scores in reading and math matter more than compassion, political and social awareness, and teaching for social justice. Even more disturbing is the cooptation of language such that now, in the United States, basic constitutional rights are sacrificed in the name of justice. This caveat is not meant to minimize the extent to which teaching for social justice is important or successful, but rather, that it cannot be divorced from the societal context. Given this limit-situation, however, we can identify conditions necessary for social justice pedagogy to emerge and thrive in schools, universities, and communities.

Conditions Enabling Teacher Education for Social Justice

Below is a list of six conditions, or proposed plans of action, which, taken together, would reseed the notions of equity and social justice throughout teacher education. They are meant to be neither exhaustive nor summative, but suggestive, and can and should be undertaken independent of one another; that is, some conditions might be easier to address for certain sites, others less so, but doubtless by engaging in dialogue around these issues and concerns, teachers and teacher educators can move forward our commitment to social justice.

Defining terms and understanding the challenge

Unsurprisingly, educators can be defensive when we are told that things are unacceptable, and that our practices, rather than widespread inequality, poverty, or regressive taxes, contribute to social inequality and injustice. Advocates for social justice need to redefine the terms of the argument, and to focus attention on structural as well as individual inequality. Just as Goals 2000 and NCLB use lofty, even unattainable goals—100 percent proficiency, for example—to structure and focus energies, so too must teacher educators set goals and benchmarks to both underscore successes and codify teaching and teacher education for social justice. For example, requiring students to complete community service projects is harder to accomplish when everyone is stressed about test scores that do not seem to relate to the service. Perhaps infusing affective components into high-stakes exams would allow schools to prepare students to both live and to test well.

Reinforcing the potential of schools to promote social justice

Throughout the history of the United States, public schools have served as a beacon, leading the country in its navigation, understanding, and amelioration of crucial social issues such as desegregation of schools, integration of curriculum, and now, the presence and rights of alternative families and students, commonly referred to as Gay, Lesbian, Bisexual, and Transgendered youth and families, or GLBT. This fact that schools are often where the country's social mettle is tested is both important and dangerous. It is important because it underscores the potential of schools to lead struggles for social justice; it is dangerous because if we do not fight this dilution now, it will ossify into the consciousness around the purpose of public schooling.

Promotion and emulation of successful programs

Although specifics of time, place, and personnel make teacher education programs for social justice difficult to replicate exactly, models such as those proposed and enacted by Cochran-Smith and Villegas and Lucas illuminate possibilities and countenance the exclusive attention on high-stakes testing and teaching basic skills. Teaching is an affective profession; if we are to learn from what has been tried already, we need models and suggestions, as well as understandings.

Dealing proactively with fear

It is impossible to deny that fear has struck the American psyche in awesome and unprecedented ways. Just as many teachers were told to allow, if not enable, their students to talk about the 9/11 attacks and their fears stemming from them, teachers and teacher educators need to be able to express both their grief and remorse for what a climate of fear does to our schools and ourselves. The country is at war in multiple locations, and there is no sense of when this wartime state might ebb. Using mindfulness rather than denial, both in teaching and in the preparation of teachers, we can approach and ameliorate more easily than if we pretend that this too shall pass. For example, by teaching about other cultures and by infusing teacher preparation with diversity and social justice strands, we can better prepare our preservice teachers to supplant fear with hope.

Increase the globalization of American curricula

This chapter began with a section on the power of teacher education for social justice, to imagine and to seek new solutions to old problems, and to empathize with those different from ourselves. Our teacher education curriculum must encourage and demand that teachers internationalize their pedagogy, beginning with themselves and their lenses, lenses colored by years of living and working within the world's now-sole superpower. Going more deeply than geopolitical awareness, however, teaching needs to be seen as a profession charged with helping students. And teacher education, with helping preservice teachers develop emerging and alternative perspectives, cognizant of context, and with a eye toward imagining better futures, not toward reducing the world to the good guys versus the bad guys.

Organize social justice advocates at the federal, state, and local levels to support and defend public schools, teachers, and teacher education programs

There is a dangerous fiction afloat from critics of university teacher preparation that anyone with subject area expertise and good verbal ability can teach, and that the programs charged with preparing our nation's teachers have monopolized and hijacked the "market" of teacher education. This notion needs to be understood, addressed, and exploded. What if the American Medical Association were told it was a terrorist group because its doctors refused to provide only abstinence-only sex advice to minors? Teachers and teacher education programs need to constantly improve, to forge new connections, and to reevaluate, but this change can and must come from within.

Conclusion

This chapter has presented the imperative of teaching and teacher education for social justice in a broad context. Beginning with the value of creative and visionary thinking, continuing with the importance of defining terms and marshalling critiques, and ending with a brief description of two programs, I have argued that to teach and educate teachers for social justice at the beginning of the Twenty-First Century is to continue to fight an uphill battle. Headlines that ascertain that the nation is polarized feed an insatiable media appetite for conflict and controversy. While adults and minors alike are punished and censored for cavalier use of language in creative writing and letters to the editor the nation's most powerful educator can label teachers terrorists with no reprimand from the president, let alone censure or dismissal. In many ways, it is a dismal time to work in schools and education, but for some of us, including the distinguished contributors to this volume, there is no choice but to fight for what we believe—educationally, pedagogically, politically, and artistically. As Villegas and Lucas remind us, "every small change" matters, even if, in a sea of military might and prescriptive education laws, our changes amount only to life-preserving rafts. For the good of our students, and indeed our country, we must stay afloat.

Notes

1. Maxine Greene, *The Dialectic of Freedom* (New York: Teachers College Press, 1988), 14.
2. Jonathan Kozol, *Savage Inequalities* (New York: HarperPerennial, 1992).
3. Ibid.
4. Retrieved from www.lausd.k12.ca.us/announcements/Figure_2.pdf.
5. Retrieved from www.bigclassaction.com/class_action/beverlyhills.html.
6. *Beverly Hills 90210* was a popular drama during 1990–2000.
7. Diane J. Goodman, "Motivating People from Privileged Groups to Support Social Justice," *Teachers College Record* 102, no. 6 (2000): 1061–85.
8. Pedro Noguera, *City Schools and the American Dream* (New York: Teachers College Press, 2004).
9. Kenneth M. Zeichner, "The Adequacies and Inadequacies of Three Current Strategies to Recruit, Prepare, and Retain the Best Teachers for All Students," *Teachers College Record* 105, no. 3 (2003): 490–519.
10. John Rawls, *A Theory of Justice* (Cambridge: Harvard University Press, 1999).
11. Marilyn Cochran-Smith, *Walking the Road: Race, Diversity, and Social Justice in Teacher Education* (New York: Teachers College Press, 2004).
12. Maxine Greene Preface: in Ayers, Hunt, and Quinn, *Teaching for Social Justice* (New York: Teachers College Press, 1998), p. xxix.
13. Linda Darling-Hammond, Jennifer French, and Silvia Paloma Garcia-Lopez, *Learning to Teach for Social Justice* (New York: Teachers College Press, 2002), 201.
14. Greene, in Ayers, Hunt, and Quinn, 1998, xxix.

15. Zeichner, 511.
16. Roderick Paige, *No Child Left Behind Fact Sheet* (Washington, DC: U.S. Department of Education, 2002).
17. Zeichner, 514.
18. L. T. Hobhouse, cited in R. W. Connell, *Schools and Social Justice* (Philadelphia: Temple University Press, 1993), 16.
19. Walter Parker, *Teaching Democracy: Unity and Diversity in Public Life* (New York: Teachers College Press, 2003), 65.
20. Frederick M. Hess, "The Case for Being Mean," *Educational Leadership* 61, no. 3 (2003): 22–26.
21. Spencer Johnson, *Who moved my Cheese?* (New York: Putnam, 1998).
22. Marilyn Cochran-Smith, *Walking the Road: Race, Diversity, and Social Justice in Teacher Education* (New York: Teachers College Press, 2004), 12.
23. Cochran-Smith.
24. Cochran-Smith, 21–22.
25. Earley, p. 174, in Cochran-Smith, *Walking the Road*.
26. Howard Zinn, *You Can't Be Neutral on a Moving Train* (Boston: Beacon Press, 1993).
27. Hugh Sockett, *The Moral Base for Teacher Professionalism* (New York: Teachers College Press, 1993), 65.
28. Parker, 179.
29. Cochran-Smith, 139.
30. Cochran-Smith, 64.
31. Cochran-Smith, 66–77.
32. Cochran-Smith, 88.
33. Ana Maria, Villegas, and Tamara Lucas, *Educating Culturally Responsive Teachers: A Coherent Approach* (New York: SUNY Press), 60–61.
34. Villegas and Lucas, 201.

CHAPTER 3

Searching for the Common Good in Federal Policy: The Missing Essence in NCLB and HEA, Title II

PENELOPE M. EARLEY

The Constitution of the United States charges the federal government with providing for the general welfare of its citizens and grants the tools to do so to its judicial, legislative, and executive branches. Although the Constitution does not mention education, the General Welfare Clause (Art. I, sec. 8) allows the federal government to collect taxes and spend the resulting revenue on programs that are in the public interest. As Alexander and Alexander point out, the tools of taxation, budget development, and appropriation of funds have been used by members of Congress and the President to expand federal authority into a variety of areas not enumerated in the Constitution itself.[1]

In this manner, from the 1950s to the present a federal presence in education has evolved to the point where many of the large programs administered through the U.S. Department of Education now are a permanent and commonly accepted part of the policy landscape. Thus, on the surface it would appear that the federal government's commitment to promoting the nation's general welfare and assuring the rights of all children through education policy directives is deep, far reaching, and includes at its core a commitment to equity: Children with disabilities are assured the right to a free, appropriate, public education; no student may be denied a public education due to race; federally-supported programs are available for English language learners; schools serving low income populations receive targeted federal assistance; and children from families in poverty are provided free or reduced school meals. However, things are not always what they seem and when recent federal legislation is analyzed the collective benefits of schooling become less prominent and a more individualistic, market-focused approach to education policy emerges.

In this chapter the connection between general welfare, social justice, and public education is considered. Then, drawing upon writings of Peter Cookson, David Labaree, and Marilyn Cochran-Smith, relevant federal laws and pending Senate and House of Representative bills are evaluated.[2] This critique is guided by three questions: (1) What is the role of the national government in linking common good and social justice within the framework of public education? (2) What are the implications for public schools when the federal government engages in decisions that ignore social justice and democratic equality? And (3) in what way is current education policy promoting or subverting education goals grounded in civic participation and social justice? Following that analysis revisions that offer a social justice obligation are offered to purposes and provisions in the 1998 Higher Education Amendments, No Child Left Behind Act, and pending bills to revise Title II of the Higher Education Act. The chapter concludes with suggestions for education activists who share a desire to redirect governments' current approach to school transformation.

Government, Justice, Democracy, and Education

When Chief Justice Earl Warren crafted the 1954 decision in *Brown v. Board of Education* he wrote "Compulsory school attendance laws and the great expenditures for education both demonstrate our recognition of the importance of education to our democratic society. It is required in the performance of our most basic public responsibilities, even service in the armed forces. It is the very foundation of good citizenship."[3] Fifty years later a very persuasive form of the same argument—that government's power to tax and spend—is connected to civic responsibility emerged in a New York supreme court decision. Although states and localities are the primary funding source for public education, national policy has a disproportionate influence on local schools, thus this chapter focuses deliberately on the actions of the federal government. However, at this point a small detour is taken to look at how this particular state court case further illustrates the relationship between government's allocation of funds and the purpose of education.

The issues being litigated were funding levels for, and finance equalization between, public school districts. Plaintiffs, represented by the Campaign for Fiscal Equity, sued the state of New York over lack of sufficient and equal funding for schools in the state. The case was ultimately narrowed to focus on the needs of New York City and was decided in favor of the plaintiffs. One of the arguments put forward by the plaintiffs, was that receiving a basic education defined by the state as achieving only low levels of literacy, mathematics computation, and the like was not sufficient for a publicly supported school system. The court rejected the state's definition of basic education and instead accepted the argument advanced by the Campaign for Fiscal Equity that schools have an obligation "to provide students with the opportunity to acquire the skills and knowledge necessary to become productive citizens capable of civic engagement and sustaining competitive employment."[4] Michelli (this volume) contends that the Campaign for Fiscal Equity's definition does not go far enough because it implies that democratic responsibility only extends to individuals who already are U.S. citizens. His caveat is noted but it remains of interest to observe how the New York court's action echoes the 50-year-old writings of Chief Justice Warren. Although the wording of the New York case does not have the power of the Brown decision, it helps build the case that the public funding of elementary and secondary education may be characterized as representing an agreement between taxpayers and government, and the essence of that agreement is that schools must do more than provide rudimentary literacy training needed for a minimum wage job. Instead, a loftier goal is expected: preparing students to be responsible community members.

Peter Cookson makes the essential connection between government funding for schools, general welfare, and social justice by arguing that "[f]ree and universal public education is part of the social contract that citizens make with one another to protect children and ensure that successive generations of citizens have a deep and abiding commitment to democracy. There is no escape clause in the social contract."[5] But the reality of political life is not always as Cookson might envision. Although students may leave schools with a measure of civic engagement skills, that alone does not mean they will have a deep understanding of the connection between democracy and social justice. In a society, like the United States, market forces are very powerful and individuals are rewarded for promoting self-interest over the community or common good. Deborah Stone brings this problem into sharp focus with the observation that "the market model of society envisions societal welfare as the aggregate of individuals' situations. All behavior is explained as people striving to maximize their own self-interest. The market model therefore gives us no way to talk about how people fight over visions of the public interest or the nature of the community—the truly significant political questions underlying policy choices."[6] Clearly the U.S. Constitution and the form of government it establishes create a paradox: the expectation that government will provide for the nation's collective general welfare while at the same time protecting each person's individual rights.

David Labaree offers a useful framework to consider the education system's dilemma of how to balance the constitutional guarantees of individual rights and the general welfare or common good.[7] He suggests that squabbles about how to fix schools miss the key point. He believes that, for the most part, educators and citizens have a solid grasp on what needs to be done to make schools better, the problem is fundamental disagreement about "what goals schools should pursue." Labaree identifies three competing aspirations for public education: democratic equality, social efficiency, and social mobility. In the same vein as arguments put forward by the Campaign for Fiscal Equity and Cookson, Labaree defines democratic equality as how society "prepares all of its young with equal care to take on the full responsibilities of citizenship in a competent manner."[8] The goal of social efficiency assumes that schools will educate children for the purpose of gaining needed credentials to sustain the nation's economy. Both democratic equality and social efficiency, according to Labaree, are *public* goods "where benefits are enjoyed by all the members of the community whether or not they actually contributed to the production of this good." Social mobility, on the other hand, assumes that "education is a commodity, the only purpose of which is to provide individual students with a competitive advantage in the struggle for desirable social positions."[9] Social mobility is aligned with personal opportunity and as such is a *private* goal. It is the extreme of the market model described by Stone in which individuals are attempting to maximize their own self-interest with no concern for the needs of the broader community.[10] When social mobility is the purpose of education, general welfare becomes no more than a compilation of what individuals want for themselves. Labaree asserts that the three competing goals of democratic equality, social efficiency, and social mobility should always be present but warns that at times one may become significantly stronger than the others, placing their essential tension in a state of imbalance.

Moving from a broad consideration of constitutional intent and conflicting national goals, Marilyn Cochran-Smith explores the nexus of social responsibility as a political construct and how this affects the daily work of teachers. She rejects the idea that assimilating children into the prevailing culture and values is the essence of preparing them to live in a democratic society.[11] Promoting social justice is infinitely complex, she argues, and it requires thinking in new ways about the role of teachers and how they are prepared. Her argument is organized around three key ideas: "teacher education occurs in the context of inquiry communities wherein everybody is a learner and a researcher; inquiry is an intellectual and political stance rather than a project of time-bounded activity; and, as part of an inquiry stance, teacher research is a way to generate local knowledge of practice that is contextualized, cultural, and critical."[12] Cochran-Smith's model puts into operation the link between publicly supported schools and sustaining the nation's general welfare by preparing thoughtful individuals capable of engaging in democratic practice.

Public schools are the bond that unites general welfare to democratic participation and to social justice. When the federal government passes education laws and supports them with public money drawn from tax revenue it is fulfilling an obligation to promote the general welfare. This social contract between citizens and government confirms that public schools are agents to offer, as a collective benefit to society, the knowledge and skills children and youth will need to participate in all aspects of self-government. Understanding civic responsibilities requires that individuals recognize that when society tacitly accepts inequality, it undermines and corrupts everyone's personal and collective rights. During a period in U.S. history when there is considerable discussion about exporting democratic values to other parts of the world, one might expect that this nation's domestic policy would be grounded in a construct of general welfare that promotes democratic equality. The analysis of federal legislation that follows tests this theory.

Goals Reflected in Federal Law and Pending Federal Education Legislation

The following analysis of federal-level attention to public schools and the quality of teaching that occurs in them begins with the passage of the Higher Education Amendments of 1998, known as the Higher Education Act (HEA).[13] It considers provisions in the No Child Left Behind (NCLB) law and examines amendments pending in the second session of the 108th Congress to reauthorize the teacher education provision in HEA. In 1998, Title II established new programs to encourage states to scrutinize their standards for teacher credentialing and imposed reporting requirements on both institutions of higher education and states. Section 207 and

Section 208 of HEA, not only include mandatory reporting requirements but also obligate institutions that prepare teachers to be ranked by their states according to the teacher licensure examination pass rate of their students. The purpose of the HEA, Title II programs is stated in Section 201 (a)(1)—(4): "to (1) improve student achievement; (2) improve the quality of the current and future teaching force by improving the preparation of perspective teachers and enhancing professional development activities; (3) hold institutions of higher education accountable for preparing teachers who have the necessary teaching skills and are highly competent in the academic content areas in which the teachers plan to teach, such as mathematics, science, English, foreign languages, history, economics, art, civics, Government, and geography, including training in the effective uses of technology in the classroom; and (4) recruit highly qualified individuals, including individuals from other occupations into the teaching force."[14] These legislative goals are ones associated with characteristics of individual teachers and individual institutions of higher education, and their premise is that promoting competition will improve teacher quality. The HEA, Title II legislation, and subsequent statute, expected that teacher preparation programs would improve once a system of institutional rankings based on teacher candidate pass rates was imposed. This is not a teacher enhancement measure. Rather, it is an example of compelling the education system to accept the private purpose of social mobility. Colleges and universities are encouraged to vie with one another using a faulty measure of worth (examination pass rates) and future teachers are sent the clear message that their value is set by their personal licensure examination score, not their work in the classroom. Moreover, HEA, Title II provisions are measures that focus on the individual institution of higher education and individual teacher and as such neither teacher preparation programs nor teachers, as part of their professional practice, are encouraged to create the inquiry communities described by Cochran-Smith.[15]

Improving student learning is an appropriate expectation for schools and evaluation of student work is a necessary part of the teaching and learning process. It is equally important to have measures in place to determine if teacher candidates have the necessary preparation to assume instructional responsibilities for children. The point of view reflected in HEA, Title II emphasizes the state licensure examination for teachers to the exclusion of other predictors of teacher success. The law then makes a conceptual leap to suggest that children taught by an individual from a college or university that reports a high candidate pass rate on the teacher licensure examination will out-perform children taught by teachers who attended a college or university with a lower licensure examination pass rate even if both educators hold the same teaching credential and had exactly the same score on the licensure exam. The HEA, Title II legislation is troublesome because of the untested assumption that an institution's teacher licensure pass rate has a causal connection to a *specific* teacher's influence on P–12 student performance. When policy focuses on high-stakes, competitive testing to the exclusion of other measures of success, the message is that public education's purpose is to give one individual a competitive edge over others. This social mobility purpose is somewhat nuanced in the HEA, Title II legislative language; however, it becomes much clearer in reports presenting the Title II pass rate data prepared by the U.S. Department of Education. HEA, Title II. Section 207, requires that the secretary of education submit to the Congress an annual report based on the Title II data compiled by each state. It is in this document that the connection is established between the HEA, Title II reporting mandates and the market concept of education for social mobility.

The secretary of education's 2002 report, *Meeting the High Qualified Teachers Challenge* unambiguously ties HEA, Title II provisions to the objectives of another major federal education initiative—the 2001 Elementary and Secondary Education Amendments, or the No Child Left Behind Act (NCLB).[16] Thus, the secretary of education's report became the vehicle to reinvent HEA: Title II as a policy tool to push the goals of NCLB. With that shift, it was expected that colleges and universities would prepare teachers for classrooms where their work would be shaped by the expectations articulated in NCLB that children will continually raise their scores on the state's standardized P–12 examinations. Consequently, new teachers may face careers where their work will be technical rather than professional, and they will be expected to contribute to a dehumanizing situation where the worth of the student will merely be a score on a standardized content examination. By linking Title II of the Higher Education Act to NCLB, a private, market-driven federal purpose for public schools is solidified. It is here that the imbalance between what Labaree describes as democratic equality, social efficiency, and social mobility begins to become apparent.

The theme of social mobility is further and more explicitly expressed in NCLB.[17] NCLB presents a policy paradox. It was enacted with bipartisan support, drawing praise from liberals and conservatives in the Congress. One can speculate that liberal forces saw NCLB as a tool to promote social justice through provisions that require schools to publicize disaggregated P–12 student test score data. With these data, school leaders, teachers, members of the public, and elected officials can easily make the connection between low student performance and factors such as family poverty level, poor and unsafe buildings, or unqualified teachers. Arguably these are powerful data for conversations about whether schools offer the same quality education for all children and in doing so support a mission grounded in values of social justice and civic responsibility. For political conservatives, however, NCLB represents education policy based on economic efficiency. Under that model, results (student learning) can be measured with utilitarian scientific tools and it is expected that cross-school or cross-state comparisons can be made. When NCLB is taken as a whole, the possible benefit of attaining social justice through policy informed by more robust data on children's test scores is eclipsed by the individualistic and competitive focus of the law.

The statement of purpose that begins NCLB in Title I, Section 1001(1)—(7) is quoted extensively to illustrate the intent of the law.

> The purpose of this title is to ensure that all children have a fair, equal, and significant opportunity to attain a high-quality educa-tion and reach, at a minimum, proficiency on challenging State academic achievement standards and state academic assess-ments. This purpose can be accomplished by—(1) ensuring that high-quality academic assessments, accountability systems, teacher preparation and training, curriculum, and instructional materials are aligned with challenging State academic standards so that stu-dents, teachers, parents, and administrators can measure progress against common expectations for student academic achievement;... (4) holding schools, local educational agencies, and States account-able for improving the academic achievement of all students... (6) improving and strengthening accountability, teaching and learning by using State assessment systems designed to ensure that students are meeting challenging State academic achievement and content standards and increasing achievement overall but especially for the disadvantaged; (7) providing greater decision making authority and flexibility for schools and teachers in exchange for greater responsibility for student performance:...[18]

It is more troublesome than ironic that after listing purposes that will restrain teachers' and schools' ability to do anything other than drill students on material expected to be on the state test (nos. 1—6 above), they will ostensibly be granted regulatory flexibility for their compliance (no. 7 above). Clearly, NCLB pushes the purpose of public education fur-ther into the realm of markets, individual competition, and private ends.

NCLB encourages competition not just among children but also among classrooms, schools, and teachers. Through the federal mandate that states administer standardized examinations to P–12 students at various grades a not too subtle message is sent to children that these assessments are the primary, if not sole, criterion to measure their personal worth. The idea that knowledge may have merit and use other than that assessed on an examination or that schools have purpose other than to be a vehicle for administering tests is not to be found. Since schools must show that each year their students are attaining higher test scores to demonstrate adequately yearly progress required by NCLB, they are at once placed in competition with other schools for resources to help them meet assessment goals. These resources may be materials, instructional aides, or additional teachers, or the most precious resource, time. Even if a community and its schools held as a value developing what Marilyn Cochran-Smith describes as inquiry communities,[19] the school day would not have the time to devote to both critical reflection and fact drills deemed necessary for students to pass the state's standardized exams. Urgency is built into NCLB. Schools must show that all students meet proficiency standards within 12 years of the law's enactment. As a consequence, educators and members of the public lack the opportunity for the thoughtful discourse on the NCLB mandates one would expect in a society where social responsibility truly is valued. Perhaps as a result, much of the criticism directed toward NCLB has been superficial: lack of clear guidance on how states and school districts should carry out provisions of the law; uncertainty about timelines; or whether the NCLB programs are receiving sufficient federal funding.[20]

Initially, Department of Education spokespersons asserted that NCLB as passed by the Congress gave them no flexibility to relax testing requirements and other provisions,[21] yet several policy changes of interest were announced in late 2003 and early 2004. When NCLB was passed in 2001, states were allowed to provide alternative assessments only for those children with very severe cognitive disabilities. Yet, on December 9, 2003, Secretary of Education Roderick Paige announced new NCLB regulations that give states and school districts additional flexibility to measure certain children with disabilities by standards appropriate to their intellectual development instead of standards applied to "typical" children.[22] Advocates for English language learners put forward similar arguments asserting that children who knew little or no English needed accommodations while they gained necessary language skills. Again the Department of Education initially was unwilling to offer concessions for school districts with large numbers of English language learners.[23] However, on February 19, 2004, Secretary of Education Paige announced new policies to allow states the option of not including the scores of these children in calculations of annual yearly progress for up to two years, allowing them sufficient time to learn English and to give school districts credit for improving the students' English language proficiency.[24] On one hand, the Department of Education is to be applauded for acknowledging the needs of diverse populations by attempting to level the playing field for these children. However, it would be naïve to ignore the fact that these changes occurred within a year of a presidential election.

Perhaps it was "March Madness" because the spring of 2004 brought even more modifications to NCLB. On March 15, Secretary Paige announced that some additional flexibility would be given to rural and small schools that have a small number of teachers who have responsibility for teaching more than one subject. In these schools teachers were especially at risk for not achieving the highly qualified status required in NCLB. Paige said, "We listened to educators from across the country..." and decided that if a multiple subject teacher is qualified in at least one subject—meaning he or she holds an academic minor or has passed a rigorous content examination—the teacher will have three years to prove proficiency in any other subject he or she teaches. The secretary also announced that the U.S. Department of Education would allow states to rely on their own certification standards to establish qualifications for science teachers.[25] Of course, one might ask why state teacher credential standards are adequate for science teachers but not for teachers in other subjects.

Later in March the U.S. Department made another announcement regarding NCLB flexibility. In a press release, Secretary of Education Paige was quoted as saying, "We are listening to parents and educators and making adjustments." In this case the issue was the participation rate of students in the state standardized examination. As originally written, NCLB required at least 95 percent of all students to take the state examinations to avoid having a local school labeled as failing. The late March NCLB modification gave states the option of not including in tests any students who miss the examination because of a medical emergency and allowing states to meet the 95 percent participation rate by averaging student participation over three years.[26]

The NCLB legislation is written in a manner that allows the U.S. Department of Education little flexibility in changing requirements without amending the law itself; a step the Congress has not been willing to undertake. Even if the administration had acted sooner to relax certain provisions of the law, as noted above, these minor adjustments do little to repair a law based on the shaky premise that competition among children, teachers, schools, and states will improve learning and contribute to civic and civil behavior.

Looking beyond the broad provisions in NCLB it is important to recognize that the social mobility foundation upon which NCLB is built has a profoundly negative effect on teachers and their work. The law requires schools to employ only what it calls highly qualified teachers to teach academic content—an expectation that on its face seems most reasonable. Yet, the law goes further and includes detailed definitions of what is meant by a highly qualified elementary and highly qualified secondary teacher. In both cases the definitions stress the individual's academic credentials: a subject matter, major or minor, or a passing score on a rigorous examination. The impact of these NCLB provisions is to nudge state departments of education to revise their requirements for teacher licensure so that a candidate's academic background is the primary, if not only, consideration in determining the individual's teaching qualifications. Licensure requirements influence teacher education program approval standards and if NCLB and HEA, Title II retain their current foci colleges and universities will be expected to graduate academic technicians rather than professional educators committed to social responsibility and school transformation.

Supporters of NCLB might counter this line of reasoning by arguing that uneven student performance in P–12 schools receiving federal funds demands imposition of some form of external accountability—generally a standardized examination of facts unrelated to community norms or values. But as Elmore points out, "internal accountability precedes external accountability." A school in distress, he asserts, won't automatically become high performing due to the provisions in NCLB. The reality of school reform is much more complex. Instead it is related to "the beliefs, norms, expectations, and practices that people in the organization share, not with the kind of information they receive about their performance. Low-performing schools aren't coherent enough to respond to external demands for accountability."[27] Stated another way, personal and mutual accountability are preconditions for responding to external forces—in this case a school or district's responsibility for accepting federal funding. As will be discussed later in this chapter, attention to personal and mutual accountability would be useful architecture upon which to rethink current education policy directions.

The complications of NCLB have been public and contentious.[28] As a result, it might be expected that as the Congress began to consider reauthorization of Title II of the Higher Education Act, decision makers would reflect on the deficits of NCLB and consider how the federal role in education could recalibrate the imbalance between public and private goals for public schools. Yet, as of spring 2004 that had not happened and more significantly, civic participation and social justice were not even footnotes in education legislation pending in the U.S. Senate or House of Representatives.

Congressional discussions about reauthorization of the teacher education provisions in Title II of the Higher Education Act began in 2003 with the introduction of H.R. 2211, the Ready to Teach Act.[29] Sponsored by the chair of the House Committee on Education and the Workforce Rep. John Boehner of Ohio, this bill was passed by the House of Representatives in May 2003. In a manner similar to NCLB, this legislation identifies as its primary purpose the improvement of student academic achievement. H.R. 2211, like virtually all federal education legislation, includes language that "[n]othing in this subsection shall be construed to negate or supersede the legal authority under State law of any State agency, State entity, or State public official over programs that are under the jurisdiction of the agency, entity, or official."[30] Nonetheless, the bill's core assumption is that teacher preparation institution and state licensure requirements will be aligned with the challenging P–12 academic content as delineated in NCLB. Since HEA, Title II provisions apply to any state or institution of higher education receiving federal government funds, the impact of the proposed legislation is far reaching. If teacher licensure standards are to be aligned with the P–12 student curriculum as outlined in NCLB, does that mean arts and sciences units in colleges and universities across the nation should develop undergraduate and graduate curricula that parallel exactly what is taught in P–12 schools? Moreover, if expectations for P–12 student achievement are included in a bill to support institutions of higher education, are colleges and universities also accountable in some measure for the failure of children in an elementary or secondary school to meet testing targets? The issue is not that a strong curriculum or student achievement are unimportant, but rather it is that the unilateral emphasis on academic content, rote learning to facilitate test performance, and a market approach in both the P–12 and teacher preparation curricula leave little time to construct inquiry communities.[31]

In addition to H.R. 2211, in the winter of 2003 and spring of 2004 three additional bills to reauthorize HEA, Title II, were introduced in the U.S. Senate. Massachusetts Senator Edward Kennedy introduced the College Quality, Affordability, and Diversity Improvement Act of 2003.[32] Like the 1998 version of HEA, Title II, NCLB, and H.R. 2211, the teacher quality enhancement provisions in S. 1793 begin with the purpose that Title II programs should improve student achievement. Although there is language in Section 207(a)(2)—a grant program to develop high quality teacher preparation programs—that references creation of "a positive learning environment" and the importance of teacher collaboration, this is one of the few departures from a mechanistic form of teacher preparation in which the quality of an educator is measured by individual student achievement on standardized examinations.[33]

Because Senator Kennedy is the ranking minority member on the Senate Health, Education, Labor and Pensions Committee his legislation carries more weight than bills proposed by other Democrats, even though they also serve on the education committee. However, two other bills to reauthorize HEA: Title II, introduced by Rhode Island Senator Jack Reed and New Mexico Senator Jeff Bingaman, respectively, are of note because they each conform to the mechanistic approach to education reform characterized by NCLB, H.R. 2211 (Boehner) and S. 1793 (Kennedy). Although there is no expectation that the Higher Education Act in which these measures will ultimately be placed will be reauthorized in 2004, collectively, this pending legislation provides a preview of how the new 109th Congress will attend to teacher education policy when it convenes in 2005. On April 22, 2004, Senator Reed introduced the Preparing, Recruiting, and Retaining Education Professionals (PRREP) bill (S. 2335)[34] and on the same day Senator Bingaman introduced the Capacity to Learn for All Students and Schools (CLASS) bill (S. 2340).[35] Both of these measures attempt to further align teacher preparation accountability programs with NCLB goals. Each stresses that the quality of teacher preparation in institutions of higher education should be measured according to the pass rates of teacher candidates on licensure examinations. Senator Bingaman's bill in particular expects that the effect of new educators on the academic performance of the children they teach will be tracked and linked back to their college or university preparation program, providing another way to measure the value added of collegiate-based teacher education.

Measuring a teacher education program on student pass rates and the impact new teachers may have on student test scores has appeal for decision makers because these measures suggest that very simple metrics offer a way to evaluate how teachers are prepared and the subsequent quality of their work. That is not the case. Analysis of the student pass rate data collected in 2003 and 2004 provide no useful information to judge program quality.[36] Furthermore, linking the impact of one teacher on a particular student and that student's subsequent performance on a high-stakes examination is very problematic. Looking at teacher evaluations and individual student performance requires that school districts release what generally is considered private information. Moreover, highly sophisticated statistical models are necessary to assure that only teacher effects are being measured when student achievement is being studied. Even more telling are the lengths of the pending Title II bills when compared with the 1998 legislation. The shortest of the Title II bills now before the Congress is 26 single-spaced pages (H.R. 2211) and the longest is 42 single-spaced pages (S. 2340). The Title II bill when passed in 1998 was but 13 pages long. This illustrates the extent to which lawmakers have included provisions detailing what states should do to gather data and enact federal provisions to align teacher education programs with NCLB expectations. In attempting to legislate the minutia how states and institutions of higher education should revise what is perceived as current practice, the Congress has attended less to why. What broad societal goals are being advanced and what goals are being ignored?

Federal education legislation drafted and introduced in the 108th Congress, although not passed, continues to reinforce a market-based, social mobility focus for public education. The influence of the federal government on P–12 schools through NCLB and on how new educators are prepared through HEA, Title II is pervasive and uses the policy process to chart a course for public schools where the "benefits of education are understood to be *selective* and *differential* rather than collective and equal."[37]

Looking at federal education policy as reflected in enacted laws and pending legislation, the picture is one where education is focused on the success of the individual and on competition for social position. The policy pendulum has swung from attention to democratic equality to active promotion of the market-based objective of social mobility. Although inextricably linked to the welfare of all citizens, social justice is conspicuously absent in federal education policy and that absence is unexcused.

Framing Federal Education Policy within a Social Justice Context

This chapter began by posing three questions: (1) What is the role of the national government in linking common good and social justice within the framework of public education? (2) What are the implications for public schools when the federal government engages in decisions that ignore social justice and democratic equality? And (3) in what way is current education policy promoting or subverting education goals grounded in civic participation and social justice? Looking at current and proposed federal education legislation the answer to the final question is that social justice and democratic equality are not on the agenda. Either by design or neglect federal decision makers have not constructed policy options to encourage public schools to attend to matters of civic engagement and social responsibility. Returning to the first and second questions, assuming a modest level of political will, could federal measures such as HEA, Title II and NCLB be rethought in order to restore a balance between public and private education goals? Could democratic equality become an organizing frame to refocus these major federal laws? At this point, one might suggest that tinkering with HEA: Title II and NCLB will not be sufficient and that both should be repealed. Theoretically that could occur but it is unlikely to happen soon. Both laws had bipartisan support and it is politically unrealistic to expect there is sufficient support to abolish them. Moreover, objections to HEA: Title II were voiced only by the higher education community and were almost immediately discounted as self-serving. Even though P–12 educators have been vocal in their objections to NCLB, the Department of Education made some attempt to address their concerns,[38] and this may be sufficient to soften if not silence objections. The task then becomes to think about the 109th Congress and those who will follow, to determine how NCLB and HEA, Title II can be modified. Ten proposals are presented to amend NCLB and HEA, Title II, respectively. These proposals are suggested to help educators, members of the public, and elected officials engage in conversations that both generate legislative revisions and model civic engagement.

- When NCLB is amended, two additional purposes should be added and they should be given priority as the law's second and third purposes, respectively: to help schools provide environments in which children and youth develop personal qualities for democratic life; and to establish inquiry communities where students and teachers engage in deep exploration of issues and learn skills to inform their personal judgments.
- Parallel language should be added to the purpose of HEA, Title II when it is reauthorized.
- Schools receiving NCLB funds should be asked to demonstrate in whatever way they determine is appropriate, how their school or school district promotes critical thinking, personal and mutual accountability, and social responsibility. Evidence of this commitment may be presented through narrative, surveys, focus groups, and the like. Involvement of teachers, students, administrators, and members of the community would be required in developing this evidence and determining how it would inform future school goals.
- Schools and districts should be eligible for special grants to establish inquiry communities. This provision could easily be added to Title II of NCLB as an activity for P–12 higher education partnerships. Similar language could be added to the partnership provisions in HEA, Title II.

- The definition of highly qualified teacher in federal law should be reconsidered. Schools and districts should be expected to explain to parents and the public at large how the collective work of professionals create learning communities that prepare children and youth to think critically about the obligations of self-government and democratic equity. In April 2004, a task force of the Council of Chief State School Officers recommended that the highly qualified teacher provision of NCLB could be met if special education and regular education teachers worked in a team teaching arrangement.[39] This notion could be applied to other groupings of teachers and would be a way to address the highly qualified teacher dilemma until the definition is modified or eliminated.
- Schools' achievement gains on standardized measures should be published no more often than every three years. Furthermore, to prevent spurious comparisons, the reporting should be staggered among schools so only one-third of the schools in a school division or state will report test scores each year.
- As a condition of receiving NCLB funds, community forums should be held so citizens, educators, and local officials can build concurrence and agreement on the purpose and goals of their local schools.
- Mandatory reporting of licensure examination pass rates by colleges and universities should be eliminated. Instead, institutions should develop systems to follow the career paths of their teacher candidates and through surveys, focus groups, and other data provided by the schools in which their graduates teach. These should be semiannual reports and institutions in the state should be encouraged to develop a common reporting system, but this should not be required.
- The institutional report required under HEA, Title II should include how teacher candidates are prepared to create inquiry communities and help students engage in democratic practice. These program characteristics should be recognized throughout the teacher education program not just offered in a particular course.
- At the next reauthorization of NCLB and HEA, Title II, a provision should be added that each will sunset after ten years.

Establishing an Advocacy Agenda

Teachers, teacher educators, and others concerned about assuring that policy decisions do not limit schools' ability to educate children and youth to have a commitment to democracy and social justice, must not be silent hoping that eventually decision makers will do the right thing. The U.S. Constitution established a system where decisions are made with the consent of the governed not absent public input. On occasion, elected officials may not be as mindful of the need to make decisions that reflect the will of the electorate. When his happens it is the obligation of citizens to be vocal in reminding lawmakers of their obligations. The following five suggestions are offered to help educators begin to build an advocacy agenda.

First, be aware of which level of government has enacted a troublesome policy or needs to consider a new policy. Although this chapter has considered only federal education policy, levels of government have overlapping authority for education decisions. The U.S. Congress, for example, wrote HEA: Title II and NCLB, and the regulations to implement them were developed by the U.S. Department of Education. Nevertheless, states and localities have some flexibility in how they will carry out the federal mandates. It is not unusual for states and localities to impose additional regulations to a federal requirement. As an example, a school district might decide that every teacher in a core academic subject must spend 25 percent of each class period on test drill in the hope that students will perform well on the state exam and the federally imposed adequate yearly progress will be met. In this nonsensical case, the point of intervention would be at the district level even though the provision is linked to the No Child Left Behind Act. Fortunately, all federal education laws and regulations are easily found on the Internet; a search can help clarify the locus of an irritating policy. It is also likely that state and local provisions are available online. If an electronic search does not provide the needed information, a phone call to the state department of education, local school board, or even U.S. Department of Education can provide needed clarification.[40] An hour of research can help get an advocacy agenda on the right course.

Second, study the policy problem and decide what could be done to resolve it. Don't expect your Congressperson to return to Washington, D.C., and immediately lead the charge to repeal NCLB; that isn't politically feasible. Rather, consider what aspects of the law are most unpleasant and offer one or more options to fix them. All decision makers are busy and confronted with a number of requests from constituents. By offering policy alternatives, even if they aren't perfect solutions, the work of the elected official has been made easier. It is important to shore up your recommendation with evidence. It could be experiences, research, poll or survey data, or other kinds of supportive facts. Again the Internet may provide useful information. Virtually all interest groups have websites where they post policy statements and useful research. In addition, a number of organizations offer online versions of policy related periodicals.[41]

Third, take the opportunity to forward positive information about what is happening in education at the local and state levels to policy makers.

This may mean sending them briefing papers or other useful materials. It also is worthwhile to find time to make a courtesy call on a school board member, a local legislator, staff person at the state department of education, or member of the U.S. Congress. These courtesy contacts are important because the time may come when you need assistance from a decision maker and providing help is always easier if initial contacts were already made. Individuals working in public colleges, universities, and schools should be aware of any restrictions on contacting elected officials. If this is the case, make the contacts during personal time as a private citizen and concerned educator rather than in an official capacity.

Fourth, although an individual may be able to influence the direction of education policy, a group of individuals who share common goals and values is more powerful. Americans commonly gather in role-alike organizations, such as associations of teachers, principals, superintendents, faculty, or education deans. These groups often are important voices for issues unique to their own membership. A potentially more powerful group force is created when coalitions of individuals or groups with different roles and backgrounds are formed to promote common goals through public policy forums. Advocates should continually look for opportunities to build alliances with others who value an education system attuned to social justice and democratic participation.

Fifth, whether as an individual or as part of a group, it is always appropriate to seek opportunities to speak about the important place public education holds as transmitter of democratic values. Voicing this message may be done through letters to the editor, Op-Ed pieces, or testimony in local school board or other civic meetings. This allows educators to promote and demonstrate an essential aspect of self-government: that it is a mechanism to activate change.

A final caution is offered. Many critics of NCLB have argued that the primary problem with the law is that it isn't supported with sufficient federal funds.[42] It is important to recognize that doubling or tripling funding for any law that is built on questionable assumptions, that has unequal impact on rural, suburban, and urban schools, that dehumanizes children, that promotes an expectation that a person's education is private property, and that demeans the role of teachers cannot be fixed by higher federal appropriations.

Notes

1. Kern Alexander and M. David Alexander, *American Public School Law* (St. Paul, Minn.: West Publishing Co., 1985).
2. Jerome J. Hanus and Peter W. Cookson Jr., *Choosing Schools: Vouchers and American Education* (Washington, D.C.: American University Press, 1996); David Labaree, "Public Goods,

Private Goods: The American Struggle over Educational Goals," *American Educational Research Journal* 34, no. 1 (1997): 39–81; Marilyn Cochran-Smith, *Walking the Road: Race, Diversity, and Social Justice in Teacher Education* (New York: Teachers College Press, 2004).
3. Brown v. Board of Education. 347 U.S. 483 (1954).
4. State of New York, Supreme Court, Appellate Division, First Department, Campaign for Fiscal Equity, Inc. et al. v. The State of New York, et al.: Brief for Plaintiffs-Respondents, No. 111070/93, 2001, http://www.cfequity.org/cfereply9-28-01.PDF (accessed February 20, 2004).
5. Hanus and Cookson, 116.
6. Deborah Stone, *Policy Paradox: The Art of Political Decision-Making* (New York: W. W. Norton & Company, 1997), 10.
7. Labaree, 40.
8. State of New York, *Campaign for Fiscal Equity, Inc. et al. v. New York. New York. The State of New York, et al.*; Hanus and Cookson, 42.
9. Labaree, 51.
10. Stone.
11. Cochran-Smith, 1.
12. Cochran-Smith, 12.
13. U.S. Congress. House Conference Committee. *Higher Education Amendments of 1998: Conference Report to Accompany H.R.6.* 105th Cong., 2nd sess., Report 105–750. (Washington, D.C.: U.S. Government Printing Office, September 25, 1998). http://thomas.loc.gov/cgi-bin/cpquery/?&dbname=cp105&maxdocs=100&report=hr750.105&sel=TOC_0& (accessed February 20, 2004).
14. U.S. Congress. *Higher Education Amendments of 1998.*
15. Cochran-Smith.
16. U.S. Department of Education, Office of Postsecondary Education. *Meeting the Highly Qualified Teachers Challenge: The Secretary's Annual Report on Teacher Quality,* Washington, D.C., June 2002.
17. U.S. Congress, *No Child Left Behind Act of 2001: Conference Report to Accompany H.R.1,* Report 107–334 (Washington, D.C.: U.S. Government Printing Office, December 13, 2001), http://www.ed.gov/policy/elsec/leg/esea02/index.html (accessed February 20, 2004).
18. U.S. Congress. No Child Left Behind Act of 2001.
19. Cochran-Smith.
20. Education Daily, "Paige Responds in Person to Democrats' Criticisms" February 25, 2004; U.S. Department of Education, Paige Details No Child Left Behind Implementation Progress, Press Release, February 24, 2004, http://www.ed.gov/news/pressreleases/2004/02/02242004.html (accessed February 25, 2004).
21. Education Daily, "Paige Warns States Not to Lower Standards for NCLB," October 24, 2003; U.S. Department of Education, Paige Outlines No Child Left Behind Act's Ten Key Benefits for Parents of English Language Learners, Press Release, December 2, 2003, http://www.ed.gov/news/pressreleases/2003/1212022003.html (accessed February 20, 2004).
22. U.S. Department of Education," New No Child Left Behind Provision Gives Schools Increased Flexibility While Ensuring All Children Count, Including Those with Disabilities," Press Release, February 20, 2004.
23. U.S. Department of Education, "Paige Outlines No Child Left Behind Act's Ten Key Benefits for Parents of English Language Learners," Press Release, December 2, 2003.
24. U.S. Department of Education, "Secretary Paige Announces New Policies to Help English Language Learners," Press Release, February 19, 2004.
25. Robelen, Erik, "Federal Rules for Teachers Are Relaxed," *Education Daily* 23, no. 28 (March 24, 2004).
26. Michael Dobbs, "More Changes Made to 'No Child' Rules," *Washington Post,* March 20, 2004.
27. Richard F. Elmore, "Unwarranted Intrusion," *Education Next* 2, no. 1 (2002): 32.
28. U.S. Department of Education, "Paige Details No Child Left Behind Implementation Progress," Press Release (February 24, 2004).
29. U.S. Congress, House Committee on Education and the Workforce, *Ready to Teach Act of 2003,* 108th Cong., 1st sess., H.R. 2211, May 22, 2003.
30. U.S. Congress, *Ready to Teach Act of 2003,* Sec. 202 (b)(3).

31. Cochran-Smith.
32. U.S. Congress, *College Quality, Affordability, and Diversity Improvement Act of 2003*, 108th Cong., 2nd sess., S. 1793.
33. U.S. Congress, *College Quality, Affordability and Diversity Improvement Act of 2003*.
34. U.S. Congress, *Preparing, Recruiting, and Retaining Education Professionals Act of 2004*, 108th Cong., 2nd sess., S. 2335.
35. U.S. Congress, *The Capacity to Learn for All Students and Schools Act of 2004*, 108th Cong., 2nd sess., S. 2340.
36. Penelope Earley, *Title II of the Higher Education Act Revisited and Reconsidered: An analysis of the Secretary of Education's 2002 Report on Teacher Quality.* http://gse.gmu.edu/centers/edpolicy/analysis.html (2002); Earley, *Analysis of the Secretary of Educations 2003 Report on Teacher Quality: It's Déjà vu All Over Again.* http://gse.gmu.edu/centers/edpolicy/analysis.html (2003).
37. Labaree, 51.
38. "Paige Responds in Person to Democrats' Criticisms," *Education Daily*, February 25, 2004.
39. "Special Ed Team-Teaching Urged by CCSSO Task Force," *Education Daily*, April 5, 2004.
40. The U.S. Department of Education's website is: www.ed.gov and the general number for the Department is 800-872-5327.
41. Recent editions of the AERA journals are available at www.aera.net, and the Education Policy Analysis Archives has a searchable database of policy related peer-reviewed articles www.epaa.asu.edu.
42. "Paige Responds in Person to Democrats' Criticisms."

SECTION **2**
Programmatic Examples

Preparing Social Studies Teachers to Be Just and Democratic: Problems and Possibilities

BETH C. RUBIN AND BENJAMIN JUSTICE

National education policy today is dominated by the quest to test and quantify students' rote knowledge. How then might those concerned with the democratizing role of schools in general and of the social studies role in particular go about preparing teachers? In this chapter we consider approaches to social studies teacher education that provide space for and model critical analysis of and reflection upon the world around us, ways of thinking that are at the core of teaching for civic efficacy and social justice.

A concern for social justice has long been at the forefront of P–12 social studies education, although not without much debate. Training new teachers in this tradition presents its own set of difficulties and opportunities, as we have found in our work as teacher educators. In this chapter we first briefly describe some of the theoretical underpinnings of social justice teaching and review the social justice tradition in the social studies. A subsequent section outlines some of the challenges to preservice teacher training in this tradition and suggestions found in the relevant literature. The final section describes the authors' own experiences as social studies teacher educators, drawing from student writing and classroom activities to offer practice-based reflections on social studies teacher education for social justice at both the elementary and secondary levels.

Teaching for Social Justice

Paolo Freire suggests that all teaching is political and embedded in particular sets of values.[1] Theorists working in this tradition argue that teaching should be an activity committed to reducing inequalities found in our society. Cochran-Smith draws on European social and economic theory, multicultural and antiracist pedagogical traditions, critical educational theory, and critical ethnographic, sociocultural, and gender studies of schooling to outline a critique of education in the United State that underlies and motivates teaching for social justice.[2] Synthesizing the work of a variety of theorists, she argues that structural inequalities embedded in the United States's system of schooling perpetuate hierarchies of domination closely linked to race and class.[3] Within classrooms, instruction is organized in ways that systematically privilege white, mainstream cultural knowledge and disenfranchise students who are poor, working class, language minority, and of color. "Animated by these understandings," she writes, "teaching for social justice is teaching that is committed to a more just social order."[4]

Drawing upon this critique, Cochran-Smith outlines six principles of practice for social justice teaching: (1) enabling significant work for all students within learning communities, (2) building upon what students bring with them to school, (3) teaching skills, (4) working with individuals, families, and communities, (5) diversifying modes of assessment, and (6) making activism, and analysis of power and social inequities part of the curriculum.[5] Similar principles can be found in the work of other writers on this topic and throughout the various chapters in this volume.

The Social Justice Tradition in the Social Studies

In social studies, teaching for social justice draws upon these critiques and principles. Indeed, teaching for social justice has often found a "home base" in the P–12 social studies classroom and curriculum. Social studies is arguably the content area most immediately conducive to the aims of social justice teaching. Often those drawn to social studies teaching are motivated by a belief in social and/or political engagement and a concern for local, national, or global issues. Many of the suggestions for teaching and curriculum development found in the social justice education literature are most easily accommodated within a social studies framework. And, indeed, insofar as policy makers, researchers, and teachers and their organizations (including the National Council for the Social Studies) identify fostering active citizenship as a vital component to the social studies, social justice will continue to be at its core.[6]

Nevertheless, the social justice tradition is just one of the competing ideas within the social studies discourse. Ross argues that social studies education is characterized by the "lack of consensus and contentiousness over its goals and methods."[7] Indeed, the area is so fraught with controversy that scholars of social studies can neither agree on the intentions of early social studies promoters nor even on how to describe the major debates in the field. In general, however, it is safe to say that the contemporary social studies curriculum emerged from two late Nineteenth-Century movements: the movement to include the study of history in public schools and the social welfare and improvement movements.

Stanley and Nelson provide a compelling description of the field today, outlining three distinct yet nonexclusive categories of thought in social studies education: subject-centered, civics-centered, and issues-centered.[8] Within each of these three strands there exists an array of views, ranging from the more conservative conception of social studies as purveyor of cultural traditions to a more activist view of social studies as aimed at fostering social action. As this implies, the social studies curriculum can serve contradictory purposes, "fostering oppression, racism and prejudice *or* [ibid] liberation and cultural equality."[9]

Among those who promote a strong social justice mission for social studies, there have been varying emphases. Noffke locates issues of racial and economic justice as central to the goals of social studies education.[10] Ladson-Billings argues for a "culturally relevant" approach to teaching social studies in which knowledge is created and shared among students and teachers, course content is viewed critically, teachers are passionate about their subject matter, students learn prerequisite knowledge and skills, and student diversity and individual differences are taken into account in planning and assessment.[11] Epstein contends that students' racial, ethnic, gender, and class identities "shape their knowledge of and perspectives on social studies subjects," she argues that teachers should strive to create lessons that are not in conflict with the knowledge and perspectives of students of color.[12] Vinson asserts that social studies teachers are complicit in maintaining oppressive social conditions and calls for them to "challenge the implications of their own instruction, to envision an education that is democratic to the core."[13] Ross suggests that those committed to social studies for social justice should create curricula that empower all citizens, engage students in active learning, accommodate diverse learners, build learning support strategies, and foster collaboration within schools and with families and communities.[14]

We are in agreement with many of these general principles and suggest that critical inquiry—teaching students the skills, knowledge, and habit of mind necessary to examine, understand, and theorize about historical, social, and political issues—is at the heart of what the social studies have to offer to the more general quest to foster democratic thinking and social justice in the classroom. Closely related is the notion that social studies classes should involve more "participation" than "transmission," in order to cultivate individuals with the skills and inclinations to engage actively in our democracy.[15] There are, however, many challenges to training new teachers in this tradition, challenges that we believe differ between preservice elementary generalists and secondary social studies specialists.

The remainder of this chapter will consider some of the challenges facing those who wish to train future teachers of social studies in a social justice tradition. We draw upon research exploring the hurdles facing teacher educators and their students and reflect upon our own experiences as social studies teacher educators. We probe the differences between training elementary teachers and secondary social studies specialists, and offer suggestions from practice for working with each of these groups.

Challenges and Suggestions for Social Studies Teacher Education for Social Justice

Teacher education for social justice faces a number of hurdles, and social studies teacher education for social justice confronts its own particular set of issues. Smylie, Bay, and Tozer argue that preservice teacher education programs "typically provide insufficient opportunity for teachers to develop the capacities they need to manage dilemmas effectively as agents of change."[16] John Goodlad's five-year study of teacher education programs in 29 institutions of higher education in the United States indicated that teacher education programs were typically focused on the development of skills and techniques, without connection to the theoretical and research perspectives presented in social foundations and educational psychology courses.[17] These programs tended to emphasize preparing teachers to conform to existing structures rather than encouraging them to act as agents of change within their schools. Others are concerned about the lack of racial and socioeconomic diversity in the teacher education pool, given the rapidly increasing numbers of urban students, low income students, and students-of-color attending public schools in the United States.[18]

Teacher education in the social studies confronts a particular set of issues that go beyond those associated with social justice teacher education writ large. Owens, for example, drew six major issues from his study of 562 preservice elementary education students in seven different institutions of higher education.[19] He found that preservice elementary teachers had negative past experiences with social studies, lacked interest in teaching social studies, were confused about what the social studies are, held ideologically inconsistent beliefs about social studies, had trouble selecting what social studies content to teach, and had encountered social studies teaching in their field experiences that ran counter to what they were learning in their education courses and to the goals of social studies education. We have also found these qualities in many of the preservice elementary teachers in our classes.

Secondary level preservice teachers in social studies education face a different set of issues, in our experience. While fairly well versed in their content area, these students (predominantly history majors) are less familiar with sociocultural perspectives on learning, youth issues, and how to build on young people's prior knowledge, abilities, and experiences to construct meaningful learning opportunities for students. They also tend to be unfamiliar with debates in the content fields and with how historians do their work.

These issues for social studies teacher education at the elementary and secondary levels have implications for social studies teacher education for social justice as well. Lack of content knowledge and little sense of the purposes of social studies on the part of preservice elementary teachers can translate into a lack of confidence about constructing socially aware curriculum. Some researchers argue that these candidates lack "multicultural literacy," which holds them back from understanding their students and creating social justice curriculum.[20] Ukpokodu reports that a lack of multicultural knowledge limits students in understanding multiple and global perspectives and in infusing such perspectives into their teaching, noting that her students tend to be parochial and ethnocentric and resist teaching from a critical framework.[21]

At the secondary level, preservice teachers' limited understandings of student and peer cultures can inhibit their abilities to construct curriculum that resonate with their students. Students bring complex experiences and identities to bear on their work in classrooms.[22] A sociocultural approach to understanding classroom life and constructing curriculum can enrich the interaction between students and the social studies curriculum. Epstein posits that such an approach would "support the ways in which children's and adolescents' social identities—i.e., their racial, ethnic, gender, and class identities—shape their knowledge of and perspectives on social studies subjects."[23]

A simplistic understanding of the work of historians can prevent new secondary teachers from constructing the very sort of activities that would engage students most: contentious and meaty debates over key historical dilemmas that call upon skills of research, analysis, synthesis, writing.[24] Preservice teachers often shy away from controversy, although the discussion of controversial issues is often an effective method for engaging older students and can cultivate competencies in critical thinking and expression that are essential to citizens in a democracy.[25] Finally, preservice teachers' lack of experience in democratically run classrooms may result in their discomfort with the implementation of democratic practices in their own classrooms, practices that have the potential to help students experience democratic thinking in action. The following section offers suggestions for addressing these challenges within the context of the elementary and secondary social studies methods course, with an eye toward promoting social justice teaching in the social studies.

Tales from the Teacher Education Classroom: Preparing Elementary and Secondary Teachers for Social Justice Social Studies

Evangelism and Boot Camp: Training Preservice Elementary Teachers To Teach Social Studies

It was the second week of "Teaching Social Studies in the Elementary School," and fear had set in. Students have read Herbert Kohl's classic essay, "Rosa Parks and the Montgomery Bus Boycott," and were showing signs of cognitive dissonance. Some were outraged that they had been misled for their entire P–12 education—about Parks (that she was a poor, tired seamstress), about the bus boycott (that it was spontaneous), and about the entire traditional approach to social studies education that downplays ugly social realities and the role of social activism in challenging them. The class discussion was intense and animated. (Every semester a show-of-hands vote suggested that the majority of students agreed that there was something dishonest and unjust about how social studies is taught). A few students displayed a cool, level-headedness. "I don't see what the problem is," said one woman. "We should just teach the kids the truth." The dissonance—and fear—came when students imagined trying to figure out what the truth was, what the point of social studies in general is, and how (and whether) to teach it to elementary school children. This fear led some students to knee-jerk conservatism. Several questioned age appropriateness. "I agree with [Kohl's argument]," one woman confessed, "but I'm not sure elementary school children are ready to learn about racism." Another was more resistant. "As for Kohl," she wrote in her weekly reflection, "I don't know what his problem is."

As the course proceeded through the semester, students continued to face the same question in different ways. We read about Columbus, Barbie, and Babar. We looked at case studies from Ruth Charney's book, *Habits of*

Goodness, and Levstik and Barton's *Doing History*.[26] Students marveled at Tarry Lindquist's *Seeing the Whole Through Social Studies*. The class largely agreed that traditional approaches to social studies cause critical thinking skills to atrophy and, more importantly, reinforce social injustice. Even the few hard-core resisters, who were often politically conservative, began to agree with the importance of shaping children into just and democratic people. But most students still wondered *how* they could actually make a difference, and whether, in the long run, it was even worth the trouble of teaching social studies at all.

Fortunately, the students were not shy about the nature of their concerns. In written assignments, as well as during class discussion, they identified the reasons for their fear and skepticism. In general, the challenges they saw fell into three categories. First, students worried about their own content knowledge. Second, they feared censure from parents and administrators who might resist any revision of the age-old social studies methods and curriculum. Finally, they saw (and felt) the crush of state-mandated testing. In each case, many of the students felt trapped between what they understood on an intellectual level to be good social studies instruction and what they felt capable of accomplishing as actual classroom teachers. The challenge of teaching these future teachers is finding ways to address these very real concerns without compromising the vitally important goal: affecting social studies instruction for critical analysis and civic competence in actual elementary classrooms.

Lack of Content Knowledge

The most immediate challenge to teaching any social studies to future elementary teachers is their lack of content knowledge. In the elementary social studies methods course that one of us teaches, any given class of 35 students has, on average, five students majoring in social sciences, American studies, or history. Most are psychology majors and have taken only one college-level history course as part of the state certification requirements. While a few students are well-trained, talented young historians, sociologists, and anthropologists, the vast majority of the students are not. Their knowledge of social studies content comes from their own P–12 experience, which, not surprisingly, is often quite limited.

They are also fairly jaded. In our opening class each semester, we do a word association exercise about social studies. Out come the words "boring," "pointless," and "dittos." In a later reflection, a woman wrote that

All throughout my schooling, social studies has been my least favorite subject because I learned facts straight from textbooks.

> The social studies are an area that I am least knowledgeable in because I memorized facts for tests and then soon forgot them afterward. ...This week's reading made me want to teach social studies and almost wish that I had taken more history classes in college. I feel so unknowledgeable in this area, that I'm not comfortable with the idea of teaching social studies in the future.

Another explained,

> I too suffered from this useless act of memorization during my elementary social studies classes. My second grade teacher, Mrs. Lacey, forced us all to memorize the presidents in order of when they served, and our reward was a piece of Bubble Yum. All I can remember now is "Washington, Jefferson, Adams," and I'm not even sure if that is correct! I did not understand the purpose of this activity, and so it had no long-lasting effects on my understanding of social studies on a whole [sic].

These types of comments are common. Not only do most of the elementary students know little about social studies content, but they also have strong negative feelings about the whole project.

To address the poor educational experiences of most future elementary school teachers, the elementary social studies education course is a weird combination of evangelism—that is, convincing students that social studies and history are exciting, alive, and vital to elementary education—and boot camp—quickly and efficiently teaching key content and concepts in social studies and history. Evangelism is the easy part. Boot camp is harder.

In the context of a teacher education course, at least, social studies is an easy sell. As we have argued above, one effective tool for fostering justice and democracy in education is encouraging students to take individual and collective ownership of their education. To that end, this course requires students to coteach one week's lesson. After years of dittos and textbooks, students are pleased and excited by the possibilities for coteaching each week's theme. They run simulations, hold debates, do jigsaws and fishbowls, and write poems for two voices.[27] Classmates respond enthusiastically, and there is wide agreement that social studies, methodologically at least, is very exciting stuff. Moreover, recent events in history—the 9/11 attacks, the invasion of Iraq, and the Bush administration's "war on terror," even gay marriage—provide students with rich content material to make our classes interesting on an adult level, even as we consider how to teach controversial issues to children.

Making the fun meaningful, however, is a tougher challenge, and the "boot camp" function of the elementary course is an ongoing project. The difference between a fun lesson and an intellectually meaningful one is not always clear to the students. In one instance, for example, a group of coteachers wanted to lead the class in making a quilt. The week's theme was "Understanding Understanding," and draws on Bloom's taxonomy and a chapter from Wiggins and McTighe's book, *Understanding by Design*. During our planning meeting, it became clear that the students simply did not understand the week's content. Together we figured out how to create a meaningful quilting activity for their classmates without being a wet blanket. This was only one single class activity. What key concepts do they need to understand about social studies in order to make learning meaningful for their own students? What common denominators will suit the content needs of all of our future teachers of grades P–7?

In general, the course focuses on three main themes in social studies. The first is that history, the backbone of most social studies instruction, is not simply a set of known facts, but rather an open landscape full of explorers with different perspectives, opinions, and understandings.[28] Students need to understand not only that historians often cannot agree on what the "facts" are, but also that every historical narrative has, built into it, a present-day agenda. We read Peter Seixas's, "Schweigen! Die Kinder! Or, Does Postmodern History Have a Place in Public School Social Studies."[29] Whether or not they swallow the postmodernist pill, students at least recognize the limitations of what Seixas calls the "best story" approach to history that so many social studies texts employ. They also begin to understand the relationship between "real history" and actual pedagogy. One student teacher wrote that

> [Before this course] I have always thought of history as a science of sorts. You look through artifacts and try to piece together a puzzle of what happened before now. However, because of this inclusion of human interpretation into the mix, history will never be a science. It will never have exactly right answers; it can never be proven through experimentation or theory. It will always be a subject that is examined, discussed, debated, and questioned. So why shouldn't we let our children join in on that fun? We talk and talk about how we want our children to think critically and make inferences and yet we go about this by throwing useless dates, facts, and stories at them....Without that essential analysis, history then becomes nothing but a fairy tale or legend, passed down from generation to generation. Teaching elementary school kids to understand multiple

perspectives isn't just more fun; it's more honest. Good history is, in itself, conducive to education for social justice.

The second major theme in boot camp is related to the first: that the aim of social studies education is not the mere acquisition of facts, but the development of cognitive abilities that enhance civic competence. In small groups, students begin the first day of class developing definitions of what social studies is, in theory at least, *for*. Their paragraph definitions mention "critical thinking" and "good citizens," and to a large degree conform to the National Council for the Social Studies's (NCSS) definition, which they read afterwards.[30] Yet as their understanding of history and social studies grows, they begin to see that these seemingly straight-forward goals push hard against how the discipline is typically taught. They worry most about their textbooks. One student wrote, "We depend on textbooks to give us the facts about events and if they become fabrications of the truth, what can we depend on to teach?" Given their weak content knowledge, students often fear that they will have no alternative but to teach straight from the text. Weekly reflections and class comments have returned again and again to the question: How can we teach social studies the "good way"? If textbooks cannot be trusted, what can? Where should content come from? Is *that* content any more accurate? For those who do not have strong history backgrounds, the sinking feeling sets in again. They can do Columbus. They can do Rosa Parks. But how can they do the Civil War? Or Mesopotamia? Or New Jersey history? There are no easy answers for them. But at least many have begun down that road of discovery, armed with a sense of what social studies and history can be and knowing that acquiescing in the traditional approach is not a neutral act.

Pressure from Parents, Administrators, and Peers

Even when elementary education students recognize the importance of teaching social studies for critical inquiry, however, they often express another concern: will they be allowed to do so? Can teaching for democratic thinking and social justice get young teachers in trouble? Students feel pressure from several sides, including parents, administrators, and their own peers. Much of the pressure is self-imposed, or abstract. This is especially true in the case of parents. One student asked, wryly, "I wonder what the parents will say about teaching kids that Columbus was a villain?" Others expressed excitement that focusing multiple perspectives and letting students make up their own minds would be parent-proof. But not all students felt so comfortable. One woman wrote:

The one question that I raised while reading [Lindquist] (and what always seems to be on most future teachers' minds) was what about the parents? What if parents who represent some of the possible perspectives that the class would be investigating disagree with the material or lesson at hand but you, as the teacher, feel as though it needs to be addressed?

Fear of administrators is similarly abstract, since our students have not yet done their student teaching, and have limited experience with administrators from observations. In class discussions and reflections in the first half of the course, students typically ask the question bluntly, and repeatedly: will the administration let us teach this way? Can we deviate from the textbook? A few students share anecdotes about teachers' great freedom in teaching social studies, while others suggest that there are unstated "rules" about avoiding controversy in the classroom. Referring to a case study on teaching Columbus from multiple perspectives,[31] one woman wrote:

Students were only in first grade when she [the teacher] did this with them, which did surprise me at first, but at the same time encouraged me that I should also do this. I was always a little nervous about controversial issues like Columbus but what [sic] she did didn't seem at all controversial she just presented her students with two different points of view.

But another is more concerned:

Like the teachers in the [Levstik and Barton] book, I would love to teach children history from different perspectives. But I worry that the administration and the principal will not allow me. At the preschool that I work at, they teach that Columbus was a great discoverer. They teach that he discovered America and that the Europeans came here and lived in peace with the Indians. I am happy that I never had to do circle time around Columbus Day and talk about his amazing discoveries. I would have definitely mentioned something about the unjust treatment of Native Americans and have gotten myself in trouble. At my job we are supposed to go by the curriculum book and if the supervisor would see a teacher teaching something controversial, the teacher might get in trouble.

The "might get in trouble" is telling, and in fact students rarely report actual evidence of administrative pressure to teach traditional social studies.

Sadly, however, the reason for the lack of administrator/teacher conflict resides, at least in part, on the fact that teachers tend not to teach the kind of social studies that we preach in our teacher education program. Research on social studies instruction suggests that most social studies instruction comes straight from textbooks.[32] In one assignment, students observe a social studies lesson and write a critical analysis of what they saw. Despite a few exciting reports, every semester the majority of students see social studies lessons that rely on the same old dittos and textbook chapters. Elementary school children memorize names and dates. One humorous, and typical, essay began with the following disclaimer: "WARNING: This paper contains material that is both questionable and offensive to those who find great importance in the teaching of social studies. Reader discretion is advised." In our class discussions, a few students express concern that deviating from this standard practice may alienate the other teachers, or that in their student teaching, they will be discouraged from doing anything "controversial."

As with lack of content knowledge, the problem with pressure from parents, administrators, and peers has no easy solution in a one-semester course. Our approach is less direct. If evangelism and boot camp have been successful, at least students believe that there are effective and ineffective ways to teach social studies and that, more important, there are necessary, fundamental goals relating to civic competence that they cannot ignore. Class discussions and readings assure students that they are not alone. The NCSS, for example, outlines clear guidelines for social studies instruction; class discussions tend to reinforce students' convictions that the "old" way that most of them learned social studies was a waste of time. We counsel students to seek jobs at schools that will support the kind of teaching that they care about. Ultimately, however, it is the caring itself—the understanding of what social studies can be—that will help students feel the confidence to resist pressure, real and imagined, against the kind of social studies instruction that we preach.

Standardized Testing and Social Studies Instruction

The most disturbing finding in student observation essays is not that most elementary social studies instruction continues to follow traditional patterns, but that recent trends in high-stakes state testing is squeezing out social studies of *any* sort. New Jersey, like other states, has implemented statewide testing programs focusing on basic reading and math skills. In third and fourth grades, students take the NJASK (New Jersey Assessment of Skills and Knowledge). Elementary schools in our area have responded by cutting back on social studies and science instruction. Students report that the effects of state testing of social studies are depressing and dis-heartening. Their cooperating teachers often do not make enough time for quality instruction. In a typical observation, one student wrote that

> When I explained to my cooperating teacher that I would be con-ducting an observation of that day's Social Studies lesson, she exclaimed, "Oh you are so lucky! We are actually going to do social studies today. You see, with the test (ASK4) coming up, we have been skipping social studies in order to allot more time to the language arts period."

Another student said that teachers at her school have "given up social studies for Lent." Scaling back social studies leaves a few students each semester in a bind. Their assigned cooperating teachers simply do not teach a social studies lesson during the observation cycle, and in some cases our students have to scramble to see any social studies instruc-tion at all.

Our primary text for the class, Tarry Lindquist's *Seeing the Whole Through Social Studies*, emphasizes the compatibility of our methods and state standards. The key, she argues, is integrating social studies and other subjects as a way to buy time, enhance interest, and foster higher-order skills and understanding.[33] While we emphasize the idea of integrating social studies for these laudable goals, the pressure of standardized tests can result in an entirely different type of integration. Several students reported on the following lesson, intended to address Black History Month:

> [The teacher] began the class by going over the answers to a ditto they had done for homework. Students were looking through their folders in search of their homework. The ditto was called "Famous Black American." The children had to solve a number of math problems in order to get the answer to who the famous black American was.... Math is being integrated into all their subjects as much as possible. Since all 100% of last year's fourth graders failed the math section of the standardized test, the schools, goal is to change that.

In our first round of practice, students' attempts at creating integrated lessons within our classroom tend toward similar types of "integration." Some lessons include opportunities for children to make connections, such as having them calculate the number of hours of the Montgomery Bus Boycott, based on the number of days that it lasted. As we discuss this and other examples, though, students begin to see that integration needs to be intellectually meaningful, and not "cheesy." In the case of the Montgomery bus boycott, having students use math to calculate the economic impact of the boycott—both for the city and for the protesters—is a far more useful and poignant approach.

The challenge of state testing is by far the most worrisome for the teachers because they see the effects of high-stakes testing firsthand in their school placements. It's one thing for Tarry Lindquist to suggest that excellent social studies instruction can actually help students do better on state tests. It's another, however, for students to see their cooperating teachers and school administrators panicking about the NJASK Once again, we have no easy answers for them. The bottom line for many elementary education students is the bottom line: getting a job and keeping it. Our hope is that we can instill a sense of social justice in these future teachers that inspires them to overcome the difficulties they face: One future teacher summed up this attitude in her reflection:

> I really feel that all children should learn about slavery, the civil rights movement, and other cultures that have been suppressed, such as Native Americans, for all students to learn about their history and why our country and world is the way it is today. I think that all students need to be validated. I really do not understand how our world is supposed to change for the better, for everyone to live in peace, if we do teach limited and biased history.

Evangelism and boot camp do, by the end of the course, change the tone of class reflections and conversations as many students are trained and converted. It's not certain whether or not this attitude will help them overcome the barriers faced by teachers wishing to teach intellectually challenging, socially just elementary social studies, but surely it's a start.

Walking the Walk: Democratic Teacher Education for Preservice Secondary Social Studies Teachers

In contrast with their preservice elementary peers, preservice secondary teachers face a different set of issues. The students in our joint master's degree and teaching credential program in secondary social studies education begin their training with much better content area preparation than do the elementary education students. The majority of the secondary level students have completed or are in the process of completing majors in history, with a few students majoring in other social science areas. Many have minors in an additional social science area. These students are fully convinced of the importance of the social studies as a school subject (although many interpret "social studies" as "history") and feel that they are well prepared with the content knowledge they will need to teach social studies at the middle and high school levels.

Most of these students, however, have little experience working with adolescents, with sociocultural perspectives on education, or with democratic education. Their disciplinary training has left them narrowly focused on history and underexposed to both theoretical and practical understandings of the daily experiences of adolescents in schools. Their college level history coursework has generally been on the large lecture with periodic testing model, and they have not experienced a range of teaching strategies. These are some of the key challenges to preparing secondary social studies teachers to be just and democratic in their teaching practices.

Lack of "Kid Knowledge"

Rather than a lack of content knowledge, many preservice secondary social studies teachers have a lack of "kid knowledge"—inadequate preparation in understanding adolescents as social, political, and academic beings. In her book of advice from high school students to teachers, Cushman notes that

> In a 2001 national survey, 65 percent of students agreed with the statement, "My teachers don't understand me," and 33 percent of the teachers reported inadequate preparation to reach students with backgrounds different from their own.[34]

With their notions of teaching largely defined by a focus on content knowledge and traditional teaching methods, preservice secondary teachers have often given more thought to *what* they will be teaching than *who* or *how* they will be teaching.

We begin to work with this shortcoming the first day of the methods course, by drawing upon students' personal classroom experiences. At the start of the semester, students write and talk about their own best and worst school experiences, beginning this reflection in the classroom, and continuing it on a web-based discussion board. There has been, over several years, a surprising level of consistency in the experiences students share. Analysis of these experiences reveals the disjuncture between the teaching the preservice teachers feel they should be doing and the teaching they most benefited from when they were students themselves.

Many students have cited positive experiences with teachers who made learning active, challenging and fun, and who take care to connect personally with their students. One student wrote:

> Early on in life school was not something I looked forward to going to. Every subject was boring and all I wanted to do was run home and play with my buddies. This all changed in the fourth grade when I met the new social studies teacher. She was amazing because she made history come alive. She was energetic and made us learn through hands-on activities that made learning fun.

Another student mentioned a teacher who was caring and patient:

> I was another one of those math haters in school....My instructor took notice of my problems fairly quickly and he offered me hours of his time to help in understanding the concepts that I just couldn't get. Slowly, I actually started to understand what he was talking about, and we both looked forward to the next test to see how I would do. I took it and was so happy that I actually knew what I was doing.

Yet another student described a college classroom where the teacher used a variety of methods to help students make meaning of the material, challenging students to really tackle the material:

> Each and every class of his involved student participation and students fleshing out the material in order to develop meaning....Professor M. would use a variety of methods—video, music, readings, and art—for us to study the subject. He just guided us and created an environment for us to create our own theories and concepts on the subject. Professor M.'s method of teaching is very challenging and he has high expectations for his students.

Most of these positive experiences involved active learning, academic challenge, and caring investment by the teacher.

Negative school experiences raised by students frequently involved unprepared and uninspired teachers, inflexible teachers with unreasonable expectations, and teachers who made students feel badly about themselves.

> My worst experience was with Prof. A. He was very knowledgeable, but just seemed to have contempt for his students. He had his own

take on history and may have been 100% right, but his lack of openness for other possible views really stifled the learning process. After failing his midterm, I went to his office for some help. I waited outside for an hour as he spoke with someone about how bad the students nowadays are. After an hour of this I decided I would find my help elsewhere....I never felt comfortable, and in the end I learned very little about a subject that I was interested in.

Despite his historical expertise, Prof. A failed to reach this student because of his dogmatism and inapproachability. Other students wrote about teachers who did not take the time to get to know them:

My worst experience hands down was in Mrs. B's 10th grade English class. She would always brag about her daughter and how she was going to retire soon. It was very evident she did not care about our class. She could not distinguish any of the students, but especially the Asian ones. She would always call my Asian friend Amy by my name, and would always refer to me [The student is also Asian] as Amy. This happened throughout the semester. She also could not get my Pakistani friend's name right. Every single time she would mispronounce her name without a twinge of guilt.

Some students described traditional teaching methods that just did not work for them. This description of a facts-based social studies course is one example:

One of the more memorable bad experiences that I can recall was the majority of my freshman year world history course. This class was the typical social studies course that is described as fact driven. Information about Xerxes, Alexander the Great and Mesopotamia was shoveled to the students and momentarily digested. Multiple-choice tests on seemingly random parts of our textbooks was the prime source of evaluation. How much of the multitude of acts that I was presented with I can actually remember now is questionable.

Drawing upon the students' own examples, we compile a list of the characteristics of students best and worst classroom experiences. This list is revealing—almost without exception best experiences involve active learning and teachers who connect personally with students. The worst experiences are almost exclusively those of boredom, humiliation, and lack of understanding. It is clear from the list drawn from the students' own experiences that content knowledge and a transmission approach to teaching do not guarantee good learning experiences for students. This becomes a launching point for a discussion of what makes for meaningful social studies teaching and learning, pushing preservice teachers to consider aspects of the learning experience that go beyond their previous ideas about content and method, which is a necessity for preparing social studies teachers to be just and democratic in their teaching practices.

Limited Experience Analyzing and Theorizing Aspects of Classroom Life

Preservice secondary level teachers being trained in a social justice tradition can benefit from observing in different classrooms and then putting those observations into critical context. Many methods courses require such observations, but if they are not used as a launching point for critique and theorization of classrooms and schools they tend to reinforce traditional practices, as mentioned earlier. To this end, during their weekly observations in social studies classrooms, our secondary methods students make note of how the teachers run their classes, what teaching and management strategies appear to be most and least effective, what students are doing in the classroom, and how the teacher runs group work and discussion, among other issues. Students discuss these observations on a web-based discussion board, getting a sense of the range of approaches and experiences found in different schools and classrooms. In class we continue to discuss these observations in light of their course reading, beginning to develop the analytical attitude toward classroom life that is part of social justice teaching.

Putting course readings and topics into play against what students observe in their field placements is particularly productive. For example, after a number of readings and class activities about discussion leading, students reflected on how the teacher they were observing in their field placement conducted discussion in his or her classroom. One student observed:

> The "discussions" that take place in a classroom may grossly differ from the "discussions" that many educators envision. What Passe, Evans, Weinstein, Parker and numerous others have delineated, sadly may be a far cry from what is executed in a class. Unfortunately, much of what I have witnessed is a distinct deviation from what has been advocated by the above authors. Mr. B's classes are the more glaring example of how the word "discussion" can get distorted in a classroom setting. Mr. B's concept of discussion seems to only entail the repetition of a couple of aimless questions. "What else?" and "What else have you guys noticed?" seem to be staples in trying to elicit conversation. The most upsetting aspect of this method of

questioning is that there are times when the students will raise some really interesting points. However, instead of building upon these salient questions or transitioning to some meaningful note regarding history, students are met with the same two questions mentioned above. A circular pattern establishes itself, as no point is ever really addressed. Referring to Passe and Evans, I think that part of the problem is that a conducive atmosphere for discussion is not being created.

Similarly, students put their observations of groupwork in real classrooms into tension with our methods class' readings and discussion about the strategy.

> I have been rather unimpressed with the groupwork I've seen so far in my placement....[The] times I've seen it used is similar to the experiences the student teachers had in the book where the kids are grouped, and then the teacher can't seem to understand why they don't just fly off to academic wonderland on their own. It seems that the kids are grouped haphazardly or get with their friends....
> I guess the conclusions I have drawn from this is that groupwork really does take a lot more planning than just counting off in threes and then expecting your students to be off to the races.

In this way students use course readings to begin to critique and theorize what they observe in the classroom, rather than accepting observed practices as "the way things must be." Students develop a language to describe what they see in the classroom (e.g., "recitation," "participant structure," "official" and "unofficial" practices) so they can plan classroom activities from a more theory-driven perspective.

Students also critically examine what they see in their field placements through a weekly activity called the "daily dilemma." Each week, a different student group presents the "daily dilemma" and leads the class in activities relating to this dilemma. This assignment serves multiple purposes: giving students the opportunity to analyze critical issues emerging from the field placements, allowing students a chance to plan and lead class, and opening up leadership of the class to create a more democratic atmosphere. Over the years students have addressed a wide variety of topics through the daily dilemmas: intolerance, bullying and outcasting, learning disabled students, classroom management, tracking, school violence, lesbian/gay/bisexual/transgendered students, plagiarism, drug use, suicide ideation, physical and sexual abuse, eating disorders, group work, discussion leading, and assessment. By allowing students to set the agenda for this portion of the course, we find that students treat a wider, more relevant, and frequently a bolder set of topics than a methods instructor could come up with by him- or herself. This activity, which takes place at the start of each class session, sets a tone of critical examination of facets of classroom life that are often treated more as hindrances than as part of the work of teaching.

The methods course is designed to model and teach the tools for the critical inquiry that lie at the heart of social justice teaching in the social studies, supporting students' quests to pursue and contextualize aspects of classroom life that they find troubling. An example of this is the ongoing discussion of tracking that took place one year.

This topic began with a web-based discussion of the issue initiated by a student who had observed differences in the teaching of high- and low-tracked classes during her field placement.

> I am really troubled by what I see in terms of tracking. It's just really disappointing to see the attitudes of teachers in the inclusion classes and the kind of instruction/work those kids are given. During my last field observation I sat in on a U.S. history class that gave the exact same assignment to 10th graders that the 9th graders in the world cultures class had the week before (write a paragraph or two on an invention and draw/print out a picture). It's disturbing on two levels—I mean, first of all, what is the challenge in this? Just having kids copy facts off the web or from a book means nothing. And secondly, why are they repeating the same skills, same level of thinking, with the older kids and the younger kids? It's just sort of wild to me. The change of attitude between the inclusion classes and the honors classes is so palpable, no wonder some of the kids feel disengaged. Then again, I wonder what I would do if I were teaching in the situation—I guess it's easy to be critical when you don't have to get up there every day.

Another student had observed something similar in her field placement at a different school.

> I am definitely troubled about some aspects of tracking by ability level....I have seen lots of classes of all different ability levels so far. It is SO troubling to me that kids in the lower ability level classes are mostly asked to do busy work (copying terms out of the textbook for example). What I find even more problematic and

pervasive, however, is that subtle and not-so-subtle ways that low expectations are communicated to the lower achievers. Many teachers that I observed so far expect very little from the lower tracked students.

A third student added his observations from a different school, writing:

My first week at my school I viewed a "skills" 11th or 12th grade U.S. History II class that was playing the stock market game. I personally remember playing that game when I was in 9th grade. The class gave out bookwork after the stock market game. There was no real teaching or interaction between the students or teacher.

These postings generated a flurry of discussion on the issue, from a variety of perspectives.

Perhaps in response to this web-based discussion, the following week's daily dilemma group chose "Tracking: The Impact on Students" as their daily dilemma topic. The group began by dramatizing two contrasting scenarios of teaching in a low and a high- and low-tracked class. They next divided the class into small groups and gave the groups questions to consider, including "Do you believe that tracking has a negative effect at your school. And if so, is it a teacher's or administration's fault for labeling students?" "Are there positive aspects of tracking?" "Do you think the students feels stigmatized by the label the school assigns to them according to their academic achievement?" "How much of an effect does the teachers' attitudes have on their students' attitudes and their performance?" After 15 minutes of small group discussion the leaders brought the group back together for a general discussion of the issue, starting with observations from their field placements. As students talked, the group leaders kept track of key issues on the board and followed up on student responses with probing questions.

The class enjoyed this daily dilemma and engaged eagerly in the discussion. In his feedback to the group leaders (written by each class member after each dilemma) one student wrote:

[I] enjoyed having other opinions on the idea of tracking. I agreed with it until I heard other sides of the topic. I have developed more of a compassionate attitude for the students in the inclusion class I observe. They are not challenged enough and this discussion allowed me to focus on their feelings a lot more.

The daily dilemma was an opportunity for students to deeply consider the issue of tracking, with some students reconsidering previously held opinions.

The topic of tracking became an ongoing theme in the class, frequently mentioned in web postings and class discussions. As we learned about various teaching methods throughout the semester, students considered how tracking or heterogeneous grouping might affect a particular method or activity, and brought in research-based articles on the topic. Closely linked to issues of democracy and social justice and embedded both in school structure and classroom practice, tracking was a perfect issue for sustained consideration by the class. More than this, however, the ongoing analysis of tracking provided students with an example of how individual classrooms were connected to larger school structures and, indeed, to issues facing society beyond the schoolhouse.

Lack of Familiarity with Methods for Fostering Critical Inquiry

Preservice teachers have some basic questions and concerns: How do I plan a lesson? How do I keep control of my class? How do I grade students? Preservice teachers wonder how to construct in our methods class the sorts of learning experiences that they read about. These fundamental classroom matters are far less simple and obvious then they might first appear. Such questions are inextricably tied to the quest for social justice teaching; the particulars of teachers' lesson plans, classroom management strategies, assessment tools, and learning activities can make the difference between classroom environments and learning experiences that empower students or those that disenfranchise them.

To this end, we begin the semester with a unit called "Framing Learning," that includes a consideration of these basic lesson and unit planning and classroom management issues. First we discuss how to plan units around meaningful, critical questions rather than solely around regions or time period, and learn about "culminating projects" as a means of organizing a large unit of study. We then consider the flow of a single class period, focusing on creating opportunities for students to learn essential skills and to create meaning for themselves, notions that are central to the social justice project. Finally, we consider the issue of classroom management, considering how to create a classroom structure that maximizes participation, exploring means of disciplining students that do not resort to humiliation, and learning how to use lesson planning and meaningful classroom activities as integral parts of a classroom management strategy. These aspects of the course satisfy some of the most pressing concerns of preservice teachers within the framework of just and democratic teaching.

The course then moves on to systematically consider specific techniques and activities to build such skills in middle and high school students. For each method considered, students participate in a simulated lesson, debrief, and create their own lesson using that strategy. Students first participate in a sample lesson using primary documents pertaining to the bombing of Hiroshima and Nagasaki during World War II; then they analyze and write accounts of the event, drawing from the multiple perspectives presented in the documents and then comparing their accounts with a standard textbook account. Students then learn about various forms and purposes of classroom talk and gain familiarity with a variety of discussion strategies including seminars, deliberations, continuums, and debates. Finally, we take on the tried-and-true social studies research paper, working to understand how teachers can employ this long-used strategy to its best advantage, discussing the skills, knowledge, and structural support that secondary students will need to successfully carry out such an endeavor and reading about how to guide students through a research process that is analytical, reflective, and emerges from students' own issues and concerns.[35] Such activities form the basis of social-justice-oriented social studies teaching, and preservice teachers need to experience and practice them before they can implement them in their own classrooms.

Conclusion

We have found that training social studies teachers to be just and democratic is an endeavor as ripe with possibility as it is fraught with challenge. The preparation of elementary teachers, who are generalists, to teach social studies differs considerably from the preparation of secondary level social studies specialists. The former group needs to be convinced of the very worth of teaching social studies and to be given some basic grounding in the subject. The latter group needs to be challenged to consider how teaching social studies entails much more than transmitting content knowledge to passive recipients.

The approaches described in this chapter make use of the "iterative" nature of the teacher education classroom to help preservice teachers experience, reflect upon, and practice an approach to teaching grounded in analysis of and engagement with significant and meaningful topics.[36] "Never is a method something outside the material," wrote Dewey.[37] The reverse holds true as well: never is a material outside of the method. Social studies teacher education for democracy and social justice should thus embody those very concerns in the methods of instruction used, engaging students as full participants in a consideration of critical social and educational issues.

Throughout both of these methods courses we strive to balance the need to provide a living example of a democratic classroom, while at the same time honoring the students' (and our own) reasonable desire to finish the semester feeling prepared for student teaching. The daily dilemma described earlier is one such effort, opening up the lines of authority and expertise in the methods class by having students take charge of how we spend part of our time together, both in terms of topic and activity. The coteaching that takes place in the elementary methods course plays a similar function, allowing students to take ownership of a portion of the class material and develop activities that draw on their own experiences and ideas. In the secondary methods course, students' lesson and unit plans become part of our course materials. Students post their plans on the class's web-based discussion board and share them in class. Culminating projects generated by previous classes are shared and discussed. In these, and other ways, we attempt to balance the need to provide guidance to new teachers with the opportunity for them to participate fully in the shared endeavor of learning to teach for social justice.

Notes

1. Paulo Freire, *Pedagogy of the Oppressed* (New York: Continuum, 1970).
2. Marilyn Cochran-Smith, "Learning to Teach for Social Justice," in *The Education of Teachers*, ed. G. Griffin (Chicago: University of Chicago Press, 1999), 114–44.
3. Cochran-Smith, 116–17, mentions the following thinkers in her synthesis of the theories underpinning teaching for social justice: Marx, Gramsci, Ladson-Billings, Tatum, Banks, Sleeter, Freire, Apple, Anyon, Giroux, McLaren, Pinar, McDermott, Heath, Cazden, Mehan, Erickson, Weiler and Grumet.
4. Cochran-Smith, 117.
5. Cochran-Smith, 117–18.
6. National Council for the Social Studies, *Expectations of Excellence* (Washington, D.C.: National Council for the Social Studies, 1994).
7. E. Wayne Ross, "Social Studies Teachers and Curriculum," in *The Social Studies Curriculum*, ed. E. W. Ross (Albany: State University of New York Press, 2001), 4.
8. William Stanley and Jack Nelson, "The Foundations of Social Education in Historical Context," in *Inside/Out: Contemporary Critical Perspectives in Education*, ed. R. Martusewicz and W. Reynolds (New York: St. Martin's Press, 1994), 266–84.
9. E. Wayne Ross, "Remaking the Social Studies Curriculum," in *The Social Studies Curriculum*, ed. E. W. Ross (Albany: State University of New York Press, 2001), 316.
10. Susan Noffke, "Identity, Community and Democracy in the New Social Order," in *Democratic Social Education: Social Studies for Social Change*, ed. D. W. Hursh and E. W. Ross (New York: Falmer, 2000), 73–83.
11. Gloria Ladson-Billings, "Crafting a Culturally Relevant Social Studies Approach," in *The Social Studies Curriculum*, ed. E. W. Ross (Albany: State University of New York Press, 2001), 201–15.
12. Terrie Epstein, "Racial Identity and Young People's Perspectives on Social Education," *Theory Into Practice* 40, no. 1 (2001): 42.
13. Kevin D. Vinson, "Oppression, Anti-Oppression, and Citizenship Education," in *The Social Studies Curriculum*, ed. E. W. Ross (Albany: State University of New York Press, 2001), 81.

14. Ross, 325.
15. Walter Parker, "Educating Democratic Citizens: A Broad View," *Theory Into Practice* 40, no. 1 (2001): 6–13.
16. Mark A. Smylie, Mary Bay, and Steven E. Tozer, "Preparing Teachers as Agents of Change," in *The Education of Teachers*, ed. G. Griffin (Chicago: University of Chicago Press, 1999), 47.
17. John Goodlad, *Teachers for Our Nation's Schools* (San Francisco: Jossey-Bass, 1990).
18. Sonia Nieto, *Affirming Diversity: The Sociopolitical Context of Multicultural Education*. (Reading, Mass.: Addison Wesley, 2000).
19. William T. Owens, "The Challenges of Teaching Social Studies Methods to Preservice Elementary Teachers," *Social Studies* 88, no. 3 (1997): 113–20.
20. Marilynne Boyle-Baise, "Multicultural Social Studies: Ideology and Practice," *Social Studies* 87, no. 2 (1996): 81 87; Gloria Ladson-Billings, "Coping with Multicultural Illiteracy: A Teacher Education Response," *Social Education* 53, no. 3 (1991): 186–89; Omiunota Nelly Ukpokodu, "Breaking Through Preservice Teachers' Defensive Attitudes," *Multicultural Education* 9, no. 3 (2002): 15–32.
21. Ukpokodu.
22. Elena M. Silva and Beth C. Rubin, "Missing Voices: Listening to Students' Experiences with School Reform," in *Critical Voices in School Reform: Students Living Through Change*, eds. B.C. Rubin and E.M. Silva (London: Routledge Falmer, 2003), 1–7.
23. Epstein, 42.
24. Sam Wineburg, *Historical Thinking and Other Unnatural Acts* (Philadelphia: Temple University Press, 2001).
25. Joseph Kahne and Joel Westheimer, "Teaching Democracy: What Schools Need to Do," *Phi Delta Kappan* 85, no. 1 (2003): 34–66; Walter Parker, *Teaching Democracy* (New York: Teachers College Press, 2003).
26. Ruth Sidney Charney, *Habits of Goodness: Case Studies in the Social Curriculum* (Greenfield, Mass. Northeast Institute for Children, 1997); Linda S. Levstik and Keith C. Barton, *Doing History*, 2nd ed. (Mahwah, N.J.: Lawrence Erlbaum Associates, 2001).
27. Tarry Lindquist, *Seeing the Whole Through Social Studies* (Portsmouth, N.H.: Heinemann, 2002).
28. John Lewis Gaddis, *The Landscape of History* (New York: Oxford University Press, 2004).
29. In Peter Sterns, Peter Seixas, and Sam Wineburg, eds., *Knowing, Teaching, and Learning History* (New York: New York University Press, 2000).
30. *Expectations of Excellence*.
31. Levstik and Barton, 57–74.
32. Paul Goldstein, *Changing the American Schoolbook* (Lexington, Mass.: D.C. Heath, 1978; J. Y. Cole and T. G. Sticht, eds., *The Textbook in American Society* (Washington, D.C.: Library of Congress, 1981), 9. For general discussion, see James Loewen, *Lies My Teacher Told Me* (New York: Simon and Schuster, 1995), 288–91.
33. Lindquist, 29–31.
34. Kathleen Cushman, *Fires in the Bathroom: Advice for Teachers from High School Students* (New York: The New Press, 2003), x.
35. Beth C. Rubin, "Beyond 'I': Critical Literacy, Social Education and the 'I-Search,'" *University of Pennsylvania GSE Perspectives on Urban Education* 1, no. 2 (2002).
36. Parker and Hess note the "iterative" nature of the teacher education classroom in Walter Parker and Diana Hess, "Teaching with and for Discussion," *Teaching and Teacher Education* 17 (2001): 273–89.
37. John Dewey, *Democracy and Education* (New York: Macmillan Company, 1916), 165.

CHAPTER 5

Where's the Joy? Justice and Caring in Science Education

MARIA S. RIVERA MAULUCCI AND
ANGELA CALABRESE BARTON

It was May 2003, and Randi and I (Maria) were discussing the uncertainty of the next school year. Under the Children First Initiative, the community school districts in New York City had been consolidated into ten super regions. District personnel were being redeployed, and my position as a district science staff developer was no longer going to exist. I had decided to take a teaching position, but was encountering principals who questioned my desire to teach after being out of the classroom.

Randi laughed and said, "Well the greatest part is, you get to be with kids. That's the best part. You know people have asked me, 'Are you going to go into administration?' That's like the next logical thing, but no! Because then, you're not with the kids and if you can't be with the kids.…"

I added, "Where's the fun?"

Randi said, "Yeah. Where's the joy?"

I asked, "Where's the joy?"

Randi replied, "Making decisions about curriculum."

We begin this chapter with an excerpt from our field notes because we believe that it captures several of the key tensions that many urban elementary school teachers face: educational restructuring and uncertainty, the balance between focusing on children and focusing on content or curricula, and the pervasive belief that "moving up" in the teaching profession means moving out of the classroom. Implicit in these reflections is the idea that when we recast our decisions to teach with a desire to help bring about social justice for children and teachers in schools, we also recast those boundaries that frame teaching. In fact, we believe, that a social justice lens "opens up" the practice of teaching because it allows us to focus on the practices and conditions that make a difference—the joy of teaching—rather than to be paralyzed by the deficits that mark institutional practices in many inner-city school systems.

In particular, in this chapter we describe one middle school teacher's —Randi's—science teaching practice, and how her belief in a "freedom to teach" offers us one vision for what science education for social justice might look like. To tell this story we first describe the issues that a social justice lens raises in science education. Then, using a personal narratives approach, we tell Randi's story and focus on the following questions:

- What does a belief in the freedom to teach mean? How does this belief in the freedom to teach frame what science teaching looks like in a fifth-grade science classroom?
- How is this vision transformative for teachers and their students?
- In what ways does the freedom to teach challenge widely held understandings of access, agency, and achievement, and how does reformulating these constructs transform how we enact visions of "science for all" in classrooms?

Reenvisioning Science Education from a Social Justice Perspective

Current policy initiatives and discussions that focus on urban education and student learning are largely driven by the quantitative findings that low-income urban youth are lagging in mathematics, literacy, science, and other academic subject areas. Indeed, key studies have described how urban students in low-income communities, on average, score lower on high-stakes tests and have lower participation in higher-level science and mathematics courses.[1] Other literature has shown that low-income urban students drop out of school at rates significantly higher than more affluent children,[2] less than half of the ninth graders in central city schools complete high school in four years,[3] and children attending poor, urban schools have reduced access to new textbooks, scientific equipment, science-related extracurricular activities, or qualified, certified teachers.[4] Consequently, the process of learning has become obscured by its product, and little attention has been granted to how context and the multiple purposes offer learning matter.

In New York City, policies are being written and implemented that exchange a focus on learning standards for a standard process of learning. While science education has yet to go the way of mathematics of literacy, where teachers are prescribed page-a-day teaching and teachers and students in all classrooms must be on the same page of the curriculum on the same day, one could easily imagine science education moving along the same trajectory. These policies have hit low-income communities in New York City hard, especially those communities within urban centers where poverty rates are high and where schools serve majority minority populations.

These sorts of discussions and policy initiatives rely on the deficit model. They focus on what students lack and qualitatively draw away from what students do bring to the science classroom. Even the reform initiatives in science education, which hold the egalitarian goal that all students should have equitable opportunities to learn science—Science for All—are steeped in a stance of learning that is separate from context. As the major reform-based policy statements have announced:

> All students, regardless of gender, cultural, or ethnic background, physical or learning disabilities, aspiration, or interest and motivation in science, should have the opportunity to attain higher levels of scientific literacy than they currently do. This is a principle of equity...and has implications for program design and the education system...to ensure that the standards do not exacerbate the differences...that currently exist.[5]

> When demographic realities, national needs, and democratic values are taken into account, it becomes clear that the nation can no longer ignore the science education of any student. Race, language, sex, or economic circumstances must no longer be permitted to be factors in determining who does and who does not receive a good education in science, mathematics, and technology.[6]

The Science for All initiatives in the United States and in other Western nations have been criticized, and we believe rightly so, for continuing to view the needs of poor, urban youth, non-English language background youth, youth of color, and girls through the deficit model.[7] As these critiques point out, Science for All initiatives indicate that students who come to school not versed in the culture of Western science are "lacking" and need to engage in extra efforts to catch up to their peers. They also assume that schooling operates meritocratically, and that science achievement scores are based on one's efforts and abilities rather than one's degree of enculturation into a system. As Kyle notes, "the rhetoric of 'science education for all' is juxtaposed to the reality of 'science education for the privileged'" (p. xi).[8]

Despite this criticism of Science for All, we agree with the thrust of the policy initiative that an equitable science education is both a moral and ethical imperative. Students need an opportunity to learn science. Our concerns rest in how the issues get framed and the importance this has for how we understand students' lives and how science instruction might authentically emerge from them. So, we wonder, what would it mean to refocus a discussion of science teaching and learning in low-income urban communities so that we frame teaching and learning in ways that are productively oriented, empowering, and transformative? In other words, what would it mean to reenvision science education from a social justice perspective?

A Social Justice Perspective

Our approach to social justice is grounded in three bodies of literature: a multicultural approach to students and teaching;[9] a politics of caring,[10] and critical approaches to science education.[11] Together, these bodies of literature capture four key meanings when applied to science education.

First, science education for social justice is transformative for all participants. Science pedagogy framed around social justice concerns can become a medium to transform individuals, schools, communities, the environment, and science itself in ways that promote equity and social justice. Creating a *transformative* science education implies that learning and using science are political activities. Transformative science, then, politicizes science education not only "by the provision of opportunities for students to confront a wide range of socioeconomic issues that have a scientific, technological, or environmental dimension" (p. 787),[12] but more important by the explicit belief that science must also have a social, economic, and political effect in students' lives. We claim that creating transformative science can be achieved only by recognizing the specific social, cultural, and political needs of the population doing the science.

Second, science education for social justice is grounded in critical awareness. In supporting this critical awareness of structures and power relations at play in their lives, we see *critical* science education as nurturing student voice and encouraging students to articulate their critical understandings. Critical science education encourages students to see themselves as agents of change in their lives and their community. That is, it supports student agency. So, by providing opportunities for students to gain a critical understanding, articulate a position, and take action, science education should play a role in reshaping student identities with new, critical understandings.

Third, science education for social justice is only possible when learning communities foster caring relationships between students and their teachers, and among students, so that a sharing of ideas, skills, and experiences in and around the curriculum, or learning, can occur. Noddings explains that caring is more than "a warm fuzzy feeling that makes people kind and likable. Caring implies a continuous search for competence."[13] This means believing that all children can learn and organizing the educative process around ensuring that all children do learn.

Fourth, an empowering education in low-income urban schools is one that is grounded in the lives of the teachers and learners who learn in those schools. We believe that the foundations (the needs, experiences, and ideas) or the seeds for change rest in the lives of ordinary people—and in particular in the lives of those people who ordinarily have been marginalized. It is our duty as professional developers and researchers to struggle with people to learn more about those needs, experiences, and ideas. In short, students and teachers must be valued for the wealth of experience, knowledge, and skills they bring to the classroom both as members of the learning community and as learners.

Reenvisioning the Goals of Science Education Through a Social Justice Lens

We specifically use the term *reenvision* to acknowledge that the teachers and students possess and express visions for caring, science, and science education, although these may or may not be well articulated. In addition, the term *reenvision* incorporates an integral part of our roles in the classroom as professional developers, teacher educators, and researchers to move teachers and students from their current locations toward actively developing classroom communities that foster respect, caring, inquiry-based learning, problem-solving, and student achievement. This is not to imply that some or all of these aspects are not already present. Thus, we also recognize that reenvisioning caring, equity, science, and science education is an ongoing process that in a real sense never ends; we grow and change and reenvision these realities alongside those with whom we work.

Valenzuela[14] documented how schooling becomes a subtractive process in which immigrant students gradually lose their language, culture, and educational values, ultimately leading to low levels of achievement. While her study was with Mexican immigrant youth, schooling may also be a subtractive process for any students whose cultures do not match that of the school, including poor, inner-city students.[15] One of the main disconnects that Valenzuela uncovered was a difference in the ways that students and teachers perceived caring. Specifically, teachers expected students to care about school while students expected teachers to care about them. As a result, Valenzuela contends that educators must become sensitive to the "politics of caring" as a first step in developing a "more relevant and authentic pedagogy."[16]

Drawing from Valenzuela's work, it is clear that it is not enough to say that science is for all students. Instead, we believe it is important to reenvision the ways in which students access science, how we measure student achievement in science, and the role of agency in the science classroom.

Access

The ways that students access, or gain entry to science typically position students as outside science and require that they assimilate the content, processes, histories, norms for participation, and discursive practices of science. Hodson explains that assimilation "sees its goal as the perpetuation, transmission, and promotion of the cultural beliefs and norms of the dominant community. It is a one-way process, through which members of an ethnic group give up (or have taken away) their original cultural identity."[17] Our own research and teaching in urban classrooms suggests that access ought to be thought about in a much more fluid and interactive manner.[18] Accessing science, whether it be in the classroom or in daily life is a reflexive process that always involves students playing active roles in shaping the science in their lives. In other words, accessing science is in part about getting into the scientific canon, which most certainly plays a gatekeeping role.[19] But part of accessing science is critically transforming the form and function of science by situating science as a sociopolitical and cultural practice.[20] As Ladson-Billings asserts, students must "develop a broader sociopolitical consciousness that allows them to critique the cultural norms, values, mores, and institutions that produce and maintain social inequities."[21]

Achievement

Similarly, rather than focusing solely on traditional measures of achievement, such as performance on high-stakes exams, or paper and pencil classroom assessments, achievement in science should be expanded to include students' self-esteem or self-efficacy with respect to science, the degree to which students elect to take advanced courses,[22] and, ultimately, greater representation of poor, urban students in science-related careers. Thus, methods of assessing what students know and are able to do must align with how teachers are expected to teach as well as how students are expected to show what they have learned.[23] In addition, in order to align with reenvisioned equity goals, assessments must be reflective of science as a sociocultural activity, include students' worldviews and perspectives, and foster agency.[24]

Agency

Agency in the science classroom has three key elements. First, agency refers to students' active role in the production and reproduction of scientific knowledge both inside and outside the classroom. Second, by providing students with an active role or voice in the process of producing scientific knowledge, science becomes responsive to their individual and collective needs, struggles, and cultures. Third, commitment to caring and social justice reformulates our roles as teachers and researchers, wherein agency "refers to the conscious role we choose to play in helping bring about social change for the collective benefit of all, especially those in lower hierarchical power or disadvantaged positions than ourselves."[25] In our teaching and research, we are consciously there to bring about changes that may be necessary, including changes in teachers' philosophies and practices, changes in students' attitudes toward science, motivation, behavior in the science classroom, and ultimately, student outcomes. Thus, it is not enough for teacher educators or researchers to gather data about teaching and learning; we have to make a substantive difference in the lives of the children and teachers we serve.

Transforming Science Learning in Middle School Science through a Social Justice Perspective: A Case Study

In the remainder of this chapter we use the social justice framework to tell a story about how teaching relationships built on caring can serve as the basis for a transformative science education practice. In particular, we tell the story of one teacher, Randi, a fifth-grade teacher in a large middle school, located in a low-income community. We use the case of Randi to explore the relationships between the teacher's lived experiences and beliefs and the enacted science curriculum within a particular urban context. In addition, this study explores critical issues, unique to the context and constituents, that arise and ultimately shape the students' and teacher's transformative pathways. The story that we tell is part of a larger set of studies that explore the interplay between the theory and practice of caring and social justice in the context of an urban science professional development lab.

The qualitative methods employed include narrative inquiry and life history. Narrative inquiry draws upon the natural role of stories in the way we make sense of our lives and experiences both in and out of the classroom.[26] By situating these stories within teachers' lived experiences, we gain a greater sense of the intersections between teachers' beliefs, motives, practices, and contexts.[27] Also, by drawing from narrative inquiry, we gain a more authentic first-hand experience of how it is that the teacher in our study understood what social justice and science education were about. Taking our cues from other narrative inquiry researchers, we therefore draw upon lengthy quotations in an attempt to remain true to the voice and perspective of the teacher with whom we worked.

Data for the study were obtained through a series of semistructured interviews focused on the teacher's life history, beliefs, and experiences, as well as classroom observations and journal entries spanning the 2002–2003 school year. As in praxis-oriented research, a primary goal was to help participants reflect upon and transform their situations.[28] As a result, the methods draw upon principles of reciprocity and collaborative theorizing, or mutual negotiation of meaning.[29] In addition, there is a blurring of the roles of researcher and researched, such that our interactions are characterized by an ability to listen to and learn from each other and to reflect candidly upon our experiences together.[30]

A guiding purpose for this study was to construct narratives that help us understand how students' and teachers' participation in urban science professional development lab programs may allow them to reenvision science in their lives, their position with respect to science, and their roles in the science classroom. Specifically, we were interested in describing what a transformative science lesson might look like in a fifth-grade, urban, science classroom to address the following questions: What does a belief in the freedom to teach mean? How does this belief in the freedom to teach frame what science teaching looks like in a fifth-grade science classroom? How is this vision transformative for teachers and their students? In what ways does the freedom to teach challenge widely held understandings of access, agency, and achievement, and how does reformulating these constructs transform how we enact visions of "science for all" in classrooms? The following is Maria's story.

Investigating Owl Pellets

I work as a district staff developer, in a model science lab, in a large, K–8 school in New York City. The school enrolls more than 1500 students, 90 percent of whom are eligible for free lunch. About 4 percent of the students are recent immigrants and 14 percent are designated as English Language Learners. 64 percent of the students are Hispanic students and 34 percent are Black. The school is divided into a Primary School for grades K–4 and an Upper School for Grades 5–8. While each school has its own principal, the two principals work closely together to facilitate a unified vision of teaching and learning across grades K–8. Nevertheless, the school struggles with low student achievement on State-mandated literacy and mathematics tests, particularly at the middle school level.

Randi is a white, female teacher in her late thirties. She describes herself as an upstate New Yorker, having gown up in Rochester. She comes to teaching following a career in hotel management, explaining: "Well, in the restaurant business the thing that I was the best at was training other people and management. You know, getting the work done that needed to be done. So training, that became my thing. I can teach people how to do things."

Randi's favorite grade to teach is fifth grade—the entry grade in the middle school—because fifth graders are "very needy ... in so many other ways than any other kid." Randi explains how they go through so many changes "mentally, physically, maturity-wise, emotionally...I mean you name it. And they kind of don't know what to do with all these changes. No one really talks about it yet because they think that they're only 10 and 11. They're not teenagers yet but really they're adolescents. It starts at 10.... So they have all these things going on and they don't know how to cope with them and they don't know how to talk about them so it's my grade." While this is her first year with the Department of Education, seven years teaching experience make her a veteran teacher and the lead teacher for her grade.

When Randi asked me to visit her class because they were dissecting owl pellets, I wondered why she was doing owl pellets when the students were in the middle of their physical science unit. For the last several weeks, the fifth-grade classes had been cycling through the District's Science and Technology Lab to learn how to use triple beam balances. In class, the teachers were focusing on other aspects of measurement, such as length and volume. I had also been working with Randi and the other fifth-grade teachers to develop science centers as a way to utilize limited materials for science. Each teacher would set up a science center in their [sic] room and the students would cycle through during the course of a week. The center activities were designed so that students should be able to follow the instructions and do the activity with little or no direct assistance from their teacher. Sometimes the teacher might need to do a whole-class lesson first. Then, students could begin cycling through the activity, followed by a whole class discussion. The first center activity was designed to give students extra practice with the triple-beam balance. The students would measure equal volumes of sand and water, find the mass of the sand and water by subtracting the mass of the cup, and then compare the mass of sand and water to determine that equal volumes of different substances have different masses. The science center approach was less than ideal, but at least the students were getting some hands-on activities. Our goal was to provide students with more opportunities to learn science in their classrooms.

As I thought about the owl pellets, I could see how it might connect to their study of animals, including birds, later in the year during the life science unit, but I did not know what the connection was now. I went up to Randi's classroom the following day and arrived several minutes after the students had begun working on their pellets. I noted that each student had their [sic] own owl pellet. Since they had already started, small mounds of fur and separate piles of bones were beginning to take shape in front of the students. "Look what I found!" Liliana exclaimed, brandishing a skull complete with long, orange incisors. "I found one too!" Jason replied. "What's this?" students were asking. I watched as students laboriously teased apart bones and fur.

The excitement was contagious and I realized that I had to document this.

I ran down to the lab to get the digital camera. I returned, and for a while, I focused on capturing the images...students delicately using toothpicks to clean the fur off the tiny bones, painstakingly matching bones to skeletal diagrams, and skeletal forms of rodents and birds taking shape. I also saw Randi conferring with students, showing them how to clean the bones, helping them compare and contrast the bones to the chart to determine which part of the skeleton they came from. Periodically, she would remind students of the time and where they should be by that point in order to finish. Jasmine asked me to help her remove the bones and fur from inside the skull she found. The material was packed in tight [sic] and she didn't want the skull to break. As I held the skull, I was struck by how delicate it was. Before long, I was digging in too.

One of the students, Diana, had the idea of matching the bones directly to the skeletal diagram, like pieces of a puzzle. Soon, students at other tables caught on and began trying the same thing. I realized that there were not enough diagrams for each student to have their [sic] own, so I asked Randi if she had more. Randi said she only made one copy per group and that she didn't think the copy room staff would make more of them since you had to request copies three days in advance. I offered to make them on the copy machine down in the Lab. I quickly borrowed one of the student's diagrams and ran downstairs again. When I came back, Randi helped me distribute the diagrams. The students were enthusiastic. Now they all would be able to complete their puzzles. During this time, the principal came in. As she circulated among the students, she was positive about their engagement with the task, but queried Randi about the next steps. When she saw that I had the digital camera she said, "Great! Randi can use the pictures for her bulletin board." By this time, we were well into the second period and the students were still on task. Many students were actively helping each other. They were sharing ideas, methods, and bones so that their classmates could complete their skeletons.

Towards the end of the period, Randi distributed construction paper and began encouraging students to glue the bones of their skeletons to the construction paper. It quickly became clear that she did not have enough glue bottles to go around, since almost all the students were ready to begin gluing. Once again I ran down to the lab to get some more glue. Upon returning, I told Randi that I had to leave to prepare the lab for a class that was coming after lunch.

She thanked me for coming and helping out. I told her, "That's what I'm here for."

Later, after many conversations with Randi, I began to realize that Randi's decision to conduct the owl pellet investigation was about her desire to build an instructional program across the subject areas that were responsive to her students' needs and interests. While I initially viewed her teaching decision to conduct an owl pellet investigation as a "deviation" from the science curriculum of the moment, I began to see that this activity was not a deviation at all. Randi did not abandon the grade's instructional goals to introduce students to measurement skills in physical science to do a more exciting life science activity. Rather, as a self-contained classroom teacher, she creatively used her schedule and her knowledge of the students' progressions through each of the academic subject areas to design an emergent learning opportunity. This seemed especially powerful to me given the school's strong emphasis on test scores and subject attention to mathematics and literacy instruction at the expense of other subject areas.

Furthermore, as I reflect upon the owl pellet activity, I have come to the realization that the students were building more than skeletons that day, and they were learning more than life science that day. They were building a community of learners and ways of talking and doing science. They were learning that the boundaries of science activities are not defined by a progression through a curriculum. Randi and I were also building something. We were building a relationship that was about making science happen for kids.

The following are Randi's comments.

Freedom to Teach Equals Opportunity to Learn

So, I think the biggest barrier is just let me shut my door and let me teach my kids. Don't tell me how to teach them. Don't tell me what works best for my students. *I know.* If I'm a professional and I've done all the things that I'm trained to do. Then *I know.* Let me do what I have to do. Because if I have to spend three days talking about measurement, then I need to spend three days on it. Don't tell me I've got one day and I'm not on the pacing chart. I need to move on. Don't tell me that. So leaving me alone to do my job [laughing]… is half the battle. Because I'm not getting stuff done.

In working with Randi across the course of two school years, it has become clear to us that Randi's practice is grounded in two principled ideas: that freedom to teach equals an opportunity to learn, and that teaching is a process that is deeply contextual, involving deep knowledge of subject matter knowledge, students, and how the systems work.

The freedom to teach, as Randi alludes to in the interview transcript shared above, involves a combination of professional knowledge, a proclivity toward practicing teaching in a way that is driven by students' needs, and a desire to make a difference. Randi passionately believes that she and her students can accomplish many things together if she were "free" to teach the way she *knew* best. A closer look at Randi's practices shows us that her belief in what we refer to as "the freedom to teach" is grounded in three practices: (1) blurring the boundaries between subject areas; (2) making time for science by reframing or resisting what, when, and how one is mandated to teach science and other subjects; and (3) using specific knowledge of "how the system works" to justify one's decisions. We describe each one of these points below, offering examples from Randi's practice that help to both contextualize the points we make and advance our understanding of the importance of the freedom to teach.

Blurring the Boundaries between Subjects

The first practice that marks Randi's belief in the freedom to teach is her decision to blur the boundaries between school subjects. While Randi often blurred boundaries between many of the subjects she taught, she paid particular attention to how she could blur the boundaries between literacy and science. Making connections between literacy and science was particularly important to Randi because she teaches in a school where student scores on the high-stakes literacy exams are low, and thus the fifth-grade curriculum is supersaturated with literacy blocks.

Randi's specific knowledge of science and literacy also influenced curricular decisions that allowed science to enter into literacy instruction seamlessly. For example, read-alouds are encouraged by the school principal and are a main component of balanced literacy instruction in all fifth-grade classrooms. Randi often chose science-related books for these read-alouds that she believed would be interesting for students to read and listen to. In discussing the content of the read-alouds with her students she often looked for student ideas that might offer springboards for other activities, projects, and discussion. In fact, the owl pellet activity, described above, was a project that had its initial origin in a literacy-block read-aloud.

Randi explained that they had been reading *Poppy,* by Avi. She described the book as a "total science book" and retold the story:

> Well it's about Poppy the mouse and her family. So in the first chapter of the book Poppy and her little boyfriend are on a hill where they're not supposed to be in the forest and Ragweed steps out of the little leaf he was hiding underneath and Mr. Ocax the owl comes down and eats him....So they talk about the talons, and the owl comes down and grabs the mouse, and then later on, you found [sic] out that Poppy is in the forest under the owl's nest and sees the pile of owl pellets and notices the earring that Ragweed had in one of the owl pellets....Then, we also learn Mr. Ocax's trick that he's playing on the mice. He tells the mice that they're not allowed to leave or go anywhere in the forest without his permission. There's the irony, right? Because he hates them, but they need his permission; so they go get his permission and he's going to eat them. Well, he scares the mice into believing this because he says porcupines are in the forest and that porcupines eat mice. Well, of course we know, porcupines are not meat eaters. So that's where this survival of the fittest, and survival, and food chains, and all of that comes into play.

This read-aloud sparked numerous questions on the part of the students, as Randi explained:

> They wanted to know a lot about the porcupine. They wanted to know what a quill was, which I showed them because I have one in my room. They wanted to know how you know that a porcupine is not a meat eater. What do porcupines eat? They wanted to know all about the pellet. They think that it's puke. They're totally curious about the pellet. So when the curiosity comes out, I have a pellet in my room and I bring that out. They take it out and they get to touch it and that creates even more questions like, What's that bone? or How does it do that? How does it regurgitate it? What's digestion? Why doesn't it digest bones? What kind of animals does it eat? How many animals can be in there? Can birds be in there? I mean just all…you name it. They want to know about it.

Although Randi described the owl pellet activity as "not teacher directed," it was clear that she introduced it in a structured way and had a process in mind for how the activity would proceed.

I had to give them some brief skill information. How they were to unwrap it. How they were to pull it apart. Why they had to keep it on the mat and then separating the bones from the fur. That was their first big deal. And then we had the charts, the bone-sorting charts. They were supposed to categorize their bones so then they could put them up to the chart and see where it belonged. And then after all of them were sorted, they had to reconstruct, based on the chart, whatever creature they had found. It's not exact because I don't know the difference between a vole bone and a mole bone....

Thus, as this quotation suggests, in addition to the read-alouds, Randi explained how other tools of literacy, such as writing narrative procedures, also became a place of science investigation for students. Randi viewed this blurring of boundaries, however, as moving in multiple directions. While she was able to use literacy time to engage in science investigations with her students, she also drew upon the excitement of exploring the owl pellets as a student-generated reason for practicing methods of scientific communication. As she explained:

Then they had to write about what kind of animal they thought it was and why. So if they thought it was a vole, or mole, or whatever, they had to talk about, basically the teeth in front and the size of the skull. Those were really the only two discerning factors. If they had a bird, obviously they would have a beak. They had to talk about what kind of animal they thought it was. And then, we kind of had some discussions about the eating process again. So, I asked them to write up in step form, what happens when an owl eats something.... You know, he eats it, digests what he can, builds up the fur until it's too much, then pukes it out. So, if I'd continued the lesson and talked more about life science and the food chains and all that stuff, I could have gotten more processes out of it.

Although Randi believed that she created opportunities to blur boundaries on almost a daily basis, she also recognized that she was constrained by the system from doing so as often as she believed would be beneficial to her students. She constantly reminded us that "every subject is separate" in her school and that "it's just not set up that way." In criticizing her own teaching actions around the owl pellet activity, she stated that she could have "gotten more processes out of it" if she could have spent more time on the project in both literacy and science.

Making Time for Science

Having time to teach science was a particularly tension-filled issue with Randi and the other teachers at her school. As described earlier, Randi teaches science in a middle school formally labeled as low performing. Consequently, instructional priority has been granted to mathematics and literacy instruction. In fact, it was the case at the school that many teachers at her grade level often did not even teach science and little administrative attention was given to its absence. Having "time" to do science for Randi, though, was not always about scheduling a class block. As the previous theme of blurring the boundaries between science and literacy shows, Randi viewed subject-matter knowledge instruction as something that could emerge from any activity if the teacher is attentive enough to the interests of her students.

In addition to blurring boundaries across subject areas, Randi challenged the time to do science by actively reframing or resisting what, when, and how she was mandated to teach. In the case of the owl pellets, Randi originally introduced the book, *Poppy*, as a read-aloud for "pure enjoyment." She said, "Just a read-aloud for enjoyment, only and then all this other stuff happened. I thought, 'Well, I'll do the owl pellet now.'" Despite the fact that in science class, they were studying properties of matter, Randi decided that it was important to facilitate the students' interest in owls. Thus the "what" to teach was decided by students' interest and in order to capitalize on students' immediate desire to learn more about owls, Randi had to change "when" she would introduce the owl pellets. Likewise, by pursuing students' interests from literacy into science, Randi was forging connections between subjects in ways that the current curricular structure did not allow. Randi explained:

> I think that things need to be connected. We keep asking kids to make connections and everything is separate. This is the time for math. From here to here. That's it. We're not asked to teach science and math together even though we all know they go hand in hand. We're not asked to teach social studies and reading together. So if it's not done in that time frame you feel like you can't do it.

Randi explained that she made time for the owl pellet lesson even though it did not fit with the science curriculum at the time, and we recalled that she had used several morning periods although science was usually in the afternoon. Randi admitted to using "social studies" time to be able to fully incorporate the owl pellet experience. While Randi explained that she learned to be flexible with her teaching schedule—she has a self-contained classroom—she was also clear that she could use her knowledge of how different subjects intersected in support of curricular decisions that countered official school policy. Randi confidently stated, "Give me one of those webs, I can stretch it wherever I need to." Thus, Randi actively resisted the arbitrary borders between subjects by expanding the boundaries of what constitutes science and ultimately transforming literacy and social studies as well.

Knowledge of the System

Having knowledge of how the school system worked allowed Randi to feel confident taking teaching risks—risks she felt were necessary to provide her students with opportunities for meaningful leaning. Randi explained:

> Well, here, in this school, I feel very constrained. Here, in this school, in order for me to do that, I would have to know my reasoning behind it and be able to justify or defend why I'm doing that particular activity at that particular time, when it's not in the map. If I know that I can do that and feel confident about it, I'll do it. I'll do it any chance I get. ... I need to get my kids motivated. My kids are not motivated to learn. If they're motivated about something and I have the chance to squeeze that in somehow, I'm going to squeeze it in. What I just do is I make sure I have a defense. And I always do.

Randi explained that being able to justify or "having a defense for" what she was doing was critical to her ability to have the freedom to teach.

> We'd already been through the scientific method but I was pushing my kids last year to go beyond and start to think about variables and how we're going to change a variable for an experiment. So I brought out the everlasting gobstoppers, and I have an experiment around everlasting gobstoppers that gets them to think in this way. Now if the principal comes in to see these kids looking at candies in a bowl and every kid's got a gobstopper in their [sic] mouth, I have to be able to justify that. But there's not one kid who's not participating.

As this quotation suggests, in Randi's school the principal, and even sometimes the superintendent, made unannounced visits. She also knew that when one walked into her room during a literacy block, he or she expected to see literacy happening. Randi also recognized that her definitions of what constituted meaningful learning in literacy might not match the vision advocated by the school or the district. She knew that if she was to continue to serve her students well, she needed to be able to explain why she was teaching *what* she was teaching and *how* she was teaching it. Thus, Randi's specific knowledge of "the system" or her ability to effectively communicate why she is doing what she is doing allows her to take risks in a climate of increased teacher scrutiny.

Randi recognized that her actions to "beat the system" were tempered by the reality of her situation. Randi was the lead teacher on the grade and visitors were often brought to see her class. As she explained, "And people have said to me, 'Randi shut your door and do what you need to do.' Well, I can't shut my door. My room is too hot. It's open all the time. That's the logistics of it. And I have visitors all the time in my room. So I have to be doing it the District way. God forbid the [principal] should come into my room and I'm not doing it the District way. I'm sure it's because I have experience and I have the class that I have but it's frustrating."

Discussion: Reenvisioning Equity: Access, Achievement, and Agency

Freedom to teach, which is the source for students' opportunities to engage in meaningful learning, is at the heart of Randi's practice. The practices that make up Randi's belief in the freedom to teach provide a vision for how one teacher worked within a set of less than optimal conditions to make transformative teaching happen. If we look across the themes, we can see that freedom to teach also helps us to envision science education differently. In particular, freedom to teach reformulates our understanding of equity in terms of access, agency, and achievement.

Access

Students' access to the science of owl pellets was mediated in three important ways that contribute to teaching for social justice. First, the access was initiated by students' interest, rather than a scripted curriculum. Randi explained, "It was pure exploration based on *their* curiosity." By allowing students voice and choice in the curriculum, Randi allowed students to access science in a more reflexive way. Second, the entry to science was achieved via literacy, through a read-aloud from a fiction book, which for many students may have rendered the scientific discourse around terminology, such as regurgitation and digestion, as well as conceptual ideas, including food chains more accessible. It is important to note that none of the students in this class were designated English Language Learners, so a read-aloud in English was accessible to all students. In addition, since students were not required to read the text on their own, poor reading skills did not hinder their access to the scientific knowledge embedded in the text or the class discussions that ensued. Finally, the narrative nature of the text and the dramatic telling of the story may have allowed students to identify with Poppy the mouse and imagine the interactions between Mr. Ocax and the mice, or predator-prey relationships within the forest setting in creative ways, whereas a nonfiction description of owls and their prey might not evoke such imagery or personal connections with students.

For Randi, what makes science accessible to students is that it is "high interest." She explained, "They like doing it. These are the things that happen around them all the time and it's available. You just have to have the materials. And even with a limited amount, you can still at least get science in." So as a teacher she strategically tries to create the conditions of "high interest." The owl pellet activity is something that Randi has taught before and planned to teach again later in the year. What she did not anticipate was that the read-aloud of *Poppy* would spur such interest in the students and blur the boundaries between literacy and science. Thus, the students' opportunity to learn was facilitated by Randi's ability to reframe the boundaries of what, when, and how science would be taught in relation to other subjects, as well as her willingness to take risks and invest her own money so that every child could dissect an owl pellet. Finally, students were able to enact their own methodologies for removing the bones and constructing the skeletons. By shaping what constitutes knowing and doing in science, students were able to access science as insiders, rather than outsiders.

Agency

By being innovative in their methodologies of removing the bones, sorting them, and constructing the skeletons, students were also able to develop a sense of agency with respect to knowing and doing science. The students were innovative because they were not taught specific methodologies; they were only told to be careful because the bones were delicate. As a result, the students had to develop their own ways of accomplishing these tasks. While there was a good deal of "trial and error," when a particular student developed a really useful method, other students and even the teachers were able to imitate that method. This placed students in the roles of independent learners, co-learners, and teachers. For example, one student, Diana, was trying to construct a skeleton of a rodent and was having difficulty keeping track of where the bones should go on her mat and what she need to get next. She began to match the bones directly to the diagram, as if she were completing a primary puzzle. This idea spread very quickly.

Randi: All the years that I've done this, I've never seen that done.

Researcher: So that was really innovative of them.

Randi: Very innovative and creative and I remember the child that did it.

Researcher: Who was that?

Randi: Diana…One of the reasons that stands out is because I hadn't seen her take initiative ever, in anything up to that point, especially not in science. So to take the initiative because she wanted to do the activity…and apparently she was interested in it.…She took the initiative to do it in that particular way, by placing the bones on the chart.

Researcher: And it caught on like wildfire.

Randi: Totally. And one part of me feels like maybe that's how I should tell them to do it but on the other hand, that was really a great learning moment, teachable moment, whatever you want to call it.

Not only did Diana have an active role in the production of scientific knowledge, but for this child it was the first instance that Randi could recall her showing initiative with respect to learning. For this particular child, who initiated this way of doing science and received the acknowledgment of her peers and teacher, the owl pellet activity became a source of agency. As the teacher, Randi recognized how this became a source of empowerment for her students, particularly Diana, and as a result she explained that she would be reluctant to *tell* future students to do the skeletons the same way, even though it really worked, because of the value that discovery had as a "teachable moment."

Despite the clear parallels between the owl-pellet activity and the work of real scientists who study owls, Randi resisted labeling this activity as one in which students were positioned as scientists, although she would label it as a science-like performance.

Well I think because scientists are curious, they have to start with their curiosity. And from there they go on and make their experiment, or draw their conclusions, or make decisions and I think one of the ways that I relate science to real life is just by using it as a decision-making process. And so just under the umbrella of science and under the umbrella of owl pellets you get kids to think in that methodological way then, you've got them to be problem-solvers. And isn't that the point? I'm not raising scientists in my classroom. I'm trying to raise problem-solvers. So I think it's linked to science in that way. Having these questions. Working through the process to either have more questions because you don't have an answer yet that you need. Or just seeking more information maybe that sparked something else in you to go another avenue. So in that way, I think it's linked to scientists.

Thus, student agency derives from their ability to use science to make decisions.

From a teaching perspective, Randi's sense of agency is derived from her ability to leverage her knowledge of the system to teach in the way that she *knows* works. This primarily means that her students are motivated about learning. One of the ways Randi garners student interest is by giving them voice and choice in the curriculum. When students see that they have a role in determining the learning goals, at least sometimes, this is also a potential source of agency. However, it is important to note that part of the reason why students were allowed voice and choice in science is because it is a relatively undervalued subject. In other words, do students also have opportunities to establish learning goals in literacy or mathematics as well?

Achievement

Randi described the owl pellet activity as a "performance assessment." Specifically, she wanted to know, "Did they complete it? Were they able to follow the steps? Were they able to talk about the steps of the regurgitation process? Were they able to physically use this guide to put back the [skeleton]? Did they understand why they were doing it?" The students could have relied upon what they learned from the book *Poppy*, or read more about owls to answer their questions about owl pellets. Instead, they engaged in an authentic process of learning about what owls eat that blurred the distinction between learning and assessment. At the same time, this performance assessment communicated to the students that a broader set of skills and capacities, such as working cooperatively, gathering evidence, sorting, categorizing, thinking critically, and solving problems, were valued besides simply being able to recall information or use information to answer questions. Embedded within the owl pellet activity was attention to the process of science, which for Randi means the scientific method.

> What did I want students to learn? I think generally, getting a feel for how an experiment works, scientific method, how to get from your prediction or your hypothesis all the way through the end of an experiment. It's not the topic that you chose, or what was in the curriculum, it's just that basic knowledge. That it's not just fun and games. It's formulating questions, observing... answering your questions. Or making new questions about what you've observed.

Beyond process, Randi explained that although writing was part of how she asked students to summarize what they learned, she was more concerned with getting students to think than to write.

> Because the writing is hard for some of them. It was hard for me as a kid. So if I can get them to think about it and then we can have meaningful discussions about it and all the kids are actively participating in a meaningful discussion or dialogue. That to me is far more superior than asking them to write.

According to Randi, what makes dialogue "meaningful" is that "everyone can do it."

> Everyone can do it no matter if they [sic] can't express themselves, fully, with really good vocabulary, they can, however, express themselves somehow and a lot of kids can't do that in writing. It's difficult for them and it's a chore. Well, talking is never a chore for any of those kids. [Laughing] It's always something they want to do. That's why I hate forcing them to have to write all the time. Forcing someone to write is not making them want to do it.

Randi's primary goal is to motivate her students to *want* to learn because she feels everything else will flow from there. To make learning accessible, she tries to scaffold the process so that even students who cannot express the understandings that they have developed through writing, have the opportunity to communicate their ideas. Thus, performance assessments have the potential to individualize learning goals for students and move beyond "one size fits all" approaches to measuring student achievement in science.

Implications

Randi stands out among her peers as a leader, an innovator, a person who is willing to learn, and as an advocate for her students. To her, the joy in teaching stems from "being with kids" and "making decisions about curriculum." At the same time, being with children and making decisions about curriculum occur within the social, political, and economic aspects of schooling in general and her school, in particular. The current policy arena of NCLB points to increasingly scripting teacher activity in the classroom, including the structure of daily lessons, rigid pacing charts, specific educational programs and materials to be used, and continuous oversight. In the effort to raise literacy and mathematics scores, funds and time are spent disproportionately on these subject areas to the detriment of quality teaching in science, social studies, and the arts, sending a clear message to students and teachers that all subjects are not equal. Furthermore, the sorting and segregating of students into higher and lower tracks belies the ideal that "all children can learn."

While concerns for equity necessitate clearly identifying the problem that our schools do not currently serve *all* children, Randi's case illustrates that by removing the decision-making power from teachers, we run the risk of severely constraining teachers' abilities to motivate all students to learn. If we continue to prescribe for teachers what, when, and how they must teach, we diminish the potential for student and teacher agency in schools and classrooms and create a climate that requires teacher resistance in order for transformative science teaching and learning to occur. We also limit the pathways by which students can access science in meaningful ways. This scenario provides little hope for improving achievement of poor, urban students by any measure.

Alternatively, connected learning opens up a realm of possibilities for student access, agency, and achievement in science. It is at the nexus of authentic caring, a more "general curriculum," and teacher and student voice and choice that transformative teaching and learning can occur, teaching and learning that more closely approximate our goals of social justice. Thus, our vision of "science for all" goes beyond raising standards to creating real opportunities for all students to learn science. Oakes explains: "An effective urban teacher cannot be skilled in the classroom but lack skills and commitment to equity, access, and democratic participation. Likewise if one is to be a teacher, a deep caring and democratic commitment must be accompanied by highly developed subject matter and pedagogical skills."[31] Thus, attention to the ways in which students access science, how we define student achievement in science, and the role of agency in the science classroom help us to reenvision equity in science education. The case of Randi demonstrates the need for a contextual approach and a multiplicity of models for transformative teaching and learning in science.

Useful Sources for Teaching Science for Social Justice

Readings for Teachers

Banks, J. A., McGee Banks, C., Fennimore, B. et al.. Handbook of Research on Multicultural Education. *Journal of Teacher Education* 48, no. 2 (1997): 136–46.
Calabrese Barton, A. *Teaching Science for Social Justice.* New York: Teachers College Press (2003).
Tate, W. "Science Education as a Civil Right: Urban Schools and Opportunity-to-Learn Considerations." *Journal of Research in Science Teaching* 38, no. 9 (2001): 1015–29.
West Harlem Environmental Action Group: http://www.weact.org/

Curriculum Resources

Rekindling Traditions Cross-Cultural Science & Technology Units (CCSTU) Project. http://capes.usask.ca/ccstu/.
Linking Food & the Environment Program! An inquiry-based science and nutrition program. http://www.tc.edu/life/life.htm.
The Secret Lives of Owls. http://www.carolina.com/owls/guide/pellets.asp.
Hawks, Owls, and Wildlife: The Owl Pellet Specialist
http://www.owlpelletkits.com/pages/513061/index.htm.

Sources for Students

The Electronic Naturalist: Cough It Up: How Owls Deal with Bones and Fur
http://www.enaturalist.org/topics.htm
KidWings: Virtual Owl Pellet Dissection
http://www.kidwings.com/

Notes

1. Jeannie Oakes, *Multiplying Inequalities: The Effects of Race, Social Class, and Tracking on Opportunities to Learn Mathematics and Science* (Santa Monica: Rand, 1990).
2. Michelle Fine, *Framing Dropouts: Notes on the Politics of an Urban High School* (Albany: State University of New York Press, 1991).
3. Education Trust, *Education Watch: The 1996 Education Trust State and National Data Book,* (Washington, D.C.: Education Trust, 1996).
4. R. Ingersoll, "The Problem of Underqualified Teachers in American Secondary Schools," *Educational Researcher* 28, no. 2 (1999).
5. National Research Council, *National Science Education Standards* (Washington, D.C.: Academy Press, 1996), 6–7.
6. F. James Rutherford and Andrew Ahlgren, *Science for All Americans* (New York: Oxford University Press, 1990), 214.
7. Okhee Lee and S. H. Fradd, "Science for All, Including Students from Non-English Backgrounds," *Educational Researcher* 27 (1998); Alberto J. Rodriguez, "The Dangerous Discourse of Invisibility: A Critique of the National Science Education Standards," *Journal of Research in Science Teaching* 34 (1997).

8. William Kyle, "Toward a political philosophy of science education," in *Teaching science in diverse settings*, ed. Calabrese Barton and M. Osborne (2001, New York: Peter Lang), xi–xix.

9. James A. Banks et al., "Handbook of Research on Multicultural Education," *Journal of Teacher Education* 48, no. 2 (1997); Gloria Ladson-Billings, "What we Can Learn from Multicultural Education Research," *Educational Leadership* 51, no. 8 (1994).

10. Angela Valenzuela, *Subtractive Schooling: U.S.-Mexican Youth and the Politics of Caring* (Albany: State University of New York Press, 1999).

11. Angela Calabrese Barton, *Teaching Science for Social Justice* (New York: Teachers College Press, 2003); Derek Hodson, "Going Beyond Cultural Pluralism: Sicence Education for Sociopolitical Action," *Science Education* 83, no. 6 (1999); Alberto J. Rodriguez, "Sociocultural Constructivism, Courage, and the Researcher's Gaze: Redefining Our Roles as Cultural Warriors for Social Change," in *Teaching Science in Diverse Settings: Marginalized Discourse and Classroom Practice*, eds. Angela Calabrese Barton and Marjory Osborne (New York: Peter Lang, 2001).

12. Hodson, p. 787.

13. Nel Noddings, "Teaching Themes of Care," *Phi Delta Kappan* (May 1995): 676.

14. Valenzuela, 201.

15. Calabrese Barton; Lori A. Kurth, Charles W. Anderson, and Annemarie S. Palincsar, "The Case of Carla: Dilemmas of Helping All Students to Understand Science," *Science Education* 86, no. 3 (2002).

16. Valenzuela, 255.

17. Hodson, 776.

18. Angela Calabrese Barton, "Reframing 'Science for All' through the Politics of Poverty," *Educational Policy* 12, no. 5 (1998); Maria Rivera Maulucci and Angela Calabrese Barton, "Negotiating Relationships between Self and Science through Science Inquiry: A Critical Science Approach," (2003).

19. Lisa Delpit, "The Silenced Dialogue: Power and Pedagogy in Educating Other People's Children," *Harvard Educational Review* 58, no. 3 (1998).

20. Hodson.

21. Gloria Ladson-Billings, "But That's Just Good Teaching! The Case for Culturally Relevant Pedagogy," *Theory into Practice* 34, no. 3 (1995): 162.

22. Jeannie Oakes, Kate Muir, and Rebecca Joseph, *Coursetaking and Achievement in Mathematics and Science: Inequilities that Endure and Change* (2000) obtained April 6, 2004 from http://www.wcer.wisc.edu/nise/News_Activities/Forums/Oakespaper.htm.

23. Alberto J. Rodriguez, "From Gap Gazing to Promising Cases: Moving toward Equity in Urban Education Reform," *Journal of Research in Science Teaching* 38, no. 10 (2001).

24. Dana Fusco and Angela Calabrese Barton, "Re-Presenting Student Achievement," *Journal of Curriculum Studies* 38, no. 3 (2001).

25. Rodriguez, 344.

26. F. Michael Connelly and D. Jean Clandinin, "Narrative Inquiry: Storied Experience," in *Forms of Curriculum Inquiry*, ed. E. C. Short (Albany: State University of New York Press, 1991); M. R. Jalongo and J. P. Isenberg, *Teachers' Stories from Personal Narrative to Professional Insight* (San Francisco: Jossey-Bass Publisher, 1995).

27. R. R. Powell, "Epistemological Antecedents to Constructivist Classroom Curricula: A Longitudinal Study of Teachers' Constrasting Worldviews," *Teaching and Teacher Education* 12 (1996).

28. Patti Lather, "Research as Praxis," *Harvard Educational Review* 56 (1985).

29. Ibid.

30. F. Michael Connelly and D. Jean Clandinin, "Stories of Experience and Narrative Inquiry," *Educational Researcher* 19, no. 5 (1990).

31. Jeannie Oakes, "Research for High-Quality Urban Teaching: Defining It, Developing It, Assessing It," *Journal of Teacher Education* 53 (2002): 229.

CHAPTER 6

Many Layered Multiple Perspectives: Aesthetic Education in Teaching for Freedom, Democracy, and Social Justice

MADELEINE F. HOLZER

We are interested in education here, not in schooling. We are interested in openings, in unexplored possibilities, not in the predictable or the quantifiable, not in what is thought of as social control. For us, education signifies an initiation into new ways of seeing, hearing, feeling, moving. It signifies the nurture of a special kind of reflectiveness and expressiveness, a reaching out for meanings, a learning to learn.[1]

Lincoln Center Institute and Aesthetic Education

For the past twenty-seven years, Lincoln Center Institute (LCI) has developed and refined its own distinctive approach to the arts and education. At present, the Institute works with over one hundred P–12 schools and more than eight hundred teachers within a thirty-mile radius of New York City. The majority of these schools and teachers are in urban areas. Based on the vision of Mark Schubart, the Institute's founder, and the work of Maxine Greene, its philosopher-in-residence, the Institute's practice has been woven from a combination of philosophy and artistry.

According to Greene, "Aesthetic education…is the intentional under-taking designed to nurture appreciative, reflective, cultural, participatory engagements with the arts by enabling learners to notice what there is to be noticed, and to lend works of art their lives in such a way that they can achieve them as variously meaningful."[2] Greene's philosophy, based on the work of the pragmatist John Dewey and existential philosophers such as Sartre and Merleau-Ponty, posits that understanding a work of art takes place in the encounter between the viewer and the artwork, and neither in the work itself nor solely in the perceiver. Therefore, the Institute's practice of aesthetic education has developed into carefully planned observations and analyses of particular works of art connected to participatory activities designed by teaching artists to highlight the possible relationship between an artist's choices and the viewer's aesthetic response. Through art-making explorations in dance, music, theater, architecture, and visual arts, partici-pants are encouraged to integrate their prior experiences and their percep-tions to shape new understandings of a particular work of art as both individuals and participants in a learning community. This approach is neither teaching "art for art's sake," nor using the arts as a vehicle for teaching other subjects, but rather a third process that incorporates some of the elements of both, involving perception, cognition, affect, and the imagination.

Each exploration of a work of art is planned and executed in a partner-ship between educators and teaching artists. While each is different depend-ing on the needs, inclinations, interests, and inspiration of the particular artists, educators, students, and on the work of art itself, all teaching and learning at the Institute bears a number of hallmarks. Some of these are:

- selection of a work of art for study that is rich with possibilities for exploration;
- collaborative brainstorming of many possible entry points into the study of an artwork;
- creation of a generative question, known as the "line of inquiry," as a beginning point for the exploration;
- exploratory workshops before experiencing the work of art;
- use of contextual materials throughout the exploration process;
- conversations punctuated by questions leading to description, analy-sis, and interpretation;
- student-centered active learning that acknowledges each partici-pant's prior knowledge and life experience;
- use of multiple learning modalities in each exploration;
- creation of vocabularies—verbal, visual, and physical—that can be used to describe a work of art;

- experiencing an artwork more than once;
- group and individual reflection throughout the exploration and after a performance or a museum visit;
- validation of multiple perspectives in the creation of individual and group understanding;
- connections to the classroom curriculum and pedagogy; and opening out of new possibilities for learning that includes generating new questions to be explored.[3]

The specific practice is not a linear one, but rather one that loops and spirals, based on the teaching artists' and educators' skills and intuition. As such, it resonates with other forms of teaching and learning, such as inquiry and reader response, that help students construct meaning rather than embrace the traditionally accepted meaning of objects under study as a given.

According to Philip Anderson, executive officer of the Ph.D. program in Urban Education at the City University of New York, this kind of teaching and learning is essential in all disciplines:

> The work of art and the *work* of art are simultaneously perceptual, cognitive, emotive, and behavioral (articulated or responded); they are also humanistic and social.... Any classroom that does its job of educating humans is all of those things as well. To not recognize the role of aesthetic experience in any discipline is to present a world and a way of knowing that are not connected to the lived experience of the world. This disconnect between experience and knowledge is the fatal flaw of schooling, as Dewey argued so clearly. The experience of art changes us, it changes art, and it changes our way of seeing the world, including the world of our classrooms.[4]

The Teacher Education Collaborative

> The overall mission of Lincoln Center Institute's Teacher Education Collaborative (TEC) is to integrate aesthetic education into teacher preparation programs in order to ensure that the arts and imagination will assume an essential place in the education of all children. The more specific purpose is to enable education students to understand the power of artworks as objects of study, participate in and come to utilize an experiential process for teaching artworks, and bring the ways of knowing the world that experiences in the arts provide into the general curriculum of the classroom.[5]

The Teacher Education Collaborative began with the City University of New York (CUNY) in the spring of 1994, partly as the result of a five-year research study undertaken in partnership with *Project Zero* and Teachers College, Columbia University. Planning meetings were held with CUNY administrators and with several deans of Schools of Education in the CUNY system. After these meetings, the Brooklyn College School of Education was selected to work with the Institute to develop a model for integration of aesthetic education and teacher education.

Since then, the Teacher Education Collaborative has broadened to include eight schools of education in the metropolitan area: Brooklyn College, Hunter College, Lehman College, Queens College, and the City College of New York, all within CUNY; Bank Street College, St. John's University, and Stern College for Women of Yeshiva University. The Institute also works with in-service teachers and school administrators through partnerships with Fordham University and Teachers College, Columbia University. As a group, these schools offer programs in early childhood, childhood, middle, and secondary education, as well as graduate specialties such as educational leadership, special education, and bilingual education. Through these partnerships, the Institute touches approximately 100 Teacher Education faculty members and 3,000 teacher candidates.

Initially, the TEC developed on each campus in response to the interests of specific faculty members. Different areas and components of aesthetic education were identified and explored, and individual faculty members became deeply invested in the program. Aesthetic education was incorporated on each campus based on faculty interest, rather than as part of a rigid and predetermined sequence. Over a number of years an overall structure, common to all the participating campuses, yet flexible enough to meet individual campus needs, evolved. The components include:

- a core committee to provide on-campus leadership;
- faculty seminars, jointly developed by LCI staff and campus teacher education faculty to provide ongoing professional development for faculty;
- coursework for teacher candidates that includes aesthetic education components;
- field experience and student teaching, preferably in an LCI-affiliated school; and an on-site Resource Collection of arts and education materials housed in the campus library.

Also, as a number of the TEC campuses go through national accreditation processes, they have found ways to include aesthetics and/or aesthetic education in either their mission statements, conceptual frameworks, or both. Often statements about aesthetic education are juxtaposed or included in broader statements about valuing diversity and community. For instance, at the City College of New York, the following statement appears in its materials for accreditation:

CCNY's mission within the Teacher Education Collaborative is threefold:

- to build a caring community that honors diversity through the investigation of aesthetic education;
- to enlarge understanding and appreciation of the arts in teacher education; and
- to facilitate the ability of teacher candidates to include the arts in their curriculum.[6]

Finally, a number of cross-campus groups and events have developed. These include a faculty research advisory group that meets four times each year; affinity groups that meet periodically around areas of faculty interest, such as early childhood education and social foundations; and intensive summer and winter sessions for faculty professional development.

Aesthetic Education, Freedom, Democracy, and Social Justice

Against this backdrop, in the fall of 2003, the eight colleges whose teacher education programs participate in the Teacher Education Collaborative, along with hundreds of P–12 teachers, continued their partnership with Lincoln Center Institute. This was a year in which standardized tests continued to be rampant in the New York City Public Schools, and where a renewed emphasis on math and literacy, important in their own right, made even the most experienced teachers wonder how to include other subjects, including the arts, in their curricula. Yet, the educators partnering with LCI, who believe that aesthetic education is essential to their students' education, incorporated it in their courses and classrooms. Many believe it is essential precisely because they understand, from their own experiences at the Institute, and through readings of Dewey and Greene, that works of art can open new possibilities of freedom for their students, ones that foster democratic principles, and might lead, through empathy, to a greater sense of social justice.

They are not alone in their thinking. In his comments about the importance of aesthetic education in the preparation of new teachers at the City University of New York, Nicholas Michelli, the CUNY Dean for Teacher Education, states:

Preparation for liberty and democracy does not mean learning how to vote. It means learning how to respect and embrace each other in our everyday encounters. Aesthetics are central to this embracing. Social justice is not achieved so long as we exclude vast numbers of future citizens from aesthetic education.[7]

He goes on to cite Maxine Greene (as he does earlier in this volume):

As Greene says, rather than being a fringe or a frill, aesthetic education is "integral to the development of persons—their cognitive, perceptual, emotional and imaginative development." In this sense it is essential for the development of citizens, as well. Citizens who, through aesthetic education, avoid "passivity and boredom and come awake to the colored, sounding, problematic world."[8]

In addition, according to Benjamin Barber, "art and democracy share a dependency on one extraordinary human gift, imagination." For Barber, imagination is the key to diversity, to civic compassion, and to commonality. "It is the faculty by which we stretch ourselves to include others, expand the compass of our interests to discover common ground, and overcome the limits of our parochial selves to become fit subjects to live in democratic communities."[9]

And, on the relevance of the arts to the pursuit of freedom, Maxine Greene, in *The Dialectic of Freedom* states:

To recognize the role of perspective and vantage point, to recognize at the same time that there are always multiple perspectives and multiple vantage points, is to recognize that no accounting, disciplinary or otherwise, can ever be finished or complete. There is always more. There is always possibility. And this is where the space opens for the pursuit of freedom. Much the same can be said about experiences with art objects—not only literary texts, but music, painting, dance. They have the capacity, when authentically attended to, to enable persons to hear and to see what they would not ordinarily hear and see, to offer visions of consonance and dissonance that are unfamiliar and indeed abnormal, to disclose the incomplete profiles of the world. As importantly, in this context, they have the capacity to defamiliarize experience; to begin with the overly familiar and transfigure it into something different enough to make those who are awakened see and hear.[10]

It is this awakening, this "seeing and hearing," that Lincoln Center Institute's practice emphasizes.

Exploring *Twilight: Los Angeles, 1992*

A group of teacher candidates from a college that is part of the City University of New York prepare to see *Twilight: Los Angeles, 1992* by Anna Deavere Smith, who has created a special version of her play for students grades six through twelve as part of the repertory at Lincoln Center Institute in 2003–2004. The play, about the riots that erupted after the initial jury verdict concerning the beating of Rodney King in 1992, is enacted by four actors, each of whom plays several parts. In this production, actors play characters that are the same race and gender as they are, as well as characters from different races and opposite genders.

The preparation for experiencing the play is conducted by an Institute teaching artist (TA) who is, herself, an actor, but who is not a part of this production. As the students sit in a circle, the TA asks them what they know about the Los Angeles riots of 1992. The students in this class seem to have a fair amount of prior knowledge of the event, mentioning the beatings of Rodney King and Reginald Denney, looting of Korean American stores, and the burning of buildings. The teaching artist notes that as Anna Deavere Smith interviewed people in order to write *Twilight*, she found that they generally felt the media had not listened to them.[11] The TA asks the students to take out a piece of paper and write about a time they felt wronged because someone had not listened to them. After writing, she asks the students to turn and talk with a partner about the incident. She asks the partner to listen carefully and notice not only what the other says, but also what mannerisms he or she uses, and the rhythm and tone of his or her voice. The TA says, "You are going to take one sentence your partners said, and say it back to us—just the way your partner said it, with gestures, pauses, 'ums,' etc." There is the quiet hum of voices and self-conscious laughter as students begin their interviews.

Across the hall, another group of teacher candidates is working with a different teaching artist, this time a director, in preparation for the same performance. These students are asked to write down an incident where they were victims of, or witnesses to, racial discrimination. They are also asked to write down three or four questions a journalist might ask regarding this experience. After they have finished writing, they form groups of three to choose one story they will work on in-depth. The person whose story is chosen becomes the storyteller. Another becomes the interviewer, who is instructed "to try to get beyond the facts to the 'emotional terrain.'" The third person will document the gestures and quality of voice of the storyteller while he or she is being interviewed. The person who conducted the interview will then become the actor who will tell the story to the rest of the class.

At an LCI Focus School in Central Harlem, middle school students are finishing up a semester-long study of *Twilight: Los Angeles, 1992*. They have seen the play twice and have done a number of activities both before and after the performances, having to do with taking different perspectives and points of view. For their final activity, several of the students have interviewed members of their local community—a policeman, a candy store owner, and a laid-off worker. The interviews have been videotaped, and, in the last class with their teaching artist, the students are watching the tape and reading the transcripts of the interviews. They study the gestures of the speakers, as well as their voice patterns. Then they work in small groups to give a group portrayal of one of the three people. They present their work to the entire class using appropriate voice intonations and gestures. To the outside observer, each group seems to become a collective representation of someone much older, whose perspective is much different from its own.

These three teaching artists have tried to retrace the artistic process used by Anna Deavere Smith to create *Twilight: Los Angeles, 1992*. In so doing, they have involved their students (be they teacher candidates or middle school students) in observation, making choices, listening well, and "getting into someone else's shoes." They have worked with them on issues of empathy. These activities are examples of the kind of teaching conducted regularly by Lincoln Center Institute teaching artists, using the hallmarks, cited earlier, "in action," to prepare their students for encounters with works of art. The hope is, in line with Maxine Greene's philosophy, that this kind of preparation and encounter, combined with ongoing reflection, can help students join in community to explore different perspectives, and ask new questions about their lives, the lives of others, and their world. The idea, in the Teacher Education Collaborative, is that if teacher candidates come to appreciate what can be learned from encounters with works of art, then they are more likely to create the same kinds of experiences for their own students, once they have their own classrooms. Again, from Greene:

> We who are teachers, working with newcomers, cannot but be aware of the diverse realizations that lie ahead for the works of art we make accessible. At once, we recognize that the quality and the fullness of those realizations will depend upon the kind of attending we can make possible. So we ponder, as we must, the ways there are of providing the sorts of experiences we ourselves have had: experiences that lead to transformations, that open new vistas, that allow for new ways of structuring the lived world.[12]

In their particularity, different works of art interacting with different people can provide for infinite experiences. It can be argued, however, that, in the case of *Twilight: Los Angeles, 1992*, there is no escaping the issues of multiple perspectives, empathy, democracy, or social justice simply because of the play's subject. It could be said that no matter who you are, no matter what you know or have experienced prior to seeing the play, questions related to these topics will be raised. Yet, at Lincoln Center Institute, we believe that works of art, precisely because of their many possible interpretations, can be powerful in raising issues related to democracy and social justice without even mentioning the words. In another possible scenario, a work of art not having subject matter clearly related to issues of freedom, empathy, and social justice, might be created via processes that encourage related principles, such as the creation of community.

Exploring Intersections:
Art Making, Noticing, and Questioning

At a different college, students in a course titled Teaching Literacy and Social Studies in Bilingual Childhood Settings are studying a work of public art called *Intersections* on their campus. It includes a plaza and walkway with quotations, scientific formulae, and visual displays. All of the text and visual representations were selected by members of the college community—academics, as well as others. The artist chosen for the project, Wopo Holup, noticed that the selections seemed to cluster around six themes: The Heavens, I, We, Words, Time, and Opposition. In the words of the artist:

> The new entrance includes a walkway and plaza. The walkway features horizontal strips of etched bluestone with inscriptions that illustrate a brief history of signmaking, from ancient cave drawings to a Space Age pictograph. The walkway leads from the main gate to the plaza, where inscribed, horizontal and vertical strips of bluestone criss-cross. The intersecting quotations suggest a conversation between the speakers, a collaboration of ideas—in short, wisdom.[13]

Even though the artist has given her vision of the work, the LCI approach encourages students to interact with it individually, each from his or her own personal vantage point, in order to come together to create communal understanding. To prepare for their interaction with *Intersections*, the students work with a visual arts teaching artist who has planned a unit of study with a partnering faculty member. There is a timeline posted on a white board in front of the class. In a prior session, the teacher candidates have posted important events in their lives.

The teaching artist asks, "What do you notice about what's on the timeline?"

The students respond: "The events seem autobiographical."

"They begin in 1974."

"They are more of a personal history than a community history."

The teaching artist notes that there seem to be happy events, and that they seem to fall into categories such as birth, school, and moving. He also recalls that the instructions the students received for making the timeline were shaped toward personal events, and not societal ones. It is not surprising to the teaching artist that September 11, for instance, is not there. The students noted that they shared certain events. The TA points out that this helps create a community. He then asks them how they might create a timeline that includes other kinds of events. The students add events such as politics, working (jobs), and learning. At his urging, they include "fun" events such as relaxing, swimming, dancing, and reading books.

After the list has been expanded to include a number of new categories, the TA asks the students to visually represent the items they are going to include in a personal timeline that includes the expanded categories. He gives them construction paper, markers, glue, and pipe cleaners. The students work quietly. After twenty minutes, the TA asks them to post their work on the white board. He asks the students to circle round the front of the board. Again he asks, "What do you notice? What do you see?" He asks them to look at all the entries and then decide which one they want to talk about first, as a group. He also asks the artist whose work is chosen not to speak about it until after the group has looked at it.

The students chime in:

"I see tears."

"The face is blue."

"It's sad."

"There are cleansing tears and water."

The TA asks, "What does the blue remind you of?"

"Cold."

"Water."

"Tears."

"Sadness."

They choose another timeline. This time they notice ABCs and 1,2,3. One wonders if the piece is about starting school. The TA asks, "What numbers would you use if it were about starting college?" Immediately, they respond:

$$a^2 + b^2 = c^2 \cdot \ e = mc^2$$

The TA points out that, judging by their responses, symbols can speak to a certain period of time.

The students and the TA continue in this manner, looking at individual timelines, the students sharing what they notice while the TA asks questions and makes comments to push their perceptions forward. In one part of the conversation, they have a long discussion about the choice of a dollar bill sign ($) in the timeline, wondering if it means money in general, or money earned on a job. The TA asks why it is wavy. Students wonder if the money is in the wind. Does it come and go? They puzzle over a calculator next to the $ sign. They surmise it might indicate something practical or something that has to do with administration.

After each piece is looked at carefully, and the students have had a chance to share their individual perspectives, the TA asks, "How might these senses of self intersect? Could we cut these and rearrange them to integrate them? How do the parts fit together? How do all these parts intersect?" (He lets on he is using this word for a reason.) The students come up with ideas of making a bridge or using words to show how they might connect. The students quickly get to work. Again they practice, in Maxine Greene's words, "noticing what there is to be noticed."

From Noticing to Connections and New Possibilities

In the above description the teaching artist and faculty have decided to focus on the community process that went into making *Intersections*, and how symbols might be used to represent ideas, as they created activities to allow students to experience some of the choices the artist made in creating the work. After the students walked through *Intersections* the following week, the TA again took them through a group process of looking closely at the work. He repeated the questioning process and "guided looking" that encourages students to describe, analyze, interpret, and ask further questions about what they saw. In addition, he asked them to create a sketch, using shapes, words, and symbols from *Intersections* that spoke to the "fullness of their lives." Students shared these, broadening their reflections to connect back to their work in bilingual classrooms. In this way the students' learning spiraled from their noticings about the work of art and individual constructions of meaning to social constructions of meaning within their group.

All lessons that Lincoln Center Institute teaching artists prepare are based on what they know, have learned or researched, or can imagine, about the process that the artist went through to create a particular work of art. They, and their faculty partners, devise activities to bring students as close to that process as they can in a given classroom experience. Because the process in *Intersections* involved a community, issues of community—so important to democracy—were likely to be fostered by the TA's lessons. But a more general layer of the LCI process, applicable to the exploration of any work of art, is at play here. This is the process that starts with participants' prior individual experience and knowledge, relates that to a particular work of art (with any subject, created by many processes), and creates a safe environment where a community of understandings and questions for further research and exploration can be formed from the valuing of multiple perspectives. It is from these multiple perspectives that new possibilities might arise, which Greene relates to the pursuit of freedom.

Exploring *Two Plus One*: Embodying Interdependence

In a childhood arts education course jointly developed by LCI staff and an arts education faculty member, students experienced a dance performance titled *Two Plus One* by Pilobolus TOO. Before the performance, they worked with an LCI dance teaching artist. Their preparation included creating balanced shapes between their individual bodies and chairs, and between two individuals, while a musical selection played in the background. Throughout their explorations (as in the other classroom examples above), they paused to notice what shapes their classmates had created, guided by questions from the teaching artist. Based on this experience, just before the performance, they generated a list of questions in anticipation of what they might see. The list included:

- How many performers will there be?
- Will they lift anything?
- What kind of music will there be?
- Is the choreographer dancing?

- Does Pilobolus have a philosophy? Does it have something to do with form?
- Is there a story to the dance?
- Is there repetition?
- Will there be improvisation?

The week after the performance, at their next class session, the teaching artist and faculty member focus on getting the students to practice thinking about key concepts in preparing lessons for their own P–12 classes. The TA asks them to think back on what stood out for them about the performance, about a moment that jumped out for them. Verbally, each student shares this with a partner. Next, students choose one of the moments they discussed and physically re-create it with their partners. They quickly get on their feet, and, in pairs, move each other around, the room becoming a swirl of arms, legs, heads, and bodies. After a brief rehearsal, they share their "moments" with each other, each pair taking a turn in the center of the room.

The TA asks, "What's the key concept you see in that position? What's the key idea?"

The answers flow with each enactment:

"Flirtation."

"Flowing Movement."

"1+1=1."

"Hand movement."

"Balance."

"Playfulness."

"Control."

Next, she instructs them to form groups of four; each group will choose one key idea and create it with either music or visual arts materials. As laughter fills the room, two groups of students pick up instruments and start connecting their sounds together. Two other groups choose to draw, each person in the group adding to the process and product. When they are finished, they again go through the process of presenting their work to the total group, and of "noticing what there is to notice," while making a collective list of what they see and, in the case of the musical instruments, hear.

There is no readily apparent social agenda in Pilobolus's dance performance. In several of their dances, the work is abstract with no narrative line. Some pieces seem purely sensual, others not. The generative question that the teaching artist and faculty member chose to pursue was "How does *Two Plus One* create transformative imagery through Pilobolus's use of interdependent physical explorations?," seemingly having nothing specifically to do with democracy, freedom, community, or social justice. And yet, in subtle ways, by including the idea of interdependence in the generative question, the faculty member and teaching artist have entered their discussion of this particular dance performance via interdependence, a concept central to issues of life in a democracy.

Multiple Perspectives/Multiple Cultures/Community in the Making

In addition, the process by which the students explored this work of art, as well as the process used in other prior examples, has everything to do with issues of life in a democracy. The teacher candidates embodied the concept of interdependence and connection in their workshops. They were asked to think about their own lives, then to observe a work of art carefully. They were asked what in the work of art might justify their interpretations (similar to the lessons around *Intersections*). They shared their multiple perspectives with each other, building on others' responses (similar to *Intersections* and *Twilight: Los Angeles, 1992*). And they asked questions that could lead to further research and questions. All of these components are present in varying degrees in any curriculum developed by Lincoln Center Institute teaching artists and their educator partners.

It is also no accident that the works of art these students were studying came from artists with different cultural backgrounds. At Lincoln Center Institute, in our search for a variety of artworks with rich possibilities for exploration, we actively pursue art from many cultures. Anna Deavere Smith is an African American; Wopo Holup is of Czech descent and was adopted into the Miwok tribe of the Sierra Mountains; and the choreographers and dancers in the performance of *Two Plus One* were of European American descent. The students who interacted with these works came from backgrounds representative of a number of groups in New York City: Latino, African American, Caribbean, Indian, Pakistani, and European American. All perspectives—that of the artist and the many perceivers—are honored in the LCI process. No one perspective is privileged. When students from many different cultures have encounters with works of art from a variety of cultures, and share their perspectives in a safe educational environment, the possibilities for empathy and what Dewey and Greene call "community in the making" are endless.

Creating "Wide Awake" Citizens and Teachers

Since the democratic process needs wide-awake citizens who can justify their positions based on what they have noticed and experienced and ask questions about what they imagine is possible or don't understand; and since dialogue across diverse perspectives is bolstered by empathy and should occur thoughtfully and with care, aesthetic education is one way new teachers can begin to incorporate these concepts into who they are and what they value in teaching. Yet, how can we continue to educate new teachers to understand the value of aesthetic education, both for them and their students, at a point in education history where they and their students may spend most of their time in literacy and math blocks, and, in some grades, preparing for standardized tests?

Through the Lincoln Center Institute Teacher Education Collaborative there is a concerted effort to explore the ways in which this might happen. As teacher education faculty and LCI staff work together to create a meaningful series of courses with aesthetic education components for their students, there are conscious conversations with teacher candidates about ways to link aesthetic experiences to literacy and numeracy, as well as other subjects. In addition, teacher candidates are given help in thinking about how to locate rich works of art in their schools' communities and how to ask their school principals if they can attempt to include works of art in their classes.

In addition to having courses that include experiential exploration of works of art, and support for thinking about connections to mandated curricula, teacher candidates must also come to value aesthetic education as part of their overall educational philosophy. In her article "From Preparation to Practice: Designing a Continuum to Strengthen and Sustain Teaching," Sharon Feiman-Nemser, while not talking about aesthetic education explicitly, sees the beliefs that most preservice teachers bring to the classroom as being in need of extension or transformation. She sees teacher education faculty in exemplary preservice settings modeling "the kind of interactive, content-rich teaching that promotes and creates opportunities for pre-service teachers to experience that teaching as learners." This must be supported by opportunities "to put into words one's evolving philosophy of teaching. ..."[14] When faculty members work with teaching artists in their classes around the study of works of art, they are attempting to do just that.

Mary Bushnell Greiner, a faculty member at Queens College who teaches social foundations, has written about how her role as a learner in aesthetic education has influenced her teaching and her students' learning:

> It is not insignificant that I am a student of aesthetic education just as I am a teacher of it. This is activist teaching, as I believe what we are doing is more ethically viable than teaching students that there is one right answer, or one correct authority. … I believe aesthetic education helps students assert their view of the world and how they name the world and describe it, rather than accepting the world as it has been described to them. This stance assumes that students' power to name the world is at the heart of their own capacity and authority to engage in that world. Even more so, their direct engagements with the arts are radical actions in these "dark times" of society.[15]

If faculty members, such as Bushnell Greiner, continue to model inquiry around works of art and encourage their students to think about its value, there is hope. When Queens College teacher candidates, about to graduate yet still confused about the objectives of aesthetic education, wondered how they could justify the time, effort, and cost to their principals, the questions were posed back to them. They ultimately answered their own questions, based on their personal and collective experiences with works of art, by coming up with a list of advantages for the inclusion of aesthetic education as a regular part of classroom learning. The list contained the following:

- accommodation to different learning styles;
- increased confidence from student expression;
- asking questions;
- embracing multiple responses;
- cultivating critical thinking skills;
- creating a safe learning environment;
- enhancing linguistic skills;
- observing their teachers co-teaching; and
- exploring the intrinsic value of art.[16]

While these students experienced works of art other than *Twilight: Los Angeles, 1992, Intersections,* or *Two Plus One,* they were able to come up with a list not dissimilar from the general characteristics one can ascribe to LCI's practice of aesthetic education.

There is, of course, no way to know, at this point, how these students might use aesthetic education in their classrooms, or if they will incorporate it at all. We have no way of knowing, either, whether they see any of this as relating to freedom, democracy, or social justice. Because the practice of aesthetic education is so rooted in individual, as well as collective, meaning, some students might not make this connection at all, or not for a long time. Nonetheless, as Lincoln Center Institute continues to collaborate with teacher education programs, to try to encourage processes that not only engage students in the study of works of art but that model processes resonant with democratic culture. There are plans to try to support new teachers who wish to pursue aesthetic education beyond graduation and into the induction years. It is a challenge well worth the effort to keep multiple perspectives, questioning, and "wide-awakeness" alive. These concepts, so often spoken of by Maxine Greene, are invaluable for a vibrant democratic society.

There is a terrible passivity and carelessness to be overcome: feelings of malaise, hopelessness, and powerlessness. The arts will not resolve the fearful social problems facing us today; they will not lessen the evils and brutalities afflicting the modern world; but they will provide a sense of alternatives to those of us who can see and hear; they will enhance the consciousness of possibility if we learn how to attend. And this itself may make a difference if more and more people are awakened, if they are freed to move through openings and develop a sense that things can indeed be otherwise than they are, somehow better than they are.[17]

Acknowledgment

I would like to thank the following teaching artists and faculty members who so generously allowed me to observe their work: April Blount, Patricia Chilsen, Rachel Dickstein, Nancy Dubetz, Mary Bushnell Greiner, John Holyoke, Helen Johnson, Heidi Miller, Herb Perr, and John Toth. Also, I would like to thank Scott Noppe-Brandon, the Executive Director of Lincoln Center Institute, for his vision and encouragement. And thank you, of course, to Maxine Greene, without whom, in so many ways, none of our work would have been possible.

Notes

1. Maxine Greene, *Variations on a Blue Guitar: The Lincoln Center Institute Lectures on Aesthetic Education* (New York: Teachers College Press, 2001), 7.
2. Maxine Greene, *Variations on a Blue Guitar: The Lincoln Center Institute Lectures on Aesthetic Education* (New York: Teachers College Press, 2001), 6.
3. Madeleine F. Holzer, *Aesthetic Education Practice and Traditions: Education Traditions* (New York: Lincoln Center Institute, 2003), photocopy 1–2.

4. *Gone Fishing*. A Collage Narrative of the Queens College—Lincoln Center Institute Collaboration, 2001, unpublished manuscript.
5. *Teacher Education Collaborative Handbook for Faculty* (New York: Lincoln Center Institute, 2003), 2.
6. Catherine Franklin, letter to the author.
7. Nicholas M. Miichelli, Forthcoming.
8. Nicholas M. Michelli, Forthcoming from TC Press; Maxine Greene, *Variations on a Blue Guitar.*
9. Benjamin Barber, *Serving Democracy by Serving the Arts and the Humanities (Traditional Perspectives, Unique Modern Conditions). President's Committee on the Arts and the Humanities* (Washington, D.C., 1997), 16.
10. Maxine Greene, *The Dialectic of Freedom* (New York: Teachers College Press, 1988), 128–29.
11. *Window on the Work: Twilight: Los Angeles, 1992* (New York: Lincoln Center Institute, 2003), 8.
12. Greene, *Variations on a Blue Guitar,* 36–37.
13. Rona Ostrow, ed. *Intersections: A Guide to the Quotes, Sources, and Contributors* (New York: Lehman College, The City University of New York, 2003), 4.
14. Sharon Feiman-Nemser, "From Preparation to Practice: Designing a Continuum to Strengthen and Sustain Teaching," *Teachers College Record* 103, no. 6 (December 2001): 1025.
15. Mary Bushnell Greiner, "To Live for Art: Teaching and Learning Aesthetic Education within Foundations of Education," in *Teaching Social Foundations of Education: Contexts, Theories and Issues,* ed. Dan Butin (Mahwah, N.J.: Lawrence Erlbaum Associates, 2004).
16. Mary Bushnell Greiner, "Learning Representations and Interpretations: Aesthetic Education in Dark Times," *Educational Studies.* Forthcoming.
17. Greene, *Variations on a Blue Guitar,* 47.

Works of Art Cited in Text from the Lincoln Center Institute Repertory

Twilight: Los Angeles, 1992

by Anna Deavere Smith
directed by Liz Diamond

Two Plus One

performed by Pilobolus TOO
Robby Barnett, Alison Chase, Michael Tracy, Jonathan Wolken, artistic directors

Program

Alraune (1975)
Pseudopodia (1974)
Shizen (1978)
Solo from *The Empty Suitor* (1980)
Tarleton's Resurrection (1981)

CHAPTER 7

The Right to Be Equally Taught: Three Sites of Inquiry for Social Justice at a Diverse High School

DAVID LEE KEISER

I learned how to connect with students and relate to them. How to voice my opinion in groups and help others in a time of need. I realized that not everyone can learn on the same level and it takes patience in order to teach every students the way they need to be taught. Also, every student has the right to be equally taught whether they [sic] have a learning disability or not.

—University student who tutored a high school student with special needs

This inspirational epigraph speaks to the power of service learning as an influence upon university students' impressions of high school students and hints at the empathy that often results. The fact that this undergraduate student can articulate "the right to be equally taught" serves to introduce my second chapter of this volume. This chapter will present three examples of social justice projects within teacher education at Montclair High School, a professional development school. Professional development schools represent partnerships between university-based teacher education programs and P–12 schools. These partnerships have at their core a four-part mission: to both demonstrate and develop successful teacher preparation; to establish and maintain ongoing faculty professional development; to create and sustain a culture of educational inquiry; and to maintain a focus on student achievement.[1]

In each partnership, the roles and responsibilities are determined by the particular needs of the partners, involving constituencies such as faculty and supervisory associations and community members and groups, in addition to school and university faculty and students. Within the *New Jersey Network for Educational Renewal*, Montclair State University (MSU) has established partnerships with seven professional development schools in the service of the above, four-part mission. In my case, as the professional development school liaison to Montclair High School, our mission is ongoing, dynamic, and challenging. In addition to the rather typical battery of professional development school activities—full-time university faculty mentoring of student teachers, on-site courses, study groups, and inquiry projects—I have for two years run a service learning program that provides students from an undergraduate course as volunteer tutors for the high school's Department of Special Education.

Montclair is a partner district with the National Network for Educational Renewal, and, like the Colorado Partnership, benefits from shared commitments to the Agenda for Education in a Democracy. The school-university partnership agrees to the moral dimensions of teaching as an organizing framework, and each example to be presented—a special education tutoring program, a small learning community called the Center for Social Justice, and a university fieldwork inquiry project—relates to concepts of access, stewardship, nurturing pedagogy, and democratic education. While the examples differ in terms of the scope of the projects and the actors involved, all share qualities of engagement, vision, purpose, and service. I will briefly describe each of the programs as they relate to teacher education for social justice, the concept of simultaneous renewal, and the moral dimensions of teaching. The first example, a service-learning program I appended to a required undergraduate course, focused the course through the lens of practice. Using descriptive analysis and selected student work samples from the course, the service-learning project serves as an example of a salient and transformative by-product of the professional development school partnership.

"Hold No Bias Coming into the Building"— Service-Learning within Special Education

> For [sic] future service-learners I would say hold no bias coming into the building. Keep your head up, and remember that you are there because these kids need you there. Whatever help you can

give is not only appreciated by the teacher but has a life-long impact on the student.

—Undergraduate tutor

The professional education sequence at Montclair State University requires students to take an upper-level course titled Teacher, School, and Society. The title of the course speaks to both the flexibility and the challenge of teaching in public schools. And, with many courses, the individual course sections represent, to some extent, the preferences and priorities of the professor. As a university/school liaison and former special education teacher, I sought to imprint on my students the need to educate all P–12 students, regardless of academic challenge. In addition to the usual university assignments such as papers and midterms, I added a service-learning component. For approximately one hour a week, my students visit Montclair High School to tutor a student referred by the Department of Special Education. Like Lucas describes in her chapter on service learning, part of the pedagogy of the course requires engagement and reflection.

Over the years I have taught the course, both successes and limitations have surfaced, not least of which includes, in both categories, the extra time I require of students. While some relish the experience of working in a school prior to fieldwork and student teaching, others find the tutoring and reflective writing simply time-consuming. The high school welcomes the help but wishes that the limitations of university course scheduling permitted me to provide students each semester, rather than each fall. Suffice to say my students are generally appreciated for what they bring—in most cases, enthusiasm, good will, and a commitment to reaching students who are academically, emotionally, or behaviorally challenging.

Each course begins with a visit from the department chair, who provides introductory information about the field, sample Individualized Education Plans and tutoring protocols, and logistical information such as parking decals and contact numbers. She also answers questions from students, most of which tend to revolve around their anxiety about "teaching special-ed kids." She then schedules weekly visits with teachers who request university tutors for individual students, placed in self-contained classes, resource centers, and in-class support settings. My course meets twice weekly, and I use every fourth class for structured peer reflections, in which students discuss their work in the field and share reflective journals. At the end of the semester, I require a term paper that reflects upon and synthesizes their work in the field, and analyzes the work of their peers as well, providing opportunities not only to reflect on their experiences, but also on those of their peers.

Extending the Concept of Simultaneous Renewal to Students in Partner Schools

One of the tenets of the National Network for Educational Renewal (NNER), a national consortium of school-university partnerships of which both Colorado and Montclair State Universities are members, is the concept of simultaneous renewal—the ongoing preparation and development of excellence in teaching and learning at both P–12 and university settings. In their book, Goodlad, Mantle-Bromley, and Goodlad describe the underlying rationale:

> A core belief held by those in the NNER was that good schools require good teachers and good teacher preparation programs require good schools. This belief means that school-university partnerships would play a central role in the work and structure of the NNER. It also brought to the fore the notion of simultaneous renewal. In other words, if you really wanted to improve schools, you had to get everyone involved in the process to work together with a shared mission.[2]

"Getting everyone involved in the process" of teacher preparation is challenging. Although we have a cadre of cooperating teachers at the high school who take student teachers each year, many teachers do not, which limits the experiences university students have. Special education teachers are at an added disadvantage because currently, our undergraduate students cannot major in special education and thus cannot student teach in that area. Special education, then, needs to be infused intentionally and mindfully by teacher educators; most teachers will in their careers work with students who need modifications, and, given that knowledge of students with special needs is an essential component of teacher preparation, I try to create such opportunities for students.

By infusing a service-learning component into a required course, I ensure that students have at least one experience with, and one type of exposure to, special needs students before entering the field. By having the component take place at a professional development school, I ask both practicing and future teachers to "work together with a shared mission"; namely, the education of students with special needs. In doing so, I try to extend the concept of simultaneous renewal to include both university and high school students. In helping others, my students develop their pedagogical lenses and gain a field-based confidence difficult to develop in traditional academic courses. In working with my university students, the high school tutees get extra academic help from university students who are closer to their age and experience than their teachers are, and who do not have the power or responsibility to grade them, call home, or mete out disciplinary consequences.

"What Am I Getting Myself Into?"— University Students Reflect upon their Experiences

A key component to effective teaching is ongoing reflection, and I ask students to produce bi-weekly written reflections and then weave those into a final paper for the course. As the semester progresses, most students seem to gain both comfort and confidence as their tutees respond to their prompts, energies, and enthusiasm. While the excerpts below represent the more successful and applied tutors, they provide both inspiration and ideas for moving forward. One of the goals of the program is to encourage students to keep tutoring after the course is over, and this excerpt is from a student who stayed on to tutor after the semester ended and who enrolled to complete her fieldwork at the school. Prior to entering the field, however she expressed trepidation upon commencing the tutoring relationship:

> When [the department chair] mentioned we would be tutoring a "special ed" student, I internally freaked out. My pulse started racing and my chest felt heavy. I guess I had misconceived notions of what special education was all about. For some reason, maybe because of movies or horror stories, I instantly pictured students that would be screaming obscenities and throwing things with drool trickling down their chins. Well, now that I've been in the high school and have spent time with my student, I am almost embarrassed to admit that I had these feelings.

This reflection bespeaks the angst many students feel about going into unknown settings containing stereotyped students with special needs. As mentioned, this student ended up impressing both her tutee and the child's teacher, so much so that by the end of her first session, she.

> clicked with [her student]. Even at our first encounter, I learned so much about this boy. He opened up to me right away, and I felt privileged, even honored that he had shown me a part of his world. I still remember that first day as if it were yesterday. As I walked back to my car that September morning, I had such an uncontainable, overwhelming feeling of joy.

While her words may ring effusive to some, it is not only the emotional connection but also the cultural exposure to special education students that frames the program. That is, the classroom culture of special education often differs greatly from non–special education classrooms. Teacher education for social justice promotes the idea of, and gives students opportunities to engage with students with special needs as integral, not marginal members of the school community.

Like many schools, many of the students placed in special education at Montclair High School are African American and are overly representative of the population of African American students at the school. For many of my university students, it is their first exposure to, and interaction with two diverse student groups: students with special needs and African American students. To help prepare them for entry into the field, I assign readings that address cultural diversity and responsive teaching, including "The Silenced Dialogue: Power and Pedagogy in Educating Other People's Children."[3] Lisa Delpit's seminal article addresses power in schools and society and offers suggestions for educators as how best to navigate and harness students' power to help them succeed. One of my students, a white male with little prior exposure to diverse students, applied Delpit's analysis to what he saw in the classroom:

> I see how easy it is for me as a white male to overlook civil inequalities between whites and blacks and I have become more aware of when I was guilty of this is the past and when I see those around me guilty of it. Reflecting on how I progressed through the semester, I first became aware of this problem with class discussions about the culture of power and the silenced dialogue. But it really hit me deep during my tutoring sessions. There I witnessed firsthand, the effects of discrimination and I developed a friendship with my student, who is getting the short end of the social stick.

I harbor no illusions that this one student's experience will change the perniciousness of racism or ameliorate social inequality, but I believe that involving teacher education students and preservice teachers with diverse students early in their fieldwork is an effective component of culturally responsive teacher preparation, and, by extension, teacher education for social justice. While these experiences may be particularly important for European American university students, my students of color also accept the charge to reach and teach students with special needs. During a class that followed my students' initial visit to the high school, an African American female student stood up and tearfully shared with the class how she refused to give up on her tutee, and told him so. In her final reflection, she elucidated what she had said in class:

> When I went to sit next to him and help him with his work he told me that he don't know why I want to be a teacher because I would end up getting tired of him. When he said this it made me try harder and want to help him even more because I couldn't believe he felt I would give up on him like everyone else. I told him I was there to help him and I would do whatever in my power to make him succeed because that was my purpose for being there and I was going to make it happen. After that I think we were doing great because I showed him how much I really care.

As a teenaged parent, my student may be unable to complete the teacher education program, or may choose to pursue a field with higher compensation than teaching. The compassion she showed her student, however, by not giving up, and by reassuring him of her commitment served as a course marker for the rest of the semester. This serves as another example of the power of students' simultaneous renewal; just as she was edified and enriched by her tutoring, so too was her tutee edified and enriched by her presence and confidence in him.

Just as I assigned Lisa Delpit to introduce discussions of race and power, for example, I assigned a short piece by Robert Tremmel to introduce the concept of mindfulness in the classroom to encourage students to think about how they act and react in the field.[4] As the Sizers[5] aptly put it, "the students are watching" their teacher's every move, and it behooves future teachers to expect student scrutiny and to be mindful of their position as role models.

The same European American student that asserted teaching has a "lifelong impact on the student" at the beginning of this chapter interpreted Tremmel to mean, "the art of paying attention is key in [sic] teaching. Not only will it help to make connections with your students, but also to pay attention is to know oneself and one's limitations." The student who mentioned her "overwhelming feeling of joy" reflected that she "must be a culturally aware and responsive individual in order to meet my students' needs as best I can. In addition, it is important to be attentive and respectful of students' opinions and concerns, even if it means taking time away from the planned lesson."

Were this service-learning course to supplant a course in the professional sequence, doubtless I would focus more on the mechanics of teaching—lesson planning, classroom management, record keeping, and so forth—but as a prerequisite course taught within the context of a vibrant professional development school, the work within the department of special education serves as a practical reminder of the breadth of the challenge facing new teachers.

Within the Montclair Partnership, in a district known for its commitment to diversity, students placed in special education are rarely the benefactors of university resources yet are arguably the most needy. This service-learning opportunity may be only a small raft in a sea of possibility—marshalling undergraduate education students both to serve and learn from students who present special learning needs. In addition to invaluable experience for both tutors and tutees, service learning extends the concept of simultaneous renewal to include those for whom professional development schools are meant to ultimately benefit, marginalized students too often left out of the human conversation.[6] This second example of inquiry for social justice took place in one of the high school's small learning communities, where high school students researched the timely community issue of neighborhood gentrification.

High School Students Research the Street: The Center for Social Justice

> Teaching for social justice is teaching for the sake of arousing the kinds of vivid, reflective, experiential responses that might move students to come together in serious efforts to understand what social justice actually means and what it might demand.[7]

"What Happened to the Street," the name we gave to the research project, sought to arouse such "experiential responses" by involving students in interviewing residents, business owners, and local politicians, as well as documenting the transformation of the target neighborhood and its impact upon the everyday lives of the residents through photography.

Students involved in meaningful and relevant school-based learning develop as citizens who understand better the significance of being responsible members within a democratic society. Community-based research is one strategy to engage students in such meaningful learning. In this case, a multidisciplinary small learning community addressed issues of immigration, activism, and social movements within a history and language arts curriculum, as students gained valuable community based- experience while fulfilling academic requirements. The Center for Social Justice partners with local organizations to provide students opportunities for primary research experience studying community organizing, housing, and education. I collaborated with students from the Center for Social Justice (CSJ), a university research project designed to investigate the transformation of a neighborhood fractured by the expansion of a commuter train line. The role of the students—some of whom lived in the affected neighborhood—was to examine and document the impact of this change upon the area.

Montclair is a town that is socioeconomically and racially diverse, yet within this diversity the proverbial sides of the tracks divide the population. On one side of the tracks live predominantly middle- to upper-class residents, while the other side of the tracks includes the neighborhood targeted by the grant, and where the majority of lower-income residents of Montclair live. Unsurprisingly, the latter neighborhood was most upended by the rail extension.

The fact that the students were members of a small learning community helped prime the pump for the project. Small learning communities are institutional design structures that allow students to make connections between their lives, classroom learning, and the community at large. Students feel more responsible to their peers, their coursework, and themselves in smaller learning communities. Students build close working relationships with staff and fellow students, and become invested members of their academic community.

Community-based action research makes significant contributions to young people's learning and development by helping them cultivate long lasting academic and life skills, including having their opinions valued by adults, taking on a greater sense of responsibility and social connectedness, and by engaging all students in the process.

Inductive Research for Social Justice

Combining research by teachers with high student-interest projects, action research was in this case enacted by both students and teachers; the teachers set up the project—in terms of getting grant monies from the university, securing parental consent, and planning curriculum—and the students operationalized the project through community walks, interviews, transcriptions, photography, and documenting their findings. Unlike traditional, deductive research that begins with a testable hypothesis, teachers intended this project to be inductive. Students were encouraged to be open and flexible in their inquiry and to let their data guide their research.

This project focused on the *process* of doing research in the community, rather than on an eventual *product*. Both the nature of doing action research and the imminent status of the train line required flexibility and commitment. When students became involved with this research project, the train connection was nearly complete, and many neighborhood residents had already left the area due to raised rents and razed homes.

Prior to students entering the field, a visiting professor offered strategies to minimize obtrusiveness within the target area, and to conduct and transcribe interviews, code data, and write up findings. Students then generated a list of names and businesses in the immediate area that they might interview. Interviewees included the mayor, the township manager, landlords, business owners, nonprofit organizations, church officials, and other community residents.

Students set a timeline to implement their plans of action, to deal with obstacles that accompanied their investigation, and to report their findings orally and in writing.

Students did not have to identify an area since the writers of the grant proposal had previously decided upon one. A primary source of data collection involved students entering the community to observe changes and interview citizens. Students met with their interviewees and asked them questions that CSJ had brainstormed, as well as extemporaneous questions. They recorded and transcribed their interviews, transcribed these interviews, and submitted them to their teachers.

As with any research project, there were both roadblocks and highlights that shaped the overall experience. In conducting this ethnographic work, students faced challenges, both predictable and unpredictable. These included stereotypes about the poorer part of town, issues of voyeurism and entitlement, and the inevitable "so what" question. "If the train is coming anyway," they were asked, "why even ask people about it?" After touring the area, interviewing a broad range of community members, discussing the issue, and writing their culminating papers, a handful of students shared their opinions on Montclair Connection's impact on the target area how their perspectives changed as they entered into the community to conduct primary research.

As students asked residents about their opinions on change, they were reminded that the change had already occurred, so why question it? Some students agreed it would have been more appropriate and interesting to conduct this research project before the Montclair Connection was nearly completed. According to one student, "it would have been really, really cool to do this project a year ago."

"Making the Bad Worse and the Good Better"—Students Reflect upon Their Research

The original impression of the development in the neighborhood sounded great. It came across to the students as a project that would help workers to commute, make Montclair cleaner and safer, and put more money into the community. However, after researching the project, we as students began to realize things are not as they seem.

This student came to the project with a benevolent perspective on gentrification, yet soon realized the issues involved might be more complicated and not "as they seem." Another student voiced her opinion on the Montclair Connection, "I feel as though the train is making the bad worse and the good better." In stark detail, she represented this conundrum; instead of writing a final paper like other students, she created a small architectural model of the neighborhood that represented the division in town. On one side, she displayed homes that were sturdy, aesthetically attractive, and on top of bright green grass; on the other side of the tracks, the houses appeared dilapidated, with caved in roofs and bleak surroundings. This and other artifacts suggest that students came to a fuller understanding of community politics, the pervasiveness of stereotyping, and the importance of dismantling stereotypes to create a fairer and more effective democracy. One way to challenge stereotypes is through primary research, and the next excerpt exemplifies the power of this pedagogy.

> This is a community rich in family bonds and close friends. To many people the area is foreign and the difference makes it scary but in reality it is not horrible. It is very possible that because the area is so segregated from the rest of the town and has such a poor relationship with the police that they are, in many ways, falsely profiled.

Community-based action research can offer an opportunity for meaningful and interactive learning, and with an issue that so closely relates to social justice, the benefits are multifold. In addition to smashing stereotypes, the project increased levels of empathy among the students. For example, another student was saddened by the absence of nature in the target neighborhood, noting,

> I think it was very important for me to see… the obvious differences were that there was no grass, trees, flowers, and common nature most suburban towns are used to. After walking only one street past Pine Street, suddenly we heard birds chirping and saw all the nature that we did not see one street away. Other differences that I observed was the way the streets and sidewalks were kept. There were many cracks and missing pieces … they all looked very old and worn down.

The melancholy inherent in this sentiment serves both to illuminate the economic disparities within the town, and the power, for good or bad, of doing engaged research with high school students. Although the project yielded many positive results, both cognitive and socioemotional, others were more problematic, such as the simplistic sentiment above. Other students, however, saw the issue of gentrification and displacement of residents through the prism of race. Given that the train line would bifurcate the target neighborhood by race as well as class, viewing the change through these prisms helped students develop a social justice perspective. One student viewed the eventual displacement of residents as an injustice, declaring,

> In Montclair as opposed to many other homogenous towns there are many different races living together. Kicking families out of their homes is not going to help this town. These families live in [the targeted area], which has the largest population of African Americans in Montclair. If you kick these families out of their homes, you will be kicking out the majority of the African Americans in this town and that will affect the diversity.

While this type of pointed analysis is not unique to, or within Montclair, it bespeaks the need for this type of research—that is, students asking questions in the service of justice and drawing attention to the importance of diversity. In addition to conceptualizing diversity as strength, however, students developed leadership skills as well. One student interviewed on the university television station about the project had this summary with which to leave the audience:

> Just knowing that once the whole project is done and everything has been documented, myself [sic] and my peers will be able to look back and say, "Wow, look at what we, at 16 years old, did!" And I think that with that confidence we'll be able to do anything and that's what will create great leaders.

This student expresses how active learning is integral to education, and, given the topic of displacement and gentrification, serves as an example of partnership for social justice. Similarly, I ask my fieldwork students to carefully observe and reflect upon one element of socially just teaching: the creation and management of the classroom community.

Creating and Managing a Classroom Community: MSU Field Students' Poster Session

In the introduction to *The Professional Development Schools Handbook*, Teitel writes, "Central to the notion of the PDS is the concept of inquiry as part of professional development and as part of the definition of teaching.[8] Following this charge, Montclair State University requires students to engage in inquiry projects during both courses and fieldwork. Combining this push for inquiry with the perennial challenge of classroom management, each semester students in my fieldwork course systematically observe, inquire, and reflect on classroom management styles, systems, and techniques that they observe in classrooms. As part of a performance assessment relating to classroom management, we ask students to observe, document, inquire, and synthesize their findings from no fewer than thirty hours of fieldwork in either elementary or secondary classrooms. My students produce 10- to 25-page papers based on this fieldwork, and, both to reward the work and to further a culture of inquiry, I ask the students to create and display a tri-fold poster demonstrating some element of classroom management or community building that they found interesting and valuable to their experience. These posters are accompanied by an abstract that describes the poster. We culminate with a catered reception at Montclair High School, to which we invite colleagues, junior faculty members, and interested others. Approximately 40 to 50 visitors engage MSU students in critical discussions of their findings. Subjects have included the importance of routine, humanistic classroom management, student engagement, and the role of multiple intelligences. In addition, students placed at Montclair High School for their observations tend to focus their inquiries on issues specific to the school, including the purpose and fairness of the no-hat rule and the perseverance of the achievement gap, as well as the various classroom management techniques of the high school teachers. For instance, one student who had observed a popular social studies teacher wrote this in his abstract:

> Behavior issues in the classroom are a part of every teacher's life and a problem that cannot be ignored. When dealing with behavior issues on a day-to-day basis, it is important to remember that learning and fostering inquisitive thought (not perfect conduct) are the teacher's basic objectives.

Through observation and interviewing the social studies teacher, this student has constructed a view of classroom management dependent not only upon students following rules but also upon creating and sustaining a culture of inquiry. Another student had a similar perspective, noting that her teacher employed student-centered learning in his classroom, noting how this changes the balance of power in the classroom.

> The teacher is no longer a dominant figure in the classroom; instead, the teacher opens up the classroom to the students and lets them share control of it. The teacher is able to do this by establishing respect in the classroom. The students learn to respect their teacher as well as each other by learning about one another. The teacher plays a large role in this by asking students questions, listening to them, noticing little things about them such as their clothing, music interests, extracurricular activities, etc. Once this respect is formed, student centered learning can flourish. Students are able to actively participate in their lessons, work in [cooperative groups], and ultimately be responsible for their own learning.

This field student has already identified a key component to teaching for democracy and social justice: empowering students to take responsibility for their own learning. She cites the example of a teacher who invests time in getting to know and value his students, and while such teacher dispositions may not show up directly on standardized tests, they certainly impact preservice teachers in ways that edify, empower, and encourage them to be humane, just, and democratic in their teaching.

These three examples—tutoring, research, and inquiry—provide opportunities for students and teachers to examine issues of social justice, including access to knowledge for all students, including those with special needs; inquiry and activism with high school students in a nurturing small learning community; and studying effective stewardship through observation, reflection, and dissemination. While the projects differed across setting and participants, they shared several characteristics. In all three cases, the high school or college student stretched their empathy muscles through interactive exercises such as interviewing, observing, and crossing cultures. Within the inquiring culture of a professional development school, it is possible to infuse the teacher education curriculum and collaborative projects for simultaneous renewal with possibilities for social justice. In the three examples herein, high school and college students had opportunities to explore the moral dimensions of teaching, in addition to more typical preparation activities, and in doing so, their ideas of teaching and pedagogy were rounded out by the particularities and timings of the projects with which they were involved.

Notes

1. Lee Teitel, *The Professional Development Schools Handbook* (Thousand Oaks, Calif.: Corwin Press, 2003)
2. John Goodlad, Corinne Mantle-Bromley, and Stephen Goodlad, *Education for Everyone: Agenda for Education in a Democracy* (San Francisco: Jossey-Bass, 2004), 22–23.
3. Lisa Delpit, "The Silenced Dialogue: Power and Pedagogy in Educating Other People's Children," *Harvard Educational Review* 58, no. 3 (1988): 280–98.
4. Robert Tremmel, "Zen and the Art of Reflection in Teacher Education," *Harvard Educational Review* 63, no. 4 (1993): 434–58.
5. Theodore Sizer and Nancy Sizer, *The Students are Watching: Schools and the Moral Contract* (Boston: Beacon Press, 1999).
6. Goodlad, Mantle-Bromley, Goodlad.
7. Maxine Greene Preface: in Ayers, Hunt, and Quinn, *Teaching for Social Justice* (New York: Teachers College Press, 1998), p. xxix.
8. Teitel, 4.

SECTION 3

Strategies for Implementation

CHAPTER **8**

Fostering a Commitment to Social Justice through Service Learning in a Teacher Education Course

TAMARA LUCAS

The Nature and Purposes of Service Learning in Teacher Preparation

Continued disparities in the school success and subsequent life opportunities of racially, ethnically, linguistically, and socioeconomically diverse groups of students raise questions about social justice—specifically, about how a country like the United States, founded on principles of equality, democracy, and opportunity for all, can tolerate such disparities. The U.S. educational system as it is currently constructed does not distribute resources equitably. It does not prepare all students for equal participation in or benefit from civic life. It does not cultivate in all students a sense of agency, self-determination, and social responsibility.[1] It does not, in other words, promote social justice. The increasing diversity among students in U.S. schools will only make these inequities more glaring in the years to come unless we transform the education system, including the preparation of teachers. This chapter examines the efforts of one teacher educator to contribute to such a transformation by fostering in his students a commitment to promoting social justice. The vehicle for this professor's efforts was service learning.

Service learning, which involves organizing the content and pedagogy of a course so that community service is integrated into academic content, can lay the foundation for a commitment to social justice among prospective teachers. Through firsthand experiences in communities and schools, future teachers can develop a greater sensitivity to issues of importance to the community, to teachers, and to students. Those who spend time in schools and communities racially, ethnically, and socioeconomically different from their own have the opportunity to expand their understanding of and sensitivity to sociocultural diversity and their appreciation for the complexities of others' lives. Service learning can also heighten future teachers' awareness of their own assumptions and biases regarding cultural diversity. It can encourage them to examine social influences on people's lives[2] and inspire them to examine and question inequity in schools and society.[3] When prospective teachers have the supervision and guidance of qualified and culturally sensitive adults, their experiences can serve as fertile ground for reflection and critical examination, a process that can contribute significantly to their development as socially aware and culturally responsive teachers.

The literature about service learning as well as about the role of field experiences in preparing culturally responsive teachers identifies a number of elements that can enhance the impact of such experiences.[4] Features of powerful service learning experiences include thoughtful planning and preparation for the activities, collaboration among institutions to develop activities of benefit to all participants, engagement of students in challenging, community-based activities that contribute to community well-being, integration of the service activities into the academic curriculum, and structured opportunities for reflection.[5] Similarly, field experiences that prepare teachers to teach students of culturally diverse backgrounds are carefully planned in advance[6] and their planning is guided by a theoretical framework and clear pedagogical purposes.[7] Prospective teachers are also well prepared for the experience before they begin.[8] This preparation might involve reflection on their expectations, development of a plan of activities and questions to ask different people in the community, and practice with ethnographic techniques. In addition, to help prospective teachers make sense of their field experiences, teacher educators provide them with ongoing opportunities to engage in critical reflection on those experiences.[9] Reflective activities are designed both to challenge prospective teachers to go beyond their own perspectives and to support them through the turmoil that these experiences can produce.[10] The literature on effective field experiences indicates that schools chosen as sites for such experiences serve diverse student populations and are staffed by teachers who are already working successfully with culturally and linguistically diverse students or are actively engaged in bringing about changes to increase their success in teaching diverse student populations.[11]

The types of service learning activities incorporated into teacher education programs vary considerably. In some programs, prospective teachers tutor children early in their course work to gain initial experience in a teacher role.[12] For example, Bondy, Schmitz, and Johnson[13] describe a program in which first-semester students tutor young people in public housing projects for ten weeks to gain experience working with children who are poor and from racial/ethnic minority backgrounds. While many of the service-learning experiences for prospective teachers center around schools, there are also benefits in having them engage in other types of community activities. They can learn about diverse communities and the agencies and institutions serving them, gain experience and skills in collaborating with people in agencies and institutions, and develop a sense of various roles they might play in the lives of children. Tellez and colleagues[14] describe a field experience for prospective teachers that requires 20 hours of service in a community agency. Participants can choose from a number of agencies, including Chicano Family Centers, urban YMCA after-school programs, community health centers, and homeless shelters. A course in the University of Houston's teacher education program requires 24 hours of volunteer work in a cultural setting unfamiliar to the students.[15] Ladson-Billings[16] has her students spend a minimum of ten hours working in human service agencies such as homeless shelters, soup kitchens, senior centers, and low-income child care centers.

As these examples suggest, service learning can support the development of a social justice perspective by prospective teachers of culturally diverse students. However, the benefits can be undermined or diffused if key participants—course instructors, program staff, and community mentors—do not share a commitment to promoting social justice.[17] One of the key challenges in developing and implementing a service learning program is to articulate and nurture a shared understanding of the purposes of service learning.[18] Participants may have radically different views, seeing service learning as career development, as charity, as a fulfillment of civic responsibility, or as a means to promote social justice. It appears that the charity perspective is the *default* view of service learning; without explicit discussion of the goals of service learning, most young people—as well as many adults—perceive their activities as a process of the "more fortunate" helping the "less fortunate."[19] While some service learning initiatives engage participants in social action that can lead to social change,[20] a focus on social justice in service learning programs is rare. One reason may be the lack of clarity about how students and faculty should be prepared for and supported in addressing issues of social justice. Without preparation, reflection, and support, both students and faculty are likely to rely on stereotypes and deficit views of oppressed groups that make it impossible to move beyond the charity perspective.[21]

In this chapter, I explore one instructor's efforts to incorporate service learning into a course for prospective teachers. The professor hoped to foster among his students greater awareness of and sensitivity to social problems and their potential solutions and a commitment to bring about educational change in support of social justice. I examine the promise of service learning for fostering a commitment to social justice as it was manifested in this course and factors that influenced the extent to which that promise was realized.

Context

Bridgetown State University (BSU, a pseudonym), a comprehensive state university in an urban suburb in the Northeast, enrolls approximately 10,000 undergraduate and 3,000 graduate students. About two-thirds of the undergraduates are white and one-third are students of color. The communities surrounding the university range from highly affluent and mostly white communities to inner-city communities where the great majority of residents are people of color. One city served by the university is largely African American, while another is largely Hispanic. The town where the university is located is a racially mixed community of 39,000 people known for its history of racial integration and its relatively large middle-class African American population. From 15 percent to 18 percent of students admitted to BSU's undergraduate preservice teacher education program are students of color. Most students come from largely white suburbs and from middle-class and working-class backgrounds. Most of them have had limited experience with people of diverse racial, ethnic, linguistic, and socioeconomic backgrounds. There are several means through which the teacher education program seeks to give all candidates some exposure to diverse communities and schools, one of which is service learning.

The service learning program at BSU was initiated by faculty in 1996. A community survey conducted in that year by the United Way identified four pressing community issues: the literacy and academic development of school-age children, care for the elderly population, substance abuse prevention, and access to computer technology. To ensure that service learning activities would reflect real community concerns, faculty and staff decided to design the service learning program to focus on these issues. Rather than having students or individual faculty members find placements, the service learning office coordinates the placement of all students in agencies that have committed to an ongoing partnership with the university. The program has grown to include courses across the university—in the Business School, the College of Humanities and Social Sciences, the School of the Arts, and the College of Education. In 2001–2002, the last year for which I collected data, 706 students and 26 faculty participated in 32 service learning courses. The university has developed partnerships with more than 25 agencies where university students carry out service learning activities, including the local Board of Education, several individual schools, a Boys and Girls Club, a senior center, and an agency that delivers meals to people's homes. As part of BSU's program, students in a number of courses work with young people in schools and after-school programs to promote the development of their literacy and other academic skills.

Between 1997 and 2002, I collected data on BSU's service learning program for purposes of program evaluation. In this chapter, I examine the experiences in one teacher education course taught by one professor in two consecutive semesters. I decided to explore how issues of social justice were reflected in this professor's course because, in interviews for the evaluation, the professor ("Dan") clearly and thoughtfully articulated his commitment to social justice. When I first interviewed him in fall 1999, he was an assistant professor in educational foundations with a disciplinary background in philosophy of education who had been at the university for two years. He integrated service learning into a course called Teaching for Critical Thinking, usually taken by juniors in the teacher education program. I analyzed the following qualitative data for this chapter: interviews with Dan in spring 1999 (when he was planning the course), fall 1999, and spring 2000; student focus groups in fall 1999 and spring 2000; and, in spring 2000, an interview with the director of Volunteer Services at the community agency where the students in the course carried out their community activities. The data reported here represent a close-up snapshot, a picture of one course over two semesters frozen in time, and should not be interpreted as reflecting current practices of the professor or the program as a whole.

The Promise of Service Learning for Fostering a Commitment to Social Justice Bringing Social Justice Issues to Life

Community settings characterized by racial, ethnic, and socioeconomic diversity provide a real-world context within which future teachers can explore social justice issues. Service learning in such settings takes social justice out of the realm of academic, theoretical discussions and into the realities of the lives of people. The community agency where Dan's students carried out their community activities was just such a setting. BSU's service learning office was, for the first time in fall 1999, placing students in the agency, which had 70 different sites across the state that, according to the agency's director of Volunteer Services, provided "advocacy, education, shelter, and care for abused, abandoned, and neglected children." The sites offered a wide array of services, including special education classes, day treatment programs, after-school and Saturday programs, and group residences. Each of Dan's students was placed in one of those sites. Dan noted that spending time in the sites brought social justice issues to life, both for his students and for him:

> I talk about [social justice issues] usually in a more theoretical way in most of my classes, but [having my students in the community sites] was a nice way of … forcing me to make what we're doing relevant to very specific social issues—for example, the way people without resources get treated and the way children are treated, the power that children have and don't have, public institutions, what people do with public money in the name of service, needs that are not met. Even gender issues came up sometimes—the way gender worked out in site administration. Socioeconomic class was the biggest one. Race didn't come up that often; there seemed to be enough racial diversity in these places that my students didn't see that as a main issue. But class definitely was. And they were shocked about the lack of resources and the way the resources were being used. Yes, we're paying a salary for somebody to supervise, but they sit in their office and read and smoke, and they stick their head out when they hear a problem and just scream at the children. And the fact that they didn't think about ordering enough school buses to take all the children on a field trip. That makes social justice a burning real issue.

The exposure Dan's students had in these community sites was especially important because the great majority of them, like BSU's teacher education students overall, had had no exposure to situations like those they encountered in the sites. Most had attended suburban schools in predominantly white and middle-class communities. As Dan pointed out, his students increased their awareness of community problems "in a really vivid emotional kind of way." He noted that while some of them probably knew about these problems before, developing relationships with people who have those problems was "a lot less insulated way to learn about the problems."

As these comments suggest, the immediacy of the experiences in the community sites heightened Dan's students' sense of inequities. In order to develop a commitment to enhancing social justice, one must recognize social *in*justice. With regard to education in particular, most of us in the United States are socialized to think of schools as the great equalizers in society. We tend to explain academic success and failure in terms of individual characteristics of learners rather than inequities in the society and the educational system. If teachers believe that schools provide all students an equitable chance to succeed, there is no reason to give attention to social or educational change to foster greater social justice. The recognition of inequities by Dan's students laid the foundation for their recognition of the need for attention to social justice issues.

The prospective teachers in Dan's classes saw firsthand that the conditions in which children were expected to learn and grow made it almost impossible for them to do so. They saw very vulnerable children being discouraged from learning. Their interactions with the children in the sites helped them recognize that the problems did not come from the children themselves but from the social settings and from some of the adults responsible for those settings. He described what some of his students reported. One said, "This is so good for me as a future teacher to learn about these problems: the things some young people are going through, the bad places these kids have been institutionalized, the educational choices that are being made for these students, the way they're being taught by their teachers, the ways the tutors handle them. The structures—like having no parents around, being left behind for field trips."

Comments by some students in focus groups corroborated Dan's observations that what they were seeing—particularly, the debilitating conditions the children in the sites experienced regularly—was making an impression on them. One student reported that she asked several people at the site how the young people would "fit in with their regular communities once they left the center." She said that the response was that "there was no help for them." Another student expressed dismay at what he encountered during his first visit to one of the sites:

> The time I went to [the site], I had to find my way around, because I didn't get a tour. I had to find the three kids that were left behind [when the others went to an amusement park for Halloween]. They were left behind because they couldn't fit in the bus. I had to figure out for myself where they were and what to do.

Another student voiced frustration at not being able to try out what he was learning in the university class because of the short time he was at the site. He said, "The counselors are watching wrestling on TV and the kids are just doing whatever they want, or doing the laundry. The counselors look up and shout at the kids occasionally." These and other students expressed shock at how children were treated. Several described the young people they interacted with at the sites as curious and eager to learn, a realization that helped them see the injustice of the conditions in which the children found themselves.

In a focus group, one student offered a particularly poignant and powerful illustration of the insight that can come from the types of first-hand experiences these prospective teachers were having:

> We took the kids one Saturday morning to an ice skating rink, and it dawned on me that…we had about 20 kids with us that day and five or six counselors. And we walked in and everyone just stared at us, like we were from Mars or something. It was an affluent area; there were events going on, little ballerinas, hockey teams, and kids with bags. We were the big group with all these black kids. I said to one of my co-workers, "I think they're staring at us." The kids started saying, "What are they looking at? These kids are whacked." I said, "Just hold your head up. We're here to ice skate like everybody else." We had a great time, but when we first walked in, there were stares and people tugging at their purse. It says a lot about racism.

This future teacher experienced what it felt like to be part of a group that was viewed with distrust and disdain for no other reason than skin color and social class. The understanding that "dawned on" him in that ice skating rink will stay with him much longer and in a much more visceral way than something he might read about racism and oppression. Opportunities for such up-close experiences with social justice issues abound in service learning activities.

Promoting a Sense of Entitlement to Critique and to Make Things Better

Recognizing injustice is only one step in the process of fostering a commitment to social justice among prospective teachers. If such recognition only leads them to wring their hands, it is of little benefit to their future students. Teachers also have to see themselves as participants in the struggle to promote social justice. They have to see themselves as capable of and entitled to critique social and educational practices and to bring about social and educational change.[22] Service learning is a means through which teacher educators can cultivate these dispositions. Through service learning, prospective teachers can get to know flesh-and-blood people who experience inequity and can then be guided to reflect on and discuss those inequities. In fact, guided reflection and discussion on community experiences are essential elements of well-planned service learning courses. This combination of experience, reflection, and dialogue can be a powerful impetus for a commitment to "set things right"—that is, to foster greater social justice.

Dan had his students write weekly journals about their service learning experiences. He asked them to reflect on how the kinds of thinking they talked about in class related to what they were observing, and how they thought different ways of thinking and action could be implemented in their settings "to make things better." He had the students do a final project in which they made a proposal for an improvement at the site where they were doing their service learning. The improvement "had to relate to a way of introducing more critical processes either with the students or the administrators." Dan also devoted some class time—more in the second semester than in the first—to discussion of the students' experiences.

He reported that many of his students developed "a general critical attitude of entitlement to make changes and make things better." They reflected in class logs and discussions about why people in the sites did what they did and why many of the adults did not seem more concerned about the children. At times, they encouraged each other to ask questions about practices or problems they observed at the sites, and sometimes they did raise concerns. The director of Volunteer Services at the community agency noted that a BSU student reported to her about what the student saw as inappropriate interactions between one staff person and some children. The director took the information to the agency director, who acted to remove the staff person. According to the director of Volunteer Services, this incident "turned into something positive.... It could have been negative public relations, but [the student] spoke out and helped us and the children."

Dan was particularly pleased to find that his students were able to "critique pedagogy" at the sites. The sites served as "an immediate context for looking at the useful and not useful pedagogies [they had] been trying to construct in the class." While in other classes, he would have to ask students to imagine or remember situations or experiences, in this class the students were in educational settings throughout the course and could draw on that immediate experience. Some of what the students observed, especially in the first semester, served as examples of ineffective teaching and inspired their negative critique. One student commented that the teachers at the site were "teaching like the 1950s with multiple choice tests all the way, no critical thinking going on." Dan also reported:

> Some students were placed in classrooms and what they saw was lecturing and abuse and authoritarian browbeating and belittling the students and trying to shame the students into doing better. There was no kind of student dialogue or discussion. And some were in tutoring programs where they had mentors who were supervising the tutoring and telling them how to tutor and it was just, Help them fill in the blanks. It wasn't, Try to engage them meaningfully with whatever curriculum they're trying to get through.

On the other hand, some students observed good teaching, especially in the second semester, and this inspired their positive critique. According to Dan, students gave "beautiful testimonials about how they were seeing aspects of community of inquiry at their sites." They described how supervisors had organized some sites so that the young people engaged in problem solving. Dan was happy to see that his students used the concepts and vocabulary they were learning in his class to analyze what they saw in the sites.

Some students made comments about the possibility of using critical thinking and community of inquiry (the content and pedagogy of Dan's course) with the children at the sites. Their comments show that they were critiquing pedagogy, as Dan reported. While some gave examples of critical thinking and inquiry, others were frustrated by the lack of these practices. One said, "I don't think it's possible to bring up the community of inquiry in that context." Another agreed: "I'm using elements of [critical thinking], but it's really stretching it to say that this course relates to what we're doing [at the sites]." In the focus group, two other students in Dan's class disagreed with each other about the possibility of engaging the students at the sites in critical thinking:

> Student A: The idea that you can introduce what we're doing in this class with the kids is farcical.

> Student B: But we did. We put them in certain situations, like: You have a friend who's dating this girl, and she wants to date you, what do you do? It's a discussion about what to do, what are the issues, what are the solutions.

This exchange shows that student B was able not only to critique the pedagogy of the community sites but also to apply the concept of critical thinking to the kinds of issues that were relevant to the lives of the students in the sites.

Other student comments mirror their frustrations with what they observed. But even some of their frustrating experiences illustrated the willingness of these future teachers to be persistent in their efforts to have a positive impact at the sites. Dan described one student's efforts as follows:

> One guy noticed that there was a broken ping pong table and pad dles and asked if they could move some furniture so they could bring the table out and fix the paddles. He wanted to organize a tournament.... The kids were involved in planning and were excited. For three weeks [he showed] up ready to do it, and they hadn't set up the physical arrangements. Finally, after four weeks, they did it. That was typical. A lot of them made suggestions, but the sites were not willing to make changes, take advice, and go about doing things differently.

Not all of Dan's students were as persistent or as successful as this student at taking actions to bring about changes in the community sites. But their reflections in their logs and in some class discussions as well as comments in the focus groups suggest that their experiences led some of them to feel compelled to try to improve the living and learning conditions of the children in the sites.

Realizing the Promise of Service Learning for Fostering a Commitment to Social Justice

As we have seen, service learning can bring social justice issues to life by giving prospective teachers firsthand experiences with people of diverse backgrounds and with inequities they face. It can also foster a sense of entitlement among participants to critique practices and to seek to bring about change. Service learning thus appears to be a promising means for fostering a commitment to social justice among prospective teachers. The experiences of Dan and his students suggest that the extent to which this promise is realized depends on a number of factors, which are discussed below.

Thoughtful Planning and Implementation by the Instructor

Service learning does not work magic; like any other pedagogical approach, it requires thoughtful planning and implementation to be successful. Ideally,

an instructor of a service-learning course has a solid theoretical understanding of the nature and purposes of service learning and has given
serious attention to how to integrate community activities with the course
curriculum. Dan's planning and implementation of the Teaching for Critical Thinking course certainly met these criteria.

Dan brought to the course a sophisticated theoretical understanding of
the connection between action and learning and of problem-based learning. In particular, his thinking about service learning was grounded in the
philosophy of pragmatism. When I first interviewed him, he explained:

> From the philosophical point of view of pragmatism, the emphasis
> is on action and behavior as the final interpretation of thought.
> Ideas only mean how they're acted out; that is their meaning. And
> especially from Dewey, who sees all of education that way—as a
> matter of doing, learning by doing.... In all my classes, I make
> activism a part of it.... So this seemed like a very natural way to do
> that—to emphasize action and learning together.... Service learn-
> ing also reflects the integration of schools and society that Dewey
> argued for.

Dan had also given thought to how to integrate the community activities into the course. He envisioned service learning as an "extension" of the
curriculum. He introduced service learning to the students by engaging
them in a discussion of the connection between thought and action, and
explained service learning as applied critical thinking. He used problem-
based learning as the theme for the course; that is, he pushed students
to identify problems and to seek ways to solve them. Specifically, he
encouraged the students to look for "difficulties, problems, puzzlements
that they're seeing in the community, outside the classroom, and use what
we're learning about critical thinking processes in class toward realizing
imagined possibilities, or solving the problems" outside the class. He
wanted the students to think of ways to solve real social problems and to
"make things better" for the children in the settings where they worked.
The final project for the course was a paper in which they applied critical
thinking to make an improvement at the sites.

Dan recognized that to incorporate their community-based experiences
in productive ways his students needed structured opportunities for
ongoing critical reflection. He believed that through action and reflection,
the students would better understand social issues and develop a commitment to social justice. As described above, he assigned weekly journals in
which the students were to reflect on their experiences and relate them to
course content. He found that students in the first semester wrote a lot

about the problems they were encountering in the sites, while students in the second semester "told stories" about their experiences. Many of them also reflected on themselves as future teachers—for example, how they would handle situations differently from what they observed, or what they needed to learn in order to be a good teacher. Many reflected on working with "students of multiethnic backgrounds."

While the journals provided a place for student reflection, Dan acknowledged that he did not give the students many other opportunities for reflection. For example, he did not devote much class time in either semester to discussing students' community experiences. In the first semester, he didn't realize until toward the end that he probably should have given more class time to students' experiences. In the second semester, he intended to spend more class time on these issues, but felt the need was not as great as in the first semester. He also felt pressed for time to "fit everything in" and found that the class was able to read only half the amount of material they read in the course without the service learning component. Thus, Dan acknowledged that he could have given more attention to critical reflection on community activities. Still, his strong theoretical grounding and careful planning and implementation of the service-learning course gave the students tools for making sense of their experiences in productive ways.

Community Sites that Offer Opportunities to Explore Social Justice Issues

The nature of the participating community sites also influences the potential for service learning to foster commitment to social justice among prospective teachers. Sites that engage people of racially, ethnically, linguistically, and socioeconomically diverse backgrounds provide rich contexts for exploring issues of equity and inequity, oppression and privilege, justice and injustice. The sites where Dan's students spent time appeared to have considerable potential for promoting thinking and dialogue among prospective teachers about issues of social justice and sociocultural diversity. Dan noted that "the opportunity [to bring up social justice issues] is there in all the places where I see [the students] being sent." At the community sites, Dan's students interacted with students from sociocultural backgrounds different from their own. As he pointed out, they were especially cognizant of the social class differences between themselves and the students at the sites, and they were shocked at the way the students were treated.

Another aspect of the community sites that can influence the attention to social justice is the nature of the actions by adults in the sites. Community sites where adults are working to enhance social justice can serve as good models for prospective teachers. Some of the adults at the sites in this study—especially in the spring semester—did appear to be working successfully with students. That semester, Dan's students saw some good educational practices with students of diverse backgrounds that reflected the types of pedagogy they were discussing in the class. In these cases, the students had the opportunity to see community-based activities that were contributing to individual and community well-being.

In contrast, in the fall semester, Dan's students emphasized what they perceived as poor treatment of children and apparent inability or disinterest in teaching them by the adults at the community sites. According to Dan, the many examples of inequities students observed made "social justice a real burning issue" for reflection and class discussion. Especially in the fall semester, the students in Dan's class had few chances to observe good models for themselves as potential future teachers of children of diverse backgrounds. Instead, they observed quite a few examples of the worst of education for poor students of color—mistreatment, irresponsibility, and lack of caring by adults. While the community-based activities they observed were "keeping kids off the street," as the agency representative noted, they did not appear to be exemplary in their contribution to the well-being of the children or the community; they did not, in other words, appear to be promoting social justice. While no one would advocate purposefully selecting community sites where children are mistreated, the shock and indignation that some of Dan's students expressed seemed to heighten their sense of injustice and sew the seeds for action to combat it. Thus, prospective teachers can learn from poor models as well as good models—as long as they are guided in their reflection and critique by a knowledgeable mentor. Although Dan provided such guidance, he felt this was an area in which he needed much more skill, as discussed below.

Preparation of Faculty to Help Students Make Sense of Social Justice Issues

The third factor that emerged as an influence on Dan's success (or lack of success) in promoting a commitment to social justice among his students was his own inexperience in working with diverse children and in facilitating the sorts of interactions his students were having with diverse children. Service learning faculty who want to foster a commitment to social justice need more than theoretical understanding and careful planning; they need skills and strategies for helping their students make sense of community experiences in ways that will support such a commitment. Because the majority of teacher educators share Dan's inexperience, they need opportunities for professional development focused on helping them develop those skills and strategies.

Dan explicitly commented that he did not feel "qualified" to help students prepare for or interpret the types of experiences they had in urban settings with "abused, abandoned, and neglected children" of various racial and cultural backgrounds. His interactions with students in journals and, in the second semester, some class discussions no doubt helped some students see beyond their stereotypes and assumptions. However, to a large extent, the students interpreted their experiences through the frames they brought with them to the class. Dan could see that the experiences at the community sites were reinforcing the stereotypes of a few students, and he was frustrated by his inability to interrupt this process. In interviews in both fall and spring, Dan expressed the desire to have more discussion among service learning faculty about social justice issues, how to help students prepare for and interpret their experiences in sites characterized by sociocultural diversity, and how to incorporate community activities more successfully into courses.

He expressed at length his frustration at not being able to successfully challenge some students' entrenched stereotypes. He described one student as having "very rigid preconceived notions" about people living in urban areas. The community activities were, in Dan's eyes, "a perfect opportunity" for this student to question his preconceptions, but instead he "used the experiences to reinforce" his stereotypical ideas. Dan discussed his efforts to challenge the student's thinking.

> In the journals I would frequently question the assumptions the student was making about what was going on. He made very stereotypical, derogatory comments, using phrases like the ghetto, saying, "Why don't they just get a life." He had a superficial interpretation, saying things like, "Well, of course that's what's going on because that's where they come from." The student wants to become a teacher to make a difference in people's lives, but is casting himself as a resource for poor people. To help them. The experience just reinforced all those stereotypes.

In class discussions, other students tried unsuccessfully to challenge this student's stereotypes. Surprised by how resistant this otherwise "thinking person" was to changing his perceptions of others, Dan concluded that "it just goes to show that having an experience like this isn't necessarily going to change your attitudes." Recognizing that he was not equipped to address these issues in the deep ways he would like to, he noted that discussions among faculty teaching service learning courses might be a good way to build understanding and expertise among all of them.

> I don't feel qualified to judge what the appropriate interpretations of the urban experience are, because I have very limited experience with urban education. I'm happy that I'm getting some here at BSU, but I'm in the same learning curve that a lot of the students are. It would be great to have this cohort of service learning teachers help each other out and make suggestions for how to address these issues—other than me [sic] going into ERIC and trying to find stuff.

BSU's service learning program did provide some professional development to faculty teaching service learning courses. They had opportunities to learn about the nature and characteristics of service learning, to learn about service learning programs in other higher education institutions, to discuss ways to engage students in reflection on their community experiences, and to connect community activities to the content of a course. They did not have formal opportunities to discuss ways to help students interpret experiences outside their own cultural and social class spheres or to help them challenge their stereotypes of people different from themselves. To support teacher educators in fostering a commitment to social justice among prospective teachers, service-learning programs need to offer professional development opportunities focused on these processes.

To engage successfully with people who are racially, ethnically, and socioeconomically different from themselves, prospective teachers need to cultivate self-awareness, understanding of culture and cultural differences, and understanding of social power dynamics.[23] Developing self-awareness is a complex process. It requires future teachers to understand that there are multiple ways of seeing and interpreting the world and that their own and other's worldviews are shaped by such factors as race, ethnicity, class, and gender.[24] It also involves engaging them in critical examination of their own worldviews—including values, assumptions, and biases—and of how their worldviews influence their perspectives of people different from themselves. Understanding culture is no less challenging. Prospective teachers need to understand the nature of culture and socialization, to learn about the particular cultures of the community and the people with whom they will be working, and to become knowledgeable of the history and the current social and political situation of the community. Finally, before embarking on service learning in communities unlike their own, prospective teachers need to understand the dynamics of power in individual social interactions and in the larger society; to critically examine privilege, social inequality, and minority group membership; and to explicitly examine the inherent imbalance of power in the service relationship.[25] Ignoring these difficult issues of power is likely to reinforce the sense that those who "help" are, in fact, superior to those who are "helped."

Faculty members who teach service-learning courses cannot prepare their students in the ways just discussed without their own self-awareness, understanding of culture and cultural differences, and understanding of social power dynamics—and strategies for preparing their students in these ways. Such preparation could come from any number of sources, including ongoing discussions among faculty, as Dan had hoped for; more formal professional development initiatives organized by the faculty, the service-learning program leadership, or other institutional offices; and attending professional workshops and conferences. While Dan saw growth in these areas for many of his students, he was pained by his inability to reach the students with the most deeply entrenched stereotypes. Some professional development might have helped him make inroads even with those students.

Programmatic Support

As the above discussion suggests, in contexts such as BSU where there is a formal service- learning program with a program coordinator and resources, the nature of programmatic support can have an impact on the effectiveness of service learning in fostering a commitment to social justice. Particular types of support that emerged from this analysis as potentially important were the programmatic commitment to social justice and the attention to the selection of sites and logistical issues.

Programmatic Commitment to Social Justice. While simply stating a program's goals does not ensure that they will be met, an explicit statement of goals or a mission can help to clarify and support priorities and actions taken under the auspices of the program. The goals of the service learning program at BSU, according to the service learning program materials, were to "foster civic responsibility by focusing on critical, reflective thinking, and an appreciation of larger social issues inherent in a democracy." It could be argued that this statement implies a value for social justice without explicitly stating it. But the implicitness of the statement resulted in a vagueness about what these concepts meant or how to accomplish these worthy goals. Most of the time and energy of those involved in the coordination of the program was devoted to building and maintaining partnerships with community agencies. This emphasis was appropriate in that it both reflected the commitment to ensure that the program was responsive to needs identified by the community and illustrated the notorious and ongoing difficulty of forging successful collaborations across institutional boundaries. There was some discussion among faculty and program staff of the need for professional development for faculty related to the social issues facing the communities—for example, racial, linguistic, and social class differences and the accompanying inequities in wealth, access to services, academic achievement, and life options—and related to ways they could help their students understand these problems. While some faculty members who taught service learning courses had given considerable thought to these social issues and to enhancing students' sociocultural consciousness,[26] others had not. In the service learning courses, some faculty engaged students in critical reflection and discussion about their experiences, as the literature suggests, and some did not. In addition, as we saw above, some students came to the service-learning activities open to seeing social issues in new ways, and others came holding on tightly to their stereotypes and assumptions.

As previously explained, Dan expressed a desire for more explicit attention to social justice among service-learning faculty. He felt that such discussion was needed to ensure that those issues would be addressed in the classes. He perceived that issues of social justice were emphasized in the College of Education, but not across the university.

> In education, it's so obvious that that's part of what we're here for; we want them to have social justice on the mind as part of their preparation. And critical thinking is a way of finding social problems and working on them.... But from my experience, it's not something that people across the campus have in mind as part of their work as faculty members.... In fact I'm discouraged about that. I think that a lot of faculty are looking for sites where students can learn more about content, and not giving a lot of thought to whether they are going to see social justice issues.

> But the opportunity is there at all the places where I see them being sent. So I would like some dialogue about it.... We need a community of service-learning faculty to talk about what we want to get out of it. As a participant in that discussion, I would push the social justice aspect of it. And hopefully get some buy-in. I guess it's not a programwide expectation that social justice should be a central issue.... We need a conversation about what we're preparing students for at the university. Are we preparing citizens? A lot of colleges of education don't talk about that, but here we do. There's no reason why the whole university couldn't emphasize that.

Unclear about where the program stood with regard to social justice, Dan had concluded with some disappointment that promoting social justice was not a program priority, and he was left with little support in his efforts to foster a commitment to social justice among his students. In fairness to program leadership, the immediate priority had to be building and maintaining relationships with community agencies and insuring that all students were properly placed each semester. At the same time, they could have held some meetings to give faculty the opportunity to discuss what the program goals meant in practice. Such meetings might have been helpful to Dan.

Attention to Logistics and Selection of Community Sites. While they may seem inconsequential, the logistics of community activities and the careful selection of community sites can have an important influence on the attitudes and perceptions of students toward people at the sites. If phone calls are not returned, appointments are not kept, and students are given no welcome or orientation at the sites, they may become so angry and frustrated that they cannot see beyond those feelings. The different experiences of students in Dan's class in the fall and in the spring serve as a good example of this phenomenon.

In the fall, the relationships between the university and the individual agency sites and the procedures for placing service learning students were still being developed. Numerous problems arose that frustrated many students as well as Dan, who reported that he had to spend far too much class time dealing with the logistical hurdles students were constantly facing. The hurdles came both from BSU's service learning office and from the sites where the students were placed.

> They had hassles getting recommended to the agency, getting phone calls returned, and not being clear about what they could or could not sign up for.... [At the sites, they encountered] people who don't know what to do with volunteers. There was no orientation, no telling them what they expect, no training or advice about how to work in our organization, how to help us help the kids, no forethought about what we're going to do with these people. Several were just told to sit there and watch the class go on. Finally they'd get sick of it and start to demand to do things. In a way that was good, but not really.

One student was advised by someone at an agency to lie to a police officer about where he lived in order to get fingerprints, which were needed before students could work at the sites. Some were "yelled at and called names, treated like children, verbally abused by people in the agency." Experiences like these may support students' prejudices and stereotypes, and they certainly make it difficult for them to turn their attention to substantive issues of equity and social justice.

In the spring semester, the students encountered very few of these problems. Both BSU and agency staff had learned from the previous semester. The placements were more carefully made. Dan had identified some specific sites "not to go back to" and the agency was more involved in "recommending certain sites and not others." While the students encountered some problems similar to those in the fall, they also observed more good teaching practices in the spring, as described previously. According to Dan, students in the fall semester needed "to vent" about their experiences, while in the spring semester they generally did not. What they talked about in class was often "illustrating positive experiences" rather than criticizing what they were seeing, which was more typical of their discussions in the fall. Because the students in the spring semester were not distracted and frustrated by logistical problems, they could give more attention to the substantive issues raised by their experiences.

Conclusion

This examination of the experiences in Dan's class suggests that service learning has great promise for promoting a commitment to social justice among prospective teachers. Service learning brought social justice issues to life for Dan's students by giving them firsthand experiences with people of diverse backgrounds and with the inequities they face. It also fostered a sense of entitlement among some of these future teachers to critique the practices they saw in the sites and to seek to bring about change. Some of the elements needed to foster a social justice commitment were present in this service learning course. Dan's thoughtful planning, solid theoretical grounding for the course, integration of community service and course curriculum, and structured opportunities for student reflection contributed to helping students learn from their experiences. The nature of the community sites also provided ample opportunities for contact with students of socioculturally diverse backgrounds and rich material for discussions of social justice. In the second semester, many of the logistical issues that were problematic for students in the first semester were addressed, making it easier for the students to concentrate on substantive issues arising from their experiences. Ultimately, it appears that many students in Dan's classes became more sensitive to sociocultural diversity and to issues of social justice. He might have had even more success if he had had some opportunities to develop his skill in challenging students' stereotypes and helping them interpret experiences in community sites characterized by diversity. He and other faculty who wanted to foster social justice through service learning might also have benefited if the service-learning program had given more explicit attention to social justice in its mission statement, literature, and communication with students, faculty, and community partners. The potential of service learning to foster a commitment to social justice among prospective teachers is great. We need to do what we can to realize that potential for the sake of the children in our public schools whose futures depend on having teachers who are ready to help them break through the barriers raised by inequity and injustice in schools and society.

Notes

1. Lee Anne Bell, "Theoretical Foundations for Social Justice Education," in *Teaching for Diversity and Social Justice: A Sourcebook*, ed. M. Adams, L. A. Bell, and P. Griffin (New York: Routledge, 1997), 1–15.
2. Rahima C. Wade, "Service-Learning for Multicultural Teaching Competency: Insights from the Literature for Teacher Education," *Equity and Excellence in Education* 33, no. 3 (2000): 21–29.
3. Marilynne Boyle-Baise, "Community Service-Learning for Multicultural Education: An Exploratory Study with Preservice Teachers," *Equity and Excellence in Education* 31, no. 2 (2000): 52–60; and Laura L. Stachowski and James M. Mahan, "Cross-Cultural Field Placements: Student Teachers Learning from Schools *and* Communities," *Theory Into Practice* 37, no. 2 (1998): 155–62.
4. See Ana María Villegas and Tamara Lucas, *Educating Culturally Responsive Teachers: A Coherent Approach* (Albany, N.Y.: SUNY Press, 2002).
5. Robert G. Bringle and Julie A. Hatcher, "Implementing Service Learning in Higher Education," *Journal of Higher Education* 67 (1996): 221–39; Corporation for National Service, ed., *Expanding Boundaries: Serving and Learning* (Washington, D.C.: Corporation for National Service, 1996); Corporation for National Service, ed., *Expanding Boundaries: Building Civic Responsibility within Higher Education* (Washington, D.C.: Corporation for National Service, 1997); Janet Eyler and Dwight E. Giles, *Where's the Learning in Service-Learning?* (San Francisco: Jossey Bass, 1999); Joan Schine, "Looking Ahead: Issues and Challenges," in *Service Learning. Ninety-Sixth Yearbook of the National Society for the Study of Education*, ed. J. Schine (Chicago: National Society for the Study of Education, 1997), 186–99; and Rahima C. Wade, "Community Service-Learning: An Overview," in *Community Service Learning: A Guide to Including Services in the Public School Curriculum*, ed. R. C. Wade (Albany: SUNY Press, 1997), 19–34.
6. Joseph M. Larkin, "Curriculum Themes and Issues in Multicultural Teacher Education Programs," in *Developing Multicultural Teacher Education Curricula*, ed. J. M. Larkin and C.E. Sleeter (Albany: SUNY Press, 1995), 1–16; and Ken Zeichner et al., "A Research Informed Vision of Good Practice in Multicultural Teacher Education: Design Principles," *Theory Into Practice* 37, no. 2 (1998): 163–71.
7. Carl A. Grant, "Critical Knowledge, Skills, and Experiences for the Instruction of Culturally Diverse Students: A Perspective for the Preparation of Preservice Teachers," in *Critical Knowledge for Diverse Teachers and Learners*, ed. J. J. Irvine (Washington, D.C.: American Association of Colleges for Teacher Education, 1997), 1–26.
8. Karen Noordhoff and Judith Kleinfield, "Preparing Teachers for Multicultural Classrooms," *Teaching and Teacher Education* 9, no. 1 (1993): 27–39; and Ken Zeichner and Susan Melnick, "The Role of Community Field Experiences in Preparing Teachers for Cultural Diversity," paper presented at the annual meeting of the American Association of Colleges for Teacher Education, Washington, D.C., 1995.

9. William D. Armaline, "Reflecting on Cultural Diversity through Early Field Experiences," in *Practicing What We Teach: Confronting Diversity in Teacher Education,* ed. R. J. Martin (Albany: SUNY Press, 1995), 163–80; Kathleen S. Farber and William D. Armaline, "Examining Cultural Conflict in Urban Field Experiences through the Use of Reflective Thinking," *Teacher Education Quarterly* 21, no. 2 (1994): 59–76; Sharon S. Nelson-Barber and Jean Mitchell, "Restructuring for Diversity: Five Regional Portraits," in *Diversity in Teacher Education: New Expectations,* ed. M. E. Dilworth (San Francisco: Jossey Bass, 1992), 229–62; Ken Zeichner and Karen Hoeft, "Teacher Socialization for Cultural Diversity," in *Handbook on Research on Teacher Education,* 2nd ed., ed. J. Sikula, T. Buttery, and E. Guyton (New York: Macmillan, 1996), 525–47; and Zeichner and Melnick.

10. Nelson-Barber and Mitchell, 257.

11. Marilyn Cochran-Smith, "Learning to Teach Against the Grain," *Harvard Educational Review* 61, no. 3 (1991): 279–310; Ken Zeichner, *NCRTL Special Report: Educating Teachers for Cultural Diversity* (East Lansing: Michigan State University, National Center for Research on Teacher Learning, 1992); and Zeichner et al., "A Research Informed Vision of Good Practice in Multicultural Teacher Education: Design Principles."

12. Fred A. Korthagen and Joseph Kessels, "Linking Theory and Practice: Changing the Pedagogy of Teacher Education," *Educational Researcher* 28, no. 4 (1999): 4–17.

13. Elizabeth Bondy, S. Schmitz, and Margaret Johnson, "The Impact of Coursework and Fieldwork on Student Teachers Reported Beliefs about Teaching Poor and Minority Students," *Action in Teacher Education* 15, no. 2 (1993): 55–62.

14. Kip Tellez et al., "Social Service Field Experiences and Teacher Education Statistics," in *Developing Multicultural Teacher Education Curricula,* ed. J. Larkin and C. E. Sleeter (New York: SUNY Press, 1995), 65–78.

15. Rahima C. Wade, "Service-Learning in Preservice Teacher Education," in *Community Service Learning: A Guide to Including Services in the Public School Curriculum,* ed. R. C. Wade (Albany: SUNY Press, 1997), 314–30.

16. Gloria Ladson-Billings, "When Difference Means Disaster: Reflections on a Teacher Education Strategy for Countering Student Resistance to Diversity," paper presented at the annual meeting of the American Education Research Association, Chicago, 1991.

17. Wade, "Service-Learning for Multicultural Teaching Competency."

18. Peter C. Scales and Donna J. Koppelman, "Service Learning in Teacher Preparation," in *Service Learning. Ninety-Sixth Yearbook of the National Society for the Study of Education,* ed. J. Schine (Chicago: National Society for the Study of Education, 1997), 118–35.

19. Joseph Kahne and Joel Westheimer, "In Service to What? The Politics of Service Learning," *Phi Delta Kappan* 77, no. 2 (1996): 592–99; Wade, "Service Learning for Multicultural Teaching Competency;" and Janie V. Ward, "Encouraging Cultural Competence in Service Learning Practice," in *Service Learning. Ninety-Sixth Yearbook of the National Society for the Study of Education,* ed. J. Schine (Chicago: National Society for the Study of Education, 1997), 136–48.

20. See Francis R. Aparicio and Christina José-Kampfner, "Language, Culture, and Violence in the Educational Crisis of U.S. Latino/as: Two Courses for Intervention," *Michigan Journal of Community Service Learning* 2 (1995): 95–104; Eyler and Giles; John Saltmarsh, "Education for Critical Citizenship: John Dewey's Contribution to the Pedagogy of Community Service Learning," *Michigan Journal of Community Service Learning* 3 (1996): 13–21; and Lori E.Varlotta, "Service-Learning: A Catalyst for Constructing Democratic Progressive Communities," *Michigan Journal of Community Service Learning* 3 (1996): 22–30.

21. Farber and Armaline; Stachowski and Mahan; and Zeichner and Melnick.

22. Villegas and Lucas.

23. Wade, "Service-Learning for Multicultural Teaching Competency."

24. Villegas and Lucas.

25. Wade, "Service-Learning for Multicultural Teaching Competency."

26. Villegas and Lucas.

CHAPTER 9

Developing a Shared Vision for Schooling and Teacher Education in a Democracy: A Story from Colorado

CAROL WILSON AND ROSCOE DAVIDSON

Societies are renewed—if they are renewed at all—by people who believe in something, care about something, and stand for something.[1]

During the early 1980s, a vast wave of criticism rose to engulf the public schools. Originating in earlier decades but not quelled by responses up through the early 1980s, this wave reached a crest with the National Commission for Excellence in Education's report, *A Nation at Risk*. The unforgettable language used by the commission likened schools' efforts to an enemy taking over the country, and the report contained urgent recommendations for mobilizing education to bring the United States into the global economy's forefront.[2]

Additional critiques followed, including numerous commission reports, studies, and books. Three books, in particular, were significant and widely read, critical but balanced, less focused on schools as a means to economic success and more focused on schools' broader purposes. These looked at schools' results and effects, while also considering the circumstances of schooling—those conditions within which schools operate—and were more deliberative studies coming from long-time scholars, researchers, and educators. They included Ernest Boyer's *High*

School,[3] Theodore Sizer's *Horace's Compromise,*[4] both of which focused on high schools, and John Goodlad's *A Place Called School,*[5] which encompassed kindergarten through high school and was the most comprehensive study of schooling ever undertaken.

The three critiques complemented each other, and they gained wide attention, not only in their analyses of the circumstances and effects of schooling, which they reflected well, but also in the responses to which they pointed. All three lamented the calcified structures and expectations of schooling—structures and expectations fashioned after industry and little changed since at least the 1950s, if not earlier. Such structures included "egg-crate schools"—large schools divided into individual classrooms with one teacher responsible for many students, ability grouping and tracking, rote memorization and use of worksheets, uniform and nonengaging "frontal teaching," and more. Expectations too often based on race and class were exacerbated by ability grouping. The responses to which these critiques pointed included, among other things, the broader role of schooling in this society, requiring more enriching curriculum for all students and teachers to engage students differently in learning.

Goodlad's critique, in particular, brought his earlier inquiry and practice in California first with the League of Cooperating Schools (LCS) and then the Southern California School-University Partnership (SCSUP), to bear on the study. Goodlad had long been calling for the reconstruction of teacher preparation, professional development, and schooling.[6] The circumstances of the time reflected a huge chasm between educator preparation programs and the public schools, despite the obvious connections between the two. The primary linkage was student-teacher placement, and sometimes curriculum projects. Much more was needed.

In *A Place Called School,* Goodlad suggested closer ties between schools and universities, describing "key schools" and stating, "Key schools should be linked to universities and to one another in a communicating, collaborating network."[7] He thus began preparing ground for the development of partner schools/professional development schools as a reflection of school-university partnerships. Eventually, the Holmes Group, a collaborative effort of research institutions linked with the schools, further developed the professional development school concept. The professional development school now has gained acceptance across numerous school districts and teacher preparation programs.

Goodlad's years of research and experience, in addition to his practical insight, led to the creation of the Center for Educational Renewal (CER) at the University of Washington in the mid-1980s as a means for renewing schooling and the way we think about it. Through the CER, he launched the idea for a network of school-university partnerships devoted to the renewal of both partners with a view toward all children and youth enjoying quality schooling. Goodlad reasoned that schools renewing themselves alone would not be sufficient, as educator preparation programs would not necessarily be preparing school professionals for these schools. Likewise, educator preparation programs renewing themselves in isolation may be preparing educators for schools that do not exist. Therefore, schools and educator preparation programs must join and engage in simultaneously renewing themselves and each other.

Further, Goodlad differentiated between renewal and the more popular approach of reform. He observed that reform is most often externally determined and suggests something is broken. The problem or issue identified comes with a particular remedy or innovation to be installed within a clearly defined time frame. Renewal, on the other hand comes from within, although it can be stimulated externally, most often by an "alternative drummer," someone who brings a new lens to view what is there. It relies upon the responsible parties, working together to inquire into the circumstances in question and develop appropriate responses. Renewal implies an ongoing process—inquiry in various forms, which Goodlad described as dialogue, decision, action, and evaluation.

Colleague Kenneth Sirotnik wrote extensively about critical, collaborative inquiry propelling and sustaining renewal. Sirotnik framed a set of questions he suggested to serve as heuristics for educators in examining their practice. They included these: "What is going on in the name of "X"? How did it come to be this way? Whose interests are (and are not) being served by the way things are? What information and knowledge do we have—or need to get—that bear upon the issues? Is this the way we want it to be? What are we going to do about all this?"[8] Questions such as these and the approach they connote speak to John Gardner's observation: "In the ever-renewing society what matures is a system or framework within which continuous innovation, renewal and rebirth can occur."[9] Gardner further notes, "Exploration of the full range of his own potentialities is not something that the self-renewing man leaves to the chances of life. It is something he pursues systematically, or at least avidly, to the end of his days."[10] So it is for the self-renewing organization, be it school, college, department, program, or network.

With renewal in mind and responding to invitation, by 1986 ten school-university partnerships across the country had formed and became inaugural members of the National Network for Educational Renewal (NNER). At the time of this writing in 2004, the number has grown to twenty-three partnership settings.

Goodlad believes in and cares deeply about the public purposes and conduct of schooling in this democracy. He and colleagues Kenneth Sirotnik and Roger Soder launched NNER with a call for partnerships to address the "hard rock issues" of schooling, issues raised in *A Place Called School* pertaining to equal access to quality education—issues of social justice. From the earliest iteration, the "hard rock issues" reminded educators of their responsibility to provide stimulating, enriching schooling to all students, especially given our system of compulsory schooling.

Urging that the approach to this work reflect its aim, Goodlad advocated partnerships among those in schools and universities be formed with the parties working together as equals. As his complementary research on preservice teacher preparation began to take shape in the early 1990s, Goodlad and colleagues further developed and articulated the overarching moral principles of this work, which became known as the Agenda for Education in a Democracy. The agenda speaks to the public purposes of schooling in our social and political democracy, directing attention to our moral responsibility to provide equal access to learning for all students, use teaching practices that nurture all students' learning, act as stewards of our schools, and help equip and bring the young into full participation in our democracy.[11]

Goodlad promoted democratic ends through democratic processes. Those in schools and university teacher-preparation programs working as equal partners could contribute to each other's renewal, which would promote equitable and excellent education for all students. Working together in such a way develops strong norms of trust, tolerance, and solidarity. Associations or social structures that do so contribute to the broader civic community,[12] as well as to schools, universities, and their students. The work would contribute to a healthy civil society, both in what the partners hoped to accomplish and how they went about accomplishing it.

Although this language was not used, the concept of social capital provides another lens through which to view the partnerships and NNER. As Robert Putnam describes, "the core idea of social capital theory is that social networks have value ... 'social capital' calls attention to the fact that civic virtue is most powerful when embedded in a dense network of reciprocal social relations." Putnam further distinguishes two forms (among many others) of social capital: bonding social capital, described as "inward looking and tend[ing] to reinforce exclusive identities and homogeneous groups."[13] Manifested in groups such as ethnic fraternal organizations or church groups, bonding social capital can offer support by reinforcing the values of that group. While contributing in some ways to a healthy civil society, by its exclusive nature, bonding social capital can also limit its development. Bridging social capital is, on the other hand, inclusive, outward looking, bringing together people from various groups and across social divides. Usually both kinds of social capital are present, but one generally predominates.

From the outset, the school-university partnerships and the network of these partnerships developed bridging social capital. The structure within and among partnerships promoted different ways of working together across groups not accustomed to working together, created new roles, and offered opportunities for thinking deeply about schooling in this democracy.

While the partnerships held common values and commitments in terms of working across schools and universities for their mutual renewal and attending to the hard rock issues, each partnership was "a tub on its own bottom." That is, each had to respond to the particular circumstances and characteristics of participating schools and universities, as well as the local community context. Further, each had to find the means for supporting itself financially. Naturally this meant the partnership settings differed somewhat in composition, conduct of their business, challenges they faced, and ways in which they responded to challenges. Building social capital thrives on such differences, while also presenting issues, as differences can more easily serve to divide than cohere. As the NNER has evolved and some differences have become more visible, these differences have also served to remind participants of the reasons for coming together. Fundamental differences, such as views of equity for gays and lesbians, or the message reflected in a state's flying the Confederate flag, serve not as points on which to separate and draw lines, but as points of inquiry for the individual partnership settings, as well as the collective network. While difficult to navigate, the key to doing so has been a willingness to inquire, reflect, and act—whether the actions are small or large—in order to renew and move a little closer to the democratic principles that all value.

The Colorado Partnership for Educational Renewal (CoPER) serves as one example of the NNER school-university partnership settings. One of the initial partnerships, CoPER was helped into being through the efforts of then education commissioner, Calvin Frazier, who earlier had invited John Goodlad to Colorado to create school-university connections similar to Goodlad's prior work in California. When CoPER formed, it differed somewhat in its composition from others in the NNER. Most formed with one university and one or more school districts, which is challenging enough, given the differences in organizational culture, reward systems, and so on. CoPER began with two higher education institutions (one university and one state college) and seven school districts. It has grown to include sixteen school districts, eight higher education institutions, and the state's community college system.

Goodlad encouraged partnerships between institutions of higher education (IHE) and school districts based on experience with the League of Cooperating Schools, which he developed between the University of California at Los Angeles and eighteen area schools, and later the Southern California School-University Partnership, which included more partners. In the league, the emphasis was on the individual school cooperating with the university and other schools in other districts, which advanced the idea that the school is the unit of change. Issues with the league, however, led Goodlad to recognize the need for a supportive school district, as the district is most often the locus of decision-making regarding change. The district must support a particular school as those in the school determine what changes it needs. CoPER and the other initial partnerships, therefore, encompassed school districts and IHEs.

In the same way that school districts can provide a supportive context for schools, as well as an infrastructure for sharing what is learned across a district, including more IHEs and district partners helped set up a structure through which more people could work together. The hope was that multiple partners working together could have a greater impact in the state. In effect, it compounded the bridging social capital. As one CoPER board member, a school district superintendent, said in reference to his district having higher funding and stronger programs, "We are only as strong as our neighbors," suggesting that it is working together that helps all districts gain strength.

This statement characterizes how CoPER members have worked together, collaboratively across school districts, across higher education institutions, and the whole of CoPER. An understanding exists among members that they can do for each other what individual partners alone cannot do. Schools can speak to educator preparation and universities can speak to schools' efforts, with neither appearing self-serving. For example, when schools have been under a particularly high level of scrutiny and the target of much criticism, CoPER university leaders have come forward to speak to schools' strengths in a variety of venues—letters to the editor, opinion-editorial articles, and direct statements or testimony to the Colorado Department of Education. School leaders have done the same when IHEs have been under attack, writing to the newspapers and appearing at hearings and other forums. This mutual support has strengthened relationships over the years. The strong relationships and the sense of real collaboration caused one superintendent, new to the state and to CoPER, to proffer in an interview related to a program evaluation that he had never seen anything like these relationships and collaboration across and among higher education and schools in his thirty years in education.

The context in which this collaboration developed naturally helped shape how partners work together and toward what end. Over the past several decades, Colorado, not unlike other states, has experienced intense and sustained criticism of the schools. While the 1980s brought the critiques noted earlier, the 1990s brought a move first toward standards for teacher licensing and student content standards and then their accompanying assessments. Strong sanctions followed, with the threat of schools being taken over by charters should they not meet proscribed requirements within a particular time frame. The No Child Left Behind Act has fortified both the criticism, the focus on assessment, and sanctions. Additionally, in recent years, the critique has extended to higher education.

In its early stages, CoPER formed in this context of heightened criticism and analysis of the public schools, but also of hope for finding fresh responses to enduring problems. The early years found CoPER providing forums in which people could come together across roles and institutions to talk about some of the more recalcitrant educational issues and over time to create a shared deeper vision for schooling, particularly attuned to the public purposes of education in this country. Board meetings, special initiatives, open conversations, conferences, symposia and other forums brought CoPER members, state and local policy makers, community members, students, and others into the mix. Participants frequently commented on program evaluations and in informal conversation about the richness of thinking that accompanied the conversation with others across roles and organizations. Additionally and critically, over the years CoPER has joined with other Colorado organizations, such as the Public Education and Business Coalition, the Alliance for Quality Schooling, the Colorado Association of School Boards, the Bighorn Center for Public Policy, and others in special initiatives and to create broader forums for sharing and exploring ideas and perspectives.

This sustained activity laid the foundation for several efforts undertaken in light of CoPER and NNER's mission/goals that informed and influenced P–12 schooling and teacher education in the state. Three themes illustrate how the work began and progressed and how the effect was felt beyond CoPER. They are (1) building a strong base from which to help inform policy and practice, (2) moving to action, and (3) deepening and expanding the conversation to the broader community. Framed as such, they can appear to be distinct phases, but they have been much more overlapping, often occurring simultaneously. Assigning these categories, however, facilitates describing the work.

Building a Strong Base

> Social justice involves social actors who have a sense of their own agency as well as a sense of social responsibility toward and with others and the society as a whole.[14]

Helping inform policy and practice necessitates a strong value base from which to speak and act. In short, it means coming to integrate the value base into one's professional life. The meetings of CoPER's early years helped create this base and continuing meetings help maintain it. CoPER's board, consisting of superintendents, deans of education and the arts and sciences, and in some cases their designees, have met regularly over CoPER's eighteen-year existence to develop and continually renew a shared vision. Other standing committees, task forces, and ad hoc working groups have also shared in this most fundamental and essential conversation, which has included attention to the importance of critical thinking, the arts, history, and all the areas that, as John Goodlad can be heard to say, contribute to young people participating in the human conversation. The values and beliefs reside in support for the public purposes of schooling and include for CoPER, as for the rest of the NNER, aspects of the agenda noted earlier:

- using teaching practices that nurture all students' learning
- facilitating critical enculturation of the young into our democracy
- providing access to knowledge for all students
- practicing stewardship of our schools

The shared vision, now known as the Agenda for Education in a Democracy and described more fully in chapter 2, includes a commitment to a central strategy, that of simultaneously renewing schooling and educator preparation. Further, for CoPER it encompasses support for specific structures for advancing the work, such as partner schools, leadership symposia, special initiatives on equity, curriculum and other themes, policy symposia on topics ranging from the value of school-university partnerships to responsible assessment and fair accountability, to teacher education per se. Some of these structures are described in more detail in subsequent sections. Here these examples serve to reflect the whole of the work: values, belief, principles; central strategy; structures, all focused on renewing our educational systems and therefore helping renew our democracy. The bridging of social capital noted earlier was key as CoPER slowly created linkages in obvious, but long neglected places—schools and educator preparation programs.

Collaboration among teacher education, the arts and sciences, and the schools called for new kinds of leadership and shared responsibility that served the interests of all, and that produced outcomes that would not have occurred by any of the three partners operating independently of the other two. To advance this three-part interactive collaborative, CoPER's leadership structure evolved. As called for in the initial NNER partnership settings, a governing board, consisting of deans of education and super-intendents—and soon to include the arts and sciences—formed to set direction and oversee CoPER's work. The board, again aligning with the prerequisite conditions for the NNER, hired an executive director, one who could bridge the worlds of the public schools and the university. Consequently, the governing board comprised broad-based membership from each partner district and the IHE and operated in a spirit of openness.

Several benefits came, not the least of which was enhanced insight for all, which emerged from understanding the differing perceptions of col-leagues. Another value of the shared leadership—rotating the chair role of the governing board between the IHE and school district—unified sup-port for CoPER's values and initiatives. Among the most significant was the partner schools, primarily due to the actual, visible changes in practice that occurred for all involved.

Colloquia provided ongoing learning experiences for all involved, whereby differences in views and experiences were exploited and explored. Successful changes in program implementation and other activities were analyzed. The theme of "schools as living democracies" was a foundation stone of all CoPER conversation and activity. Examples of programs and sites driven and characterized by components of this overriding theme became a backdrop for CoPER discussions, planning, and activities.

To fund its work, CoPER partners developed a basic operating budget and a budgeting process in which each school district and higher educa-tion institution pays annual dues consisting of a base amount plus addi-tional monies predicated on size of district or institution. Over the years, an occasional school district or institution has found itself in financial straits making it impossible to pay its dues in a particular year. In these instances, the other partners have taken up the slack, sometimes voting to pay additional monies to keep the district or institution in the partnership. Often the nonpaying district or institution will find a way to make in-kind contributions by hosting the website, contributing office space, or other-wise taking on additional responsibilities.

Special initiatives require additional funding. As a large collaborative organization including urban, suburban, small town, and rural schools and a range of colleges and universities, CoPER has been successful in securing grants from the U.S. Department of Education, the Colorado Department of Education, and local foundations. These special initiatives, however, have been part of what CoPER has seen as its work, rather than projects developed to fit a grant opportunity. An example is the U.S. Department of Education funded effort titled "Finding Democracy in Standards-Based Education," which brought the need to extend and deepen the conversation and thinking about schools and democracy to the fore while responding to the emerging standards movement. This initiative is noted later in this chapter and serves to illustrate the appeal to funders of an existing infrastructure that includes a rich diversity of partners.

Recognized as the only organization in the state to bridge the public schools and higher education, over the years CoPER's leaders have been invited to serve on a variety of committees and boards. For example, when Colorado's first Professional Standards Boards were created as a part of the 1991 Educator Licensing Act, a CoPER dean and CoPER executive director co-chaired the teacher licensing board, and other CoPER leaders served on this board and on the principal and administrator board. By statute, the two boards' members were appointed by the governor, confirmed by the Senate, and served in an advisory capacity to the State Board of Education. The nomination and confirmation of a number of these leaders served to acknowledge the coherent and systemic nature of CoPER's work, encompassing educator preparation and schooling. Most important, principles from the Agenda for Education in a Democracy helped guide the development of a framework for rules and regulations governing educator licensing in the state. Although not as far reaching as initially hoped, one of the five licensing standards spoke specifically to the need for teachers to understand and engage in democratic practices in their classrooms. This standard expressed a central and critical idea long neglected in public education, one that Nicholas Michelli, in chapter 2, observes most often gets a nod of the head, but not often enough the deliberate attention it requires. Also in the standards were specific references to diversity and the importance of teaching students with differing learning needs and from diverse backgrounds.

When the state educator licensing standards were revised in 1999 as part of Senate Bill 99-154 requiring all teacher education programs to become performance based, reference to democracy and democratic practice remained as a result of broad support; but it was combined with other areas and became "Democracy, Educational Governance and Careers in Teaching."[15] The standards became more pointedly directive with emphasis on mathematics, literacy, standards and assessment, content, classroom and instructional management matching the emphasis in state testing for public schools. Not only were references to diversity eliminated, they became lightning rods for responses from state approving agencies. Most teacher education programs continued attention to diversity and democracy without the explicit language, although some institutions deliberately kept the language, and the University of Northern Colorado added its own standard to those of the state.

During this time, the Colorado Commission on Higher Education (CCHE) and the Colorado Department of Education (CDE) convened a special task force on performance-based assessment, which again consisted largely of CoPER members, including several education deans and CoPER's executive director. Working through this group, CoPER sponsored a teacher-work-sample workshop inviting experts in performance-based assessment from Oregon to lead it. Additionally, CoPER, in collaboration with CDE and CCHE convened a group of assessment experts in Colorado universities and school districts, who, in turn, created a performance-based assessment guide for teacher education programs. Ultimately, the teacher work sample became part of the performance-based assessment approach used by all programs.

The bill and resulting teacher licensing standards also required programs to include 800 hours of well-planned, supervised field experiences, with a view in early stages of the planning toward promoting partner schools. Teacher educators saw that the performance-based assessment and field experience requirements could complement one another as the extensive field experiences provide a natural setting for many, although not all, of the performance assessments that bring a stronger sense of expectation to field experience. A huge amount of paper work and revising of programs were called for. Now, several years later, teacher educators are still trying to determine how best to link the requirements with other aspects of teachers' professional lives, that is, induction of new teachers and ongoing professional development. CoPER partners are working to address this through an initiative titled Intersections, through which it is hoped the natural linkages can be developed in seamless and ongoing ways. Heeding Gardner's observation, CoPER efforts reflect that renewal "is not just innovation and change. It is also the process of bringing the results of change into line with our purposes."[16]

CoPER partners worked together assiduously to mitigate the disruption in the teacher education programs and to keep the principles they valued so highly in the programs. Having a strong democratic value base and also recognizing the risk of losing the organization's bridging capability, CoPER never became a vocal extreme advocacy group but rather assisted to help guide the work as it unfolded and step in as appropriate to fill any voids. Without knowing it at the time, CoPER attended to Chrislip's requirements for collaboration, avoiding the pitfalls of extreme advocacy. "Instead of advocacy, collaboration demands engagement, dialogue instead of debate, inclusion instead of exclusion, shared power instead of domination and control, and mutual learning instead of rigid adherence to mutually exclusive positions."[17] CoPER was therefore able to maintain credibility to help convene groups across a spectrum.

Much work remains. The current climate fueled by an emphasis on testing poses challenges for educators, both in the public schools and teacher education. Such challenges, however, serve as reminders of the importance of keeping a focus on the broader educational purposes of our schools.

Moving to Action

> For a school-university partnership to effect lasting change, a structure must be created in which all partners have equal status.[18]

A central focus for CoPER is the development of schools that sustain historic purposes of public education and promote democratic ideals and values. CoPER has promoted activities that produce students who advance civic responsibility; know and use problem-solving and analytical skills; possess basic literacy skills; appreciate human differences; and are dedicated to achieving the greatest human potential for themselves and for others.

For these goals to become embedded in the day-to-day work carried out in teacher education institutions and in public schools, effective reciprocal working relationships are needed, leading to the simultaneous renewal of both. Consequently, partner schools were developed between higher education institutions and public schools. As places that bring renewed focus on (1) providing exemplary education for all students, (2) engaging educators in ongoing professional development, (3) inquiring into the circumstances of the school, and (4) sharing in the preparation of new teachers, they include college and university faculty, teacher education students, and public school faculty and students. An example of these partner schools was one established by Flood Middle School in the Englewood School District and Metropolitan State College in Denver.

Through ongoing interactive planning sessions, this collaboration created mutually agreed upon premises for its operation, which guided the work of both the college and the public school faculty. The premises—some more explicit than others—included the following:

- commitment to operating the school as a living democracy
- devotion to learner-centered instruction

- focus on research about adolescent development
- interactive teaching and learning by college staff and public school faculty
- shared responsibility for student engagement and learning
- development and use of components of highly effective teaching
- attention to comprehensive curriculum content and skills.

Driven by these premises, the structure of the partner school took shape. To enable the college and school faculty and the teacher education students to learn from each other and to contribute their own expertise, extensive shared planning and teaching occurred. A number of features were built into the school year to create a realistic experience for the teacher preparation students. The program began with planning and preparation before the school year started. College students were direct contributors to plans for classroom and school activities, and they assumed responsibility for their implementation as quickly as the development of the skills permitted. Interactive classroom work increased to the point that observers often could not tell who was regular staff and who were teachers in training. The roles of college faculty included supervision of their students, classroom teaching, and planning with school faculty. School faculty shared teaching of the college students and had direct supervision responsibilities.

The benefits to all involved were extensive, far exceeding the outcomes of more traditional teacher preparation programs and typical school reform efforts. Benefits included the following:

- College and public school faculty benefited from interactive planning and teaching.
- The curriculum for middle school students was enriched due to the extensive experiences and expertise of all adults involved.
- Low ratios of staff to students resulted in increased individualization of instruction and support to children.
- Interaction among and shared responsibilities by faculty, as well as by the school's students, enhanced the school's ability to operate as a living democracy.
- For the college and the public schools, the quality of teaching and the effectiveness of school operation and activities represented meaningful systemic reform.
- Change was based on research and the best in professional practice.

From this partner school experience, sets of basic beliefs evolved—about learners and learning, teachers and teaching, leadership and shared responsibility, governance, research-based practice, and components of effective planning and implementation. The effectiveness of all the partner school activities was dependent upon an articulated, shared process that included attention to the definition of desired outcomes, current profile data, appropriate action steps, and ongoing assessment and feedback.

At the outset, the support and participation of the board of education, the school community, and the entire school staff were essential if departure from historical school and university roles and relationships was to be successful. The environment of support was generated by and evolved from consistent attention to the driving characteristics of the school's operation. One was a commitment to the importance of renewal. Demonstrated through a history of increased student achievement and community satisfaction, the necessity of ongoing dynamic school improvement activities gained broad support. Thoughtful change was viewed as essential for continued school improvement. A framework that includes analysis of profile data, agreed-upon desire outcomes, commitment to research-based actions, and comprehensive assessments and feedback, drives productive school renewal planning. Adherence to systemic, continuous improvement becomes a major contributor to the partner school's success.

The presence of these essential components in the ecology of school renewal not only assures success of the partner school as an effective interactive process, it also creates an environment in which children, faculty, and prospective teachers learn together for their mutual benefit, demonstrating democratic principles. Similarly, the culture of the teacher preparation program must embody commitment to these kinds of program characteristics and values if congruence in partner school goals and activities is to be assured.

Manifestations of the partner school concept varied among CoPER institutions based on contextual circumstances, such as number of part-time, nontraditional students, cohesiveness of faculty, and other considerations. Two universities, Colorado State University (CSU) and the University of Colorado at Denver (UCD) soon moved to partner-school-dependent programs, with all teacher education students (teacher candidates) in partner schools. UCD capitalized on licensing changes in the early 1990s to completely revamp its program, building on the licensing standards and the Agenda for Education in a Democracy and how these could be more fully developed in partner schools. CSU reshaped teacher preparation also heeding the agenda, as well as the required licensing standards. For teacher education faculty, this meant a certain amount of time each week was spent in partner schools working with teacher candidates and school faculty. Both CSU and UCD education deans and faculty worked closely with district and school educators to plan collaboratively how they would enact partner schools and what each party would bring to the work. These IHEs and their school partners created exemplary partner school approaches that have served as models within the state and beyond.

During the early and mid-1990s, CoPER secured several large grants, including Goals 2000 monies and a U.S. Department of Education professional development grant to support partner schools, which helped accelerate their development. Later the whole of CoPER developed an overarching set of partner school characteristics, which all agreed reflected their hopes for this way of working together. Additionally, CoPER convened an evaluation team of experts from within partner districts and IHEs and external experts. This evaluation team undertook an extensive partner school study grounded in aspects of the Agenda for Education in a Democracy and the partner school functions. To embed professional development, the team involved public school and IHE educators in data collection across partner schools, and ultimately developed a self-study for schools who wished to look more closely at themselves.

More than sixty partner schools exist among CoPER districts and IHE partners, in various stages of development. After more than sixteen years of talking about, planning for, and creating partner schools, CoPER members are currently taking stock of progress and determining how to move to the next level of development by linking partner schools with district-wide induction of new teachers, connecting the key elements of the teacher work sample to the rest of the professional life of a teacher, and address other natural intersections of schools and teacher education. Because CoPER districts and IHEs include more than half of the public school population and 80 percent of new teachers prepared in Colorado, these next steps will help inform work across the state.

As the mid-1990s brought the creation and further development of partner schools, so also the times brought a growing emphasis on content standards for public schools. With funding received from the sources noted above, CoPER initiated an effort to explore student content standards and standards-based education in light of democratic principles. When first approached about participating in such an effort, a typical response from educators was, "What does what I do have to do with democracy and democratic principles?" With the number of such responses growing, the extent of work to be done became increasingly apparent. Thus CoPER commenced a leadership initiative for teachers, principals, teacher educators, arts and sciences faculty, and other educators, which became known as Finding Democracy in Standards-Based

Education. This initiative brought educators together within and across districts and IHEs, and to several events that included more than five hundred educators at each gathering. These events featured opportunities to explore issues deeply and engage in discourse that linked the everyday lives of teachers to the larger purposes of education in and for this democracy. One of several methods had all five hundred participants in groups of approximately twenty simultaneously engaged in Socratic Seminars on critical texts. Responses were very positive toward the means of engaging as well as the substantive focus of the engagement. The link between democracy and classroom practice no longer remains a mystery for the many educators engaged in this initiative, and for the colleagues with whom they have shared their experiences.

Democracy, Social Justice, Equity

From the outset, CoPER and the other NNER settings saw the need to focus on issues of equity. In the early years, CoPER's Gender Equity Project brought school educators and IHE faculty together to delve into the schools' issues and circumstances, leading to substantive changes in those schools. Faculty study groups, inquiry projects, student-led programs, student leadership groups, and other activities brought needed attention to gender, as well as racial and cultural issues in the schools. As some of these schools were partner schools, the effects extended into teacher preparation programs. Following this effort, Partners for Parity, a group of leaders from the districts and IHEs formed to continue a focus on equity, including the recruitment and retention of underrepresented groups. CoPER joined with ten other NNER settings in the Diversity in Teaching and Teacher Education initiative, and through this work, CoPER created the Equity Cadre, a group that grew to include forty teachers across the sixteen school districts. These teachers were all recognized for their success in working with diverse student needs and backgrounds. They became leaders in their schools and districts and worked closely with the teacher preparation programs to help prospective and new teachers cultivate the understandings and practices their students needed. Equity Cadre members have helped inform teacher preparation and ongoing professional development in schools. They have presented workshops for the Colorado Council on Professional Development and have served on committees within their respective districts and for the state.[19]

Deepening and Expanding the Conversation

> The resolution of malaise depends heavily on the smallest units of the infrastructure. These must join in a collectivity of spirit and action.[20]

Since 1986, CoPER member school districts, colleges, and universities have joined purposefully "in a collectivity of spirit and action." Partner schools, the teacher leadership initiative, governing board and committee meetings, and numerous other forums over the years have continually provided venues for CoPER partners to address issues such as standards and statewide testing, licensing standards, state-required teacher-education reform, other state requirements, and most recently various aspects of No Child Left Behind, in light of the agenda. Often state officials and policy makers have participated in the more intimate discussions, as well as in the larger forums.

Special symposia in which CoPER has joined with other organizations, such as the Colorado Association of School Boards, the Public Education and Business Coalition, the Bighorn Center for Public Policy, which is a bipartisan policy center, the Education Commission of the States, and others provided the means for engaging the broader community in exploration of and discourse about the aspects of the agenda and issues viewed through the lens of the agenda. As dialogue has continued, an emerging realization for CoPER and others in the NNER is that our partnerships must engage the community as full partners if our work is to deepen and be sustained. Toward this end, one CoPER community has participated in developing a school-university-community partnership as part of the Institute for Educational Inquiry's Developing Networks of Responsibility to Educate America's Youths initiative as well as additional local conversations have added to this work. Many of these occasions have served to remind educators and noneducators alike of our fundamental purposes in schooling our nations' youths and have in no small way contributed to bridging social capital statewide. Schools and teacher preparation programs have grown and developed in our deepened understandings of schooling and teacher preparation in and for our democracy.

At the same time, the new millennium has brought increasing pressure on public schools and higher education. Manifesting itself in various forms, such as a questioning of educator licensing, and therefore a questioning of professional preparation for educators, such pressures tend to polarize groups. Additionally, Colorado's colleges and universities have suffered tremendous budget cuts, to the extent that the president of the flagship institution warned legislators that, staying the present course, universities will be financially crippled within a matter of years. Further, an "academic freedom" bill has been introduced by the legislature as a way "to protect students from being singled out, ridiculed or punished academically by professors because of their political views."[21] Schools continue to be financially strapped, as well as suffering under the crush of numerous mandates brought by state and national policies.

Such challenges suggest CoPER must continue to reflect public schooling's role in helping sustain and renew our democratic society, to continue reminding others and ourselves of that to which our work ultimately points. Doing our part in building social capital suggests we look inward to continually develop our understandings and capacity to contribute, as well as look outward to help bring together those groups and individuals whose voices must be part of finding solutions to issues and challenges. Working with others thusly helps mitigate somewhat the vicissitudes of policy making in the state.

Conclusion

This work requires the particular kinds of leadership and efficacious collaboration that have allowed the NNER, and CoPER as part of it, to exist and grow for almost two decades. It requires leaders who understand the power of collaboration and who are willing to step forward for the common good, leaders who can lead as peers and also follow as leaders. It calls for leaders who know the importance of balancing the self-interests of their respective school districts and institutions and those of the collective partnership. These leaders have credibility and positional power and can use such assets to further CoPER's effectiveness and promote the broader common good.

Leadership at different levels and across institutions is imperative. Fortunately for the CoPER and for Colorado, the deans and superintendents have been willing to step forward for the greater good, even in increasingly difficult times in which the pressure on schooling and higher education accelerates while resources decline. Such leadership is evident across the NNER. Associate superintendents, associate deans, curriculum directors, teachers, principals, arts and sciences and teacher education faculty, teacher candidates and others have been willing to work with peers and across roles and institutions and beyond to move our collective work forward. John Goodlad, Calvin Frazier, and NNER leaders have contributed significantly, reminding CoPER it is part of something still larger, something that shares the central values of democracy and schooling. Such leadership has propelled CoPER in reaching out and connecting, thereby building the bridging social capital essential for generating "broader identities and reciprocity."[22] Indeed, Goodlad's words summarize this best, "Just as it takes a whole village to raise a child, it takes everyone beyond the years of childhood to create a village worthy of raising all children."[23]

Notes

1. John W. Gardner, *Self-Renewal: The Individual and the Innovative Society* (New York: Harper & Row, 1971), 143.
2. National Commission on Excellence in Education, *A Nation at Risk: The Imperative for Educational Reform* (Washington, D.C.: U.S. Government Printing Office, 1983).
3. Ernest L. Boyer, *High School: A Report on Secondary Education in America* (New York: Harper & Row, 1983).
4. Theodore R. Sizer, *Horace's Compromise: The Dilemma of the American High School* (Boston: Houghton Mifflin, 1984).
5. John I. Goodlad, *A Place Called School: Prospects for the Future* (New York: McGraw-Hill, 1984).
6. John I., Goodlad, "The Reconstruction of Teacher Education," *Teachers College Record* (September 1970): 61.
7. Goodlad, *A Place Called School*, 301.
8. Kenneth A. Sirotnik, "Evaluation in the Ecology of Schooling: The Process of School Renewal," in *The Ecology of School Renewal* (Chicago: University of Chicago Press, 1987), 41.
9. Gardner, 6.
10. Gardner, 13.
11. John I. Goodlad, Roger Soder, and Kenneth A. Sirotnik, eds., *The Moral Dimensions of Teaching* (San Francisco: Jossey-Bass, 1990).
12. See Robert D. Putnam, *Bowling Alone* (New York: Simon & Schuster, 2000), 22–24, and David D. Chrislip, *The Collaborative Leadership Fieldbook* (San Francisco: Jossey-Bass, 2002), 29.
13. Putnam, 19–22.
14. Lee Ann Bell, "Theoretical Foundations for Social Justice Education," in *Teaching for Diversity and Social Justice*, ed. Maurianne Adams et al. (New York: Routledge, 1997), 3.
15. Colorado Department of Education, *Performance-Based Standards for Colorado Teachers*, 2000.
16. Gardner, 7.
17. Chrislip, 41.
18. Russell T. Osguthorpe et al., *Partner Schools: Centers for Educational Renewal* (San Francisco: Jossey-Bass, 1995), 3.
19. See Fred Rodriguez et al., "Professional Development for Teacher Leaders," *Partnering for Equity, Journal for Educational Equity and Excellence*, special issue (2004).
20. John I. Goodlad, *In Praise of Education* (New York: Teachers College Press, 1997), 49.
21. Ryan Morgan, "'Academic Freedom' Measure Advances," *Daily Camera*, February 26, 2004, p. 1.
22. Putnam, 23.
23. Goodlad, *In Praise of Education*, 76.

CHAPTER **10**

Critical Thinking for Democracy and Social Justice

DAVID S. MARTIN

In any work devoted to the position that critical thinking has a fundamentally important place in American education, the question of how to prepare professional educators to implement that teaching is essential to discuss. A prime historical reason, although not the only reason, for the non-systematic inclusion of critical thinking in American classrooms has been the lack of commitment to that area on the part of the institutions that prepare future educators. But this lack of commitment has its roots in the society at large, inasmuch as the shape of teacher education characteristically follows the priorities that it believes must reflect what the general society desires; this following, rather than leading, on the part of the educator-preparation profession is an unfortunate indicator of a lack of pro-active initiative on the part of that profession. Thus, any discussion of educator preparation is seamlessly bound up with a view of society's values and beliefs about what is important in educating young persons.

This chapter discusses the importance of and techniques for promoting the teaching of critical thinking by both current and future teachers, within the context of an era when the requirements of high-stakes testing is nearly universal across the United States's various state school systems, and has been amplified and strengthened now by federal mandates as well. The chapter will encompass the rationale for teachers to be teachers of thinking, some examples of methodology by which this teaching can be embedded into subject-matter instruction, how this type of teaching can indirectly assist students to succeed in some aspects of high-stakes testing, and the options that are available to both preservice education of teachers-to-be and professional development of current teachers in the domain of critical thinking. Included also are criteria and questions that can be applied in the intelligent selection of published critical thinking programs for classroom adoption. The chapter is framed within the relationship between teaching critical thinking and democratic practice, an area which is explicitly addressed at the conclusion of the chapter.

Historical Background

Historically, since the middle of the Twentieth Century in American education, we have seen alternating trends of "liberal" and "conservative" approaches to teaching and curriculum, in cycles lasting approximately 10 to 15 years each. By "liberal," we refer to divergent methodologies such as student-centered learning, individual teacher-choice about curriculum content, and decentralization of authority within schools and school systems. By "conservative," on the other hand, we refer to methodologies that are convergent in the sense of demanding strict adherence to external curriculum standards, a focus on teaching for factual memorization and recall by students, and strong central control of schools—frequently from the state level.

These "cycles" correspond roughly to different stages in the economic health of the country, a fact that has been commented upon by numerous educational columnists and other writers and thus is by no means an original observation by this writer. That is, when the country's general economy is comfortable and prosperous for a great many—particularly the vast middle class—a "liberal" approach to education follows not far behind; on the other hand, when the economy is experiencing a significant downturn, education seems to turn toward a more "conservative" bent. Commentators have speculated about the reasons for these trends; one explanation is that education is seen as the controlling and explanatory factor—when economic times are not going well, it must be because the schools are not doing their job. In actuality, such observations give perhaps more credit to the power of education than is deserved.

To take some concrete examples from the past half-century, the period of the 1950s was focused on the "basics" of education with rather strict expectations related to curriculum; it is interesting to note that this decade corresponded largely with a Republican presidential administration.

Then the 1960s was a period of significant reform, partly in response to the shocking event in 1957 of the successful launch of *Sputnik* by the Soviet Union indicating that Americans were woefully behind in mathematics and science. This period was replete with many exciting curriculum innovations sponsored by numerous government and private grants; moreover, great interest was generated in the United States by the British approach to early childhood education. It was at this time that so-called open education was experimented with by many school districts. Through the work of such luminaries as Jerome Bruner (e.g., *The Process of Education*), building on and extending the earlier work of Piaget, the beginnings of active curricular interest in teaching for thinking, "cognitive education," was now on the map.[1] Again, it is of more than passing interest to note that this decade corresponded roughly with Democratic presidential administrations.

The period of the 1970s was a time of retrenchment, and was labeled "back-to-basics" with good reason; many of the innovations of the 1960s were considered to have had either limited success and applicability or were deemed to have failed (in fact, many succeeded, but many never got the full support they needed, while others were misinterpreted and misapplied). We should note that in this decade, the country experienced a major economic recession and unusually high interest rates.

Around this time, however, the trends became more complex and interwoven. While there was some renewal of educational experimentation in the 1980s, at the same time, it was also the beginning of the present cycle known as the Reform Movement, starting with the well-known *A Nation At Risk* report, and then followed by a succession of national reports of many kinds, all calling for one or another kind of reform. These national reports that criticized American education continued into the 1990s.[2] But during the same decade, there was an interesting increase in the application of higher-order thinking skills through a variety of programs and projects; this trend served as somewhat of a balance to the effects of the numerous calls for "conservative" reform.

One milestone was the publication in the United States of Feuerstein's *Instrumental Enrichment* program, which called for an active intervention through cognitive mediation of a number of explicit cognitive strategies, although the program itself was invented originally in the 1950s in Israel.[3] Another milestone in the 1980s was the publication of Howard Gardner's *Frames of Mind*—the very same year, ironically, as *A Nation At Risk*.[4] Also, Robert Sternberg presented his theory of the "triarchic" understanding of intelligence.[5] And this period also saw the publication of other thinking projects, notably Matthew Lipman's *Philosophy for Children*.[6]

The period of the 1990s continued with calls for continuing reform, and at this time nearly all of the national professional associations in education developed voluntary national standards; during the same time, state by state began to impose state curriculum standards on their schools, in some cases utilizing the voluntary national standards developed by the associations. However, while one might have expected the higher-level thinking skills movement to wane in favor of a greater emphasis on factual learning, the thinking-skills movement somehow managed to co-exist and became solidified.

With the start of the Twenty-First Century, we witnessed the passage of perhaps the largest federal-level intervention in local schools, now not just encouraging but requiring certain passing levels of achievement on mandated examinations—to be federally implemented in places where states were not requiring such examinations—through the No Child Left Behind Act of 2002. In the 1990s, many of the high-stakes graduation tests imposed by states emphasized factual recall and multiple-choice formats; however, by the early part of the first decade of the Twenty-First Century, at least a few of the states were also including some items that demanded some constructed-response higher-order thinking rather than exclusively multiple-choice formats, which stressed only factual recall and lower-level comprehension. Thus, up to the present time, we see an interweaving of trends. Therefore, two seemingly contradictory trends actually have common ground.

The Teacher Education Profession and Critical Thinking

A clear rationale for preparing teachers explicitly to be teachers of thinking was stated by Ray Nickerson when he said:

> It is no more reasonable to expect an individual who does not know a lot about thinking to teach thinking effectively, than to expect one who does not know a lot about math, or physics, or literature, to be an effective teacher in any of those areas. In the long run, how successful institutionalized education will be in incorporating effective teaching of thinking in the typical classroom will depend to no small degree on how much emphasis teacher-training programs put on thinking in their curricula.[7]

The teacher education profession, as it has been housed within universities since the beginning of the Twentieth Century, has (with a few exceptions) focused on the preparation of teachers in teaching subject matter together with techniques of pedagogy with little or no explicit reference to embedding instruction within a cognitive-education framework.

Brandt makes important distinctions between three categories of higher-order thinking and problem solving.[8] First, he points out that teaching for thinking is quite old—it is what, for example, a successful teacher of biology does when he or she sets up a laboratory experiment that requires groups of students to create a hypothesis, collect data systematically, and draw careful conclusions based on the data. That teacher is incorporating higher-level cognitive strategies and expecting the students to apply them, but without any explicit discussion of the strategies per se and thus minimizing the chances that students will transfer these strategies to other domains; good science teachers have, however, been carrying out such instruction for a long time.

Second, the teaching of thinking is what teachers do who explicitly label the cognitive processes that they teach—for example, teaching and labeling the processes of analysis, synthesis, categorization, and so forth; in this definition, thinking becomes part of the planned curriculum of the school. This area, called cognitive education, only became a part of the classroom to a significant degree with the adoption of some published critical thinking programs beginning in the 1980s.

Third, finally, the teaching about thinking is what teachers do when they ask students to reflect metacognitively on the mental processes that they have used to solve challenging curriculum problems; this area is perhaps the most recent of these three techniques to enter the classroom, and is a part of some (but not all) of the above-mentioned critical thinking curricula. To amplify metacognition, research in classrooms has demonstrated the usefulness of at least two techniques: metacognitive reflection, and modeling.[9] Metacognitive reflection is particularly powerful because students must reflect on and share with peers how they have done a particular procedure, thus becoming aware of their own processes and internalizing them.[10,11] When a teacher models this kind of thinking for her students with an explanation of principles, the combination is powerful.[12]

In today's world of cognitive education, the teaching for, of, and about thinking, then, are all considered essential to a balanced program. Therefore, the trend toward explicit cognitive education is relatively young—20 years at this writing—which is not a long time for innovative school practices to permeate back into the teacher education curriculum. Much of the implementation of cognitive education programs, thus, have been the result of professional development of currently practicing teachers since their own preservice preparation had not equipped them to teach critical thinking.

The Knowledge Base in Teaching Thinking

We have already referred to some essential way points in the development of the knowledge base for the teaching of critical thinking—for example, the above-mentioned seminal works of Gardner in establishing that intelligence is not a single property but rather multiple, and of Feuerstein in establishing that intelligence is not fixed but rather dynamic. These two principles form the basis on which many of the critical thinking programs are founded; the message is essentially positive and hopeful—that it is, for example, never too late to increase a student's capacity for learning (what some might label to be a form of "intelligence"); yet this idea flies in the face of much conventional thinking outside of the education profession and even to some extent within it. Thus, the struggle to implement that philosophy and its accompanying practices is an uphill one.

But there are other aspects of the knowledge base that form a foundation in this area. One of these is the research that has been done on the effects of "wait-time" in the classroom. The work of Rowe established that if a teacher asks a well-phrased higher-order question, then the longer she waits for students to reply, the better the chances of an appropriate response; unfortunately, however, many teachers fill the brief gap of embarrassed silence after they ask a question by giving the answer themselves, thus sending an implicit message to the students that they do not really have to think because the teacher will do it for them.[13]

Continuing on those elements of the knowledge base related to teacher behaviors, Costa lists four major categories that enhance student thinking: questioning, structuring, responding to students, and modeling behaviors.[14] We already know much about the ways in which a learner constructs and manipulates ideas effectively. Costa gives us a useful list and explanation of teacher behaviors that produce student thinking. They include praise, the use of wait-time, making clarifying statements, accepting student responses, the use of certain types of questioning, and giving students the opportunity to apply and evaluate actions in new situations. We can now add other specific effective behaviors for teachers to use:

1. Asking questions that demand explanation responses—responses to questions such as "why" and "how"
2. Identifying the specific strategies that students have just used to solve a problem—metacognition
3. Reminding students of the cognitive strategies from which they could select in order to solve a problem
4. Establishing at atmosphere in which thinking is highly valued
5. Modeling by the teacher of reflective thought

6. Developing assessment methods that tap into higher-level problem solving
7. Structuring of the physical layout of the classroom is another consideration, related to the arrangement of student seating in order to facilitate meaningful dialogue in a critical-thinking episode
8. Responding to students by relating to them in a way that builds trust
9. Maintaining student awareness of their own thinking (metacognition)

Thus, many pathways are possible for incorporating these behaviors into a teacher's repertoire. Some may be part of the natural behavior of teachers, while others may require specific cultivation through preservice and in-service education programs for teachers. Still another exciting and burgeoning area of our knowledge base comes from ongoing neurological research. Teacher educators are becoming better aware of the possible connections between ongoing physiological and psychological brain research and classroom learning. Some have even labeled the 1990s the "decade of the brain."[15] Much, of course, remains to be done before unambiguous connections can be established. Important technologies such as CAT scans and MRIs are providing greater insights every year about brain functions. An example of work in this area of the biological basis of thinking would be the synthesis developed by Lowery, in which patterns of brain interaction are related to different forms of instruction.[16]

But, as Bruer notes, in spite of significant theoretical progress on "neural hardware" and the connection between brain structure and mental functions, "we know relatively little about learning, thinking, and remembering at the level of brain areas, neural circuits, or synapses; we know very little about how the brain thinks, remembers, and learns." However, nothing in neurological research diminishes the idea that teaching for thinking is fundamental. For now we can rely on our current understanding of learning from past research in psychology and philosophical inquiry, in order to firmly make the case for the importance of teaching thinking.[17]

Of course another area of growing interest to teachers and teacher educators is or should be the steady accumulation of data from research on how students perform when given an opportunity to work within explicit critical thinking programs in the classroom. While some of the research results are mixed, the overall trend shows significant improvement in thinking behaviors for students who practice systematic thinking using special materials in the hands of a specially prepared teacher.[18]

Also of considerable interest is the effect of teaching thinking on teacher behaviors. Teaching itself is a cognitive activity; the work of

Morine-Dershimer establishes methods for researching the thinking of teachers.[19] Renner found positive cognitive growth in teacher candidates as a result of their preservice preparation for teaching science using reasoning activities.[20] Clark and Yinger and others have studied teaching as a cognitive activity.[21] Clark and Lampert present an excellent summary of research on teacher thinking.[22] Peterson conceptualizes how teacher and student cognitions and knowledge can mediate effective teaching.[23] Shulman calls for a "paradigm shift" in research on teacher development, away from process-product approaches and toward a cognitive paradigm that looks at the effects of the thinking and decision making that teachers do while they are interacting with students.[24] And Martin looks at the effects of teaching thinking on the teachers' own thinking. In a comparison of teachers in Costa Rica and the United States who had been trained in and implemented a student-thinking program, it was found that teachers in both cultures reported changes in their own teaching styles toward more use of open-ended questioning and use of cognitive vocabulary, as well as more frequent use of preplanning in their own solutions to classroom problems.[25] (The teachers also said their personal outside-school problem-solving strategies also evolved toward more systematic use of strategies such as personal planning, sequencing, and logical thought.) Some research has also indicated that when teachers are explicitly prepared in the techniques of critical thinking and implement them, the same strategies often "spill over" to other aspects of their teaching even when critical thinking is not the overt topic of instruction—a highly desirable result; some evidence has also been found that after implementing the teaching of critical thinking, teachers also change their own views of instruction and the learner.[26]

Finally, let us briefly pursue the area of teaching itself as a cognitive activity. If we understand that successful teaching involves frequent (multiple times per day) decision making, carefully phrased verbal instructions and presentations, the ability to multitask, anticipation, organization, categorization, analysis, and synthesis, then we can easily see that teaching done well is clearly a higher-order cognitive function. It follows that a teacher who is prepared to teach thinking and becomes aware of her own cognitive processes has a good chance of becoming a better teacher in general. This area is fertile for further research.

As a result, the knowledge base for cognitive education is well established and yet also dynamically growing; it forms a strong foundation for the incorporation of thinking into the school curriculum and the teacher education curriculum.

Teacher Education and Critical Thinking

In reference to the distinctions between teaching for, of, and about thinking, historically teacher education programs have done a reasonably competent job of preparing teachers in some subjects to teach for thinking—particularly in some areas of science and social studies. Some aspects of mathematics and language teaching have also incorporated ways for teachers to teach for thinking. However, the teaching of and about thinking have yet to become comprehensively embedded in teacher preparation programs, thus necessitating professional-development seminars for practicing teachers. However, some inroads in this direction have been made, and a review of the steps taken to attempt to provide this embedding on a national level since the mid-1980s will be useful at this point.

In the early part of the 1980s the Association for Supervision and Curriculum Development (ASCD) had been one of the professional organizations that had begun to promote the systematic teaching of critical thinking. A special coalition, known as the Association Collaborative for Teaching Thinking (ACTT), was then formed, bringing together representatives of ASCD, the American Association of Colleges of Teacher Education (AACTE), and several other professional organizations. This body deliberated on ways to promote systematically and nationally the teaching of thinking. Among other actions, ACTT formally proposed critical-thinking standards for teacher preparation programs for adoption by the National Council on the Accreditation of Teacher Education (NCATE). The proposed standards asked that teacher education programs be externally and objectively assessed on the degree to which they promoted:

1. An attitude of thoughtful consideration of the problems, topics, and issues of their candidates' professional experience
2. An active working knowledge of the methods of effective inquiry, using all levels of thinking
3. The application of methods of inquiry to classroom teaching
4. An actively supportive climate that promotes the exercise, application, teaching, and learning of thinking dispositions and cognitive processes

NCATE subsequently adopted standards in 1995 (and renewed them in 2000) that require that candidates develop understanding and use of a variety of instructional strategies for developing critical thinking and problem solving.[27]

Separately, in the fall of 1987, AACTE called a special task force meeting to discuss directions for the association concerning the preparation of teachers of thinking. Twelve individuals came together, representing the fields of psychology, teacher education, curriculum, and related fields; subsequently 65 teacher educators met in 1988 to examine possible models for including thinking-skills programs in teacher education. Later in 1988 a one-week seminar was held for teacher educators who represented eight teacher-education institutions to examine in-depth models for program revision and course revision in teacher preparation and in the direction of incorporating critical thinking. From that seminar grew a network of interested individuals as well as a special resolution for AACTE as a whole; this resolution called for establishing a Special Study Group for the Infusion of Critical Thinking into Teacher Education within AACTE and also called for all programs in teacher education to incorporate preparation for teaching thinking. The resolution, after considerable debate, passed by a large margin (although not unanimously). The Special Study Group was then formed and met continuously on an annual basis at annual meetings of AACTE through 2003, providing a forum for representatives of teacher education institutions to share model programs and problems related to preparing teachers of thinking. Selected examples of some model teacher-education programs that have implemented critical thinking is provided below:

1. Marshall University, West Virginia, uses the theme of critical thinking in their teacher education program and ties assessment to it.
2. Marymount University, Virginia, has a theme of "Habits of Mind" which is applied to reflection by teacher candidates and candidates' portfolios.
3. University of Northern Iowa has a required course in inductive and deductive reasoning for its candidates, offered by the Psychology Department; the university also uses the Watson-Glaser Critical Thinking Appraisal in its program.[28]
4. Steven Foster State University, Texas, incorporates state standards that include critical thinking.
5. Wake Forest University, North Carolina, requires candidates to take a seminar in comparison of classrooms, during the practicum experience.
6. Tuskegee University, Alabama, has infused critical thinking into its education courses, and candidate portfolios must show evidence of critical thinking.
7. Mitchell State College, Colorado, incorporates critical thinking in a joint effort of the education program and the college of arts and

sciences. Thus, we see a variety of ways that institutions have implemented these practices.

Since the early 1990s, the Goodlad National Network for Educational Renewal has been a stimulus for change in teacher education, one of whose members is Montclair State University, New Jersey. Montclair has an exemplary teacher education program (see chapter 7). The program uses critical thinking as a way to enable students to become effective, functioning citizens in a political and social democracy; critical thinking is the organizing theme, and the program uses a focus on the moral dimensions of teaching with the use of critical thinking as a vehicle for examining these dimensions.[29] Critical thinking is deeply embedded into many of the professional sequences of courses in Montclair's teacher education program. For many years, Montclair required a specific course, Teaching for Critical Thinking, of all candidates—a course that was originally thought to be only temporary while critical thinking gradually became infused across many courses. That diffusion has now occurred, and the focus is on critical thinking within the disciplines and within a course on democratic practice. Critical thinking is also a core theme of the graduate program.

Thus, some explicit and coordinated efforts to institute the teaching of thinking within teacher education programs have been made and have met with some success. Yet, in fairness, the shape of different implementations of teacher preparation varies widely across different teacher education institutions; further professional efforts will be essential in order to keep the movement alive and growing dynamically.

Models for Teacher Education

When a teacher education program has become serious about the infusion of critical thinking across the program, several options are available to the university program leaders. Each of these options has different consequences, and clearly the best overall solution is some combination of all of these. The options are:

1. A single required teacher-education course in critical thinking. The difficulty with this option is that it compartmentalizes critical thinking into one candidate experience rather than infusing it across different candidate experiences.
2. Embedding critical thinking across all teacher education courses. While desirable, the challenge in this option is the faculty development that is required in order to change university faculty pedagogy as well as revise the content of their courses to include techniques of critical thinking for candidates to use with students. Another

challenge is how to spread this commitment also to university faculty in the arts and sciences, inasmuch as teacher candidates have much of their early university instruction with other than the teacher education faculty. The close relationship between arts/sciences and education that is now fostered by NCATE program-reviews could assist in the unified innovation of changes in university pedagogy toward more applications of critical thinking.

3. Course examinations requiring critical thinking. One clear message is sent to teacher candidates if course examinations require more than factual recall and regurgitation—critical thinking applies to all aspects of the life of the learner, including how one is measured as an adult professional learner at the end of candidates' course experiences.

4. Portfolios that demonstrate critical thinking. Candidates should be required to include in their teacher-education portfolios the evidence that they are, among other things, committed to and implementers of critical thinking with students. Such evidence could include lesson plans, videotapes, written units of instruction, student examinations developed by the candidate, and case studies, all of which would demonstrate some aspect of implementing critical thinking.

5. Internship placements with appropriate cooperating-teacher models. After the completion of coursework and other preparatory experiences, it is essential that in the final teacher-education experience of internship in a classroom, the candidate be placed with a veteran teacher who is herself a model of successful teaching of critical thinking. Without this important final step, all of the previous program experiences may be unused or considered by the candidate to be irrelevant to the "real" classroom setting.

What might a teacher educator do immediately in order to embark on the infusion of critical thinking into coursework for teacher candidates? Several specific strategies are available for selection, as follows:

1. Broaden the instructor's course objectives to include higher-order cognitive strategies that relate to the course topic. For example, in a philosophy of education course, candidates could be expected to take a position on a particular philosophy and logically defend it.

2. Build into the course activities the requirement for candidates to identify a particular cognitive skill (e.g., comparison) and apply it during the course, reflect on the cognitive strategies needed, and discuss how to apply that skill to the teaching of students.

3. In class sessions, foster regular dialogue, while modeling higher-order questioning and the application of wait-time, and then reflect on these strategies with candidates.
4. Connect course activities with parallel classroom observations in classrooms of teachers who have been identified as strong teachers of thinking.
5. Revise course-assessment methods to include higher-level analysis and reasoning processes.

Thus, a combined strategy rather than any single strategy from the above list, may be the most appropriate approach to take.

Thinking and High-Stakes Testing

With the implementation of state curriculum frameworks that are largely subject-matter-based as opposed to process-based, along with the state and federal mandates for high-stakes testing to be used to determine student promotion and graduation, the pressure on classroom teachers to revert to lower-level cognitive processes is extreme. Stories have been disseminated in the media about cheating on the part of both educators and students in order to achieve "passing" status on these tests. The public rating of school performance, based on such tests, is an example of a practice that adds to the pressure that falls directly on teachers. Thus it is no surprise that one response to these mandates is the elimination from the curriculum of any topic (e.g., critical thinking programs) which does not have some obvious potentially positive impact on ultimate student performance on such tests.

However, another response is possible and has occurred in enlightened school districts, some of whom have even been at first rated low performing. Although the rationale for teaching critical thinking should never rest on its potential for enhancing student performance on externally designed tests, nonetheless, a critical-thinking program that is well implemented for other purposes can indeed have a positive impact on test scores as well. An example of a demonstrated positive effect is the result in Massachusetts of the Massachusetts Comprehensive Assessment System (MCAS), their mandated high-stakes test, by students who have had instruction using the LINKS Program (Porcaro 2003), which stresses among other areas metacognitive reflection.[30] The preliminary results indicate that students who had the LINKS program, by comparison with those who had not, made significant improvement in their MCAS scores in English/language arts and mathematics.[31]

The question then becomes, how could a program of critical thinking have any effect on subject-matter-based testing, when the critical thinking program itself does not directly address subject matter? Four different answers are readily available. First, the use of such critical-thinking programs is usually embedded within the subject matter of the regular curriculum (as opposed to being taught as an outside-the-regular-curriculum topic); thus, students are applying the tools of critical thinking to their own mastery of the subject matter. When it is time to recall certain facts in a multiple-choice format, students have a framework upon which to recall those facts. Second, responding to multiple-choice formats requires that students apply an essential higher-order strategy—decision making from among alternatives; when they have to select one response from five that are presented, if they have a way to systematically eliminate irrelevant choices (rather than randomly selecting), their chances of obtaining correct responses are enhanced. Third, not all test items in all high-stakes tests are only multiple-choice; on the MCAS, for example, constructed-response items require students to construct an answer rather than respond to given options; in this context, the student who has had the benefit of a critical-thinking program focusing on planning and analysis and reflection has an advantage in constructing his or her response in a comprehensive and planned manner. Finally, one of the strategies leading to success on high-stakes tests is efficient time management; again, a student who has had experiences in critical thinking is more likely to think in an organized and sequential manner, thus managing well the use of time.

Hence, although critical-thinking programs were never designed explicitly to produce success on high-stakes tests (since most of the critical-thinking programs were developed well before the advent of the current national testing movement); nonetheless, the careful implementation of such programs can have this desirable serendipitous effect. In turn, as such results become more widely recognized, the case may be made that now more than ever, critical-thinking programs are essential in schools, but now for different reasons than before. In this way, the apparently opposing movements of higher-order problem solving and high-stakes testing can actually coalesce if the right decisions and promotions are made by educators and teacher educators.

It remains essential, however, that educators understand that critical-thinking programs still have their own intrinsic merit in a variety of contexts, only one of which is their use to enhance performance on mandated assessments. Other aspects of the life-centered rationale continue to be decision making in life situations, decision making in the future workplace of students, and the ability to consider alternative viewpoints within logical arguments posed in the media and by political candidates.

Selection of Critical Thinking Programs

Once the decision is made by a teacher or a teacher educator to adopt a critical thinking program, as opposed to developing one's own program, then a set of criteria must be applied in order that this adoption decision can be an intelligent one. Several criteria should be applied, as follows:

1. Theory-based: Does the program have a basis in sound cognitive theory, founded on research and on articulated positions taken by recognized experts in cognitive education?
2. Comprehensiveness: Does the program encompass a wide range of cognitive skills, as opposed to one or two specific processes?
3. Slow Progress: Does the program espouse the philosophy that there is truly no "quick fix" for improving cognition but rather a slow and steady progress that involves a deep changing of the habits of mind in the individual learner?
4. Teacher development: Does the adoption of the program also require that some systematic preparation of teachers (including for in-service teachers) be implemented as a prerequisite? The teaching of critical thinking, because it is a different way of teaching, should not be merely a product to be purchased and taken off the shelf to be implemented on Monday morning.
5. Tested implementation: Does the program have a reported history of successful implementation, at least in some pilot school contexts, to which the potential educator-consumer can refer?
6. Successful evaluation: Does the program material provide the results of some systematic and credible evaluation or research involving the program, with positive outcomes?
7. Follow-up support: Does the program provide some kind of ongoing support—such as free or inexpensive consultation from the publisher/trainer or a regular newsletter—that will help the implementer to answer implementation questions after the teacher-development sessions have concluded?

Some, but definitely not all, of the available published programs meet these requirements; within teacher-education programs, therefore, these criteria need to be promulgated to teacher candidates so that when they become consumers of published programs, they will have a basis for a well-reasoned decision about which program to adopt or adapt for their own classrooms.

Thinking and the Democratic Process

After considering all of the above, we need to return to the overall rationale for including critical thinking as an essential component of successful living within a democratic country. That area, separate from all arguments of curriculum and teacher education, should form the ultimate rationale for this incorporation and should transcend all specific educational and economic and political trends of the moment.

The work of John Dewey, cited in this volume, provides us with a strong platform for the process of viewing thinking as tightly tied to the democratic process; it is useful to return to his ideas as being seminal to this movement. Dewey's work is based on the idea of the human being as a "growing organism whose major development task is to come to terms…with the environment in which he or she lives," and in this process, the human being is constantly in the process of constructing adaptations for itself.[32] This process in turn requires not only active thought at high levels (e.g., analysis) but also reflection (which requires that the individual be able to stand back and look at her or his situation with some detachment—also a higher-level strategy). Dewey is also careful to point out that intellectual development not only depends on genetics but also on cultural contexts—a concept that is widely accepted today, but one which was strongly resisted in the early Twentieth Century and still has its detractors in the early Twenty-First Century. To elaborate, many adults automatically have lower expectations for a student whose culture is not the dominant culture in society than for students from the dominant culture; and low expectations, we know, are self-fulfilling. From a social-policy perspective, low expectations also become a means of preventing a so-called minority group from becoming educated and assuming power or influence in the society.

So, what benefit would accrue to anyone by detracting from Dewey's ideas in the current world? From a social justice viewpoint, the benefit would be the justification of providing inadequate resources (human and financial) to groups of people in society who are seriously disadvantaged, on the basis that they are incapable of growth into fully functioning members of society, thus preserving power and influence in the dominant culture.

For Dewey, another of the purposes of schooling is to provide educational situations through which the child becomes increasingly able to deal with more and more complex problems; the systematic provision of critical thinking opportunities is essential to enabling learners to deal with such problems in a systematic way.[33] The application of these systematic strategies is one key way that individuals and groups who have disadvantaged backgrounds may assertively rise beyond those backgrounds to become fully functioning members of society; thus, such individuals in some ways have to force the granting of social justice by others in power to themselves.

Thus, Dewey provided the basis for viewing the child not as an empty vessel to be filled, but instead one who acts upon the environment and actively creates connections and relationships and in the process can transform one's own environment. Social justice is the end result of this kind of transformation if sufficient numbers of children are educated to be able to carry out active problem solving at high levels.

It is a short step from these ideas to the notion of democratic process that Dewey also envisioned for schools; he wanted the school to become a microcosm of the society into which the learners were growing, by having schools be places where democratic processes and (in our terms today) social justice were actually practiced. A next step is to understand that Dewey's ideas also led to a problem-centered curriculum; and in today's terms, a problem-centered curriculum rather than a traditional topic-centered curriculum directly fosters higher-level problem-solving—critical thinking.

Still another of Dewey's ideas fit well with the conceptions behind this book—individualization; it is entirely inappropriate to view learners as all needing to fit into one mold, rather than to grow to become different individuals, each building on his or her own strengths.

And a final extension of Dewey's ideas is the world of school curriculum and its sources. One of the most disturbing trends, cited earlier in this book as well as earlier in this chapter, is the "top-down" prescription of curriculum. Such top-down thinking prevents the development of curricula that will fit the local needs of groups of students; while external standards are useful for general coordination, the high-stakes testing against these standards (particularly in the narrow paper-and-pencil methodology) militates against any internal development of curriculum. Instead, in order to achieve not only social justice but also the full flowering of individual students according to their needs, we need to have internal standards that are flexible and that evolve from the local needs that the school and the teacher identify.

Therefore, a huge debt is owed to John Dewey for many of the ideas about critical thinking in their original and evolved form as they relate to democracy and social justice.

What are the reasons why critical thinking is essential in a democracy today? Several reasons would be:

1. The careful consideration of choices is the essence of democracy on the part of average citizens. Without the ability to think critically and be aware of one's own thought processes in doing so, the average citizen may frequently make unwise choices from among alternatives, whether those decisions involve some aspect of family life or work life or political selection.

2. The making of intelligent decisions follows from the consideration of choices. Even a child's life is filled with decision making that requires a rational basis, not to mention adult life with its many-faceted demands. One who can analyze, synthesize, organize, find patterns, and use logic (among other processes) will be well equipped to make decisions that will stand the test of implementation.

3. The ability to consider several viewpoints on an issue, rather than just one viewpoint, is another hallmark of living in a democracy. Thus, in public debates and forums, as well as sitting in front of a televised debate among political candidates, the critical thinker is open to other views on issues and can legitimize changing his or her mind on an issue or candidate, or can empathize with another person who expresses a viewpoint different from one's own. This area also relates to the openness to changing one's mind, based on new information.

4. The ability to consider all aspects of an issue is a related area. An individual who can take a given topic or issue and systematically investigate multiple dimensions rather than a single dimension will be able to comprehend the full import of any decision that is made by oneself or by others for oneself.

5. The ability to find creative alternatives to removing barriers is still another valued skill in a democracy. A U.S. Army officer, after being trained in critical thinking as part of officer-training procedures, remarked to a critical-thinking trainer about a historical fact of World War II—the German army was highly trained and efficient, but when it encountered a barrier or lost an officer or leader, they were frequently unable to improvise; on the other hand, when the same events happened within the American armed forces, American military personnel in general were more often able to improvise, innovate, or appoint a new leader "on the spot" to replace a fallen one. In the 1940s, formal programs to teach critical thinking had not yet been developed; nonetheless, the democratic spirit reflected

by the American military was clearly a part of the society from which these soldiers came; a formal critical-thinking program in schools can only further propagate those strategies and the value that is placed on the ability to innovative through systematic and open thinking.

6. The propensity for questioning, rather than blindly accepting, is fundamental to a democracy.

At first sight, teaching students to question seems to be asking for problems because students then might not accept any authority of any kind; but that concern is ill-founded because it misunderstands what is meant by teaching students to question. Yes, we must teach students to question authority as well, but equally important, we must teach them how to ask intelligent and probing questions that may result in a better ultimate decision by those who are in authority. Silent acceptance and acquiescence are the very antitheses of life in a real democracy.

Doubtless one could develop additional points of rationale for including critical thinking as a fundamental part of schooling in America. If we are serious about preparing the coming generations to be active, questioning citizens in a political and social democracy, we must be serious about the infusion of critical thinking. Goodlad has underlined this point, in his remark that critical thinking can be potentially transforming of both the individual and society.[34] No better argument could be made for such a commitment.

Notes

1. Jerome Bruner, *The Process of Education* (Cambridge, Mass.: Harvard, 1960).
2. *A Nation At Risk* (Washington, D.C.: National Commission on Excellence in Education, 1983).
3. Reuven Feuerstein, *Instrumental Enrichment* (Baltimore: University Park Press, 1980).
4. Howard Gardner, *Frames of Mind: The Theory of Multiple Intelligences* (New York: Basic Books, 1983).
5. Robert Sternberg and J. Davidson, "A Four-Prong Model for Intellectual Development," *Journal of Research and Development in Education* 22 (1989): 22–28.
6. Matthew Lipman, *Thinking in Education* (Cambridge, England: Cambridge University Press, 1991).
7. Raymond Nickerson, "On Improving Thinking Through Instruction," *Review of Research in Education* 15 (1989): 3–57.
8. Ronald Brandt, "Foreword," in *Developing Minds*, ed. A Costa (Alexandria, Va.: Association for Supervision and Curriculum Development, 2001), xii–xiv.
9. Barry Beyer, "What Research Says About Teaching Thinking Skills," in *Developing Minds*, ed. A. Costa (Alexandria, Va.: Association for Supervision and Curriculum Development, 2001), 275–82.
10. Lev S. Vygotsky, *Thought and Language* (Cambridge, Mass.: MIT Press, 1962).
11. Cognition and Technology Group, *Anchored Instruction and Situated Cognition Revisited* (unpublished manuscript) (Nashville, Tenn.: Vanderbilt University, 1993).

12. A. Palincsar and A. L. Brown, " Reciprocal Teaching of Comprehension-Fostering and Comprehension-Monitoring Activities," *Cognition and Instruction* 1 (1984): 117–75.
13. Mary B. Rowe, "Wait-Time and Rewards as Instructional Variables: Their Influence on Language, Logic, and Fate Control," *Journal of Research in Science Teaching* 11 (1974): 81–84.
14. Arthur L. Costa, "Teacher Behaviors That Enable Student Thinking," in *Developing Minds*, ed. A. Costa, 359–69.
15. J. T. Bruer, "In Search of Brain-Based Education," *Phi Delta Kappan* 8, no. 3: 7–12.
16. Lawrence F. Lowery, "The Biological Basis for Thinking," in *Developing Minds*, ed. A. Costa, 234–43.
17. D. S. Martin and N. M. Michelli, "Preparing Teachers of Thinking," in *Developing Minds*, ed. A. Costa , 111–17.
18. D. S. Martin, A. R. Craft, and N. Zhang, "The Impact of Cognitive Strategy Instruction on Deaf Learners: An International Study," *American Annals of the Deaf* 146 (2001): 366–78.
19. G. Morine-Dershimer, *Tying Threads Together: Some Thoughts on Methods for Investigating Teacher Thinking* (New York: American Educational Research Association, 1982).
20. J. W. Renner, *Determination of Intellectual Levels of Selected Students: Final Report to the National Science Foundation* (Washington, D.C.: National Science Foundation, 1975).
21. C. M. Clark and R. L. Yinger, "Teacher Thinking," in *Research in Teaching: Concepts, Findings, and Implications*, ed. H. J. Walberg and P. L. Peterson (Berkeley: McCutchan, 1979).
22. C. M. Clark and M. Lampert, "The Study of Teacher Thinking and Implications for Teacher Education," *Journal of Teacher Education* 37, no. 5 (1986): 27–31.
23. P. L. Peterson, "Teachers' and Students' Conditional Knowledge for Classroom Teaching and Learning," *The Educational Researcher* 17 (1988): 5–14.
24. L. S. Shulman, "Paradigms and Research Programs in the Study of Teaching: A Contemporary Perspective," in *Handbook of Research on Teaching*, ed. M. C. Wittrock (New York: Macmillan, 1986).
25. D. S. Martin, "Teaching of Thinking: A Cross-Cultural Study of Effects on Professionals," *ERIC Reproduction Service* (1998): Document SP 038 049.
26. D. S. Martin, A. R. Craft, and H. Tillema, "Developing Critical and Creative Thinking Strategies in Primary School Pupils: An Intercultural Study of Teachers' Learning," *Journal of In-Service Education* 28 (2002): 115–34.
27. National Council on the Accreditation of Teacher Education (NCATE), *Standards, Procedures, and Policies for the Accreditation of Professional Education Units* (Washington, D.C.: National Council on the Accreditation of Teacher Education, 1995).
28. G. Watson and E. M. Glaser, *Watson-Glaser Critical Thinking Appraisal* (San Antonio: The Psychological Corporation, 1980).
29. N. M. Michelli, T. Jacobowitz, and R. Pines, "Renewing Teacher Education Through Critical Thinking," *Record in Educational Leadership* (1994): 45–48.
30. K. Porcaro, *LINKS Secondary: A Resource Handbook for Teaching Metacognitive Strategies*, 9th ed. (Worcester, Mass.: Viateck Publications, 2003).
31. G. Mazzola and K. Porcaro, "Implementation of LINKS Metacognitive Strategy System." Paper presented at the national conference of the Association for Supervision and Curriculum Development, San Francisco (2003).
32. E. Eisner, *The Educational Imagination* (New York: Macmillan, 1994).
33. J. Dewey, *The Educational Situation* (Chicago: University of Chicago Press, 1902).
34. J. Goodlad, "Teachers for the Teaching of Intelligence," presentation at the 5th annual Conference for the Teaching of Intelligence, San Francisco, 1999.

CHAPTER 11

External Funding: The Place of Foundations in Teacher Education for Democracy and Social Justice

CARLA ASHER WITH DIANE EIDMAN

Education is a major focus of corporate and foundation giving in the United States. In 2003, for example, funding for education represented 26.4 percent of all foundation grants of $10,000 or more, the largest share of overall foundation support. Some foundations support education because it is (or was) a special interest of their founders. For others it is a component of an interest in supporting programs for youth or low-income populations. For corporate givers, support for education may provide an opportunity to support future workers or consumers of their product or to present a positive image in a geographic area where they do business.

During the 1990s, the long-standing interest of many major foundations and corporate giving programs focused on providing support for education reform and for improvements in the teaching profession. These donors believed that their private funds could serve as catalysts for educational changes that were being called for by educators and others. Funders provided major support to the Coalition of Essential Schools, a consortium of schools seeking to exemplify the educational ideas of its founder, Theodore Sizer; to the National Board for Professional Teaching Standards (NBPTS), an effort to develop and implement a system of assessing and rewarding accomplished teaching; to the National Commission for Teaching and America's Future, a blue-ribbon panel that would examine the state of the teaching profession, make recommendations for improving the profession, and join with interest states in implementing these recommendations; to the Accelerated Schools Project, a consortium of schools organized by Henry Levin; and to the School Development Program developed by James Comer at Yale, specifically to address the needs of low-income children; and many others.

Both the DeWitt Wallace–Reader's Digest Fund, a private foundation and the Philip Morris Companies, Inc., provided significant support to the Institute for Educational Inquiry and the National Network for Educational Renewal (NNER), a coalition of teacher preparation institutions committed to a reform agenda developed by Professor John Goodlad. This chapter explores the reasons for that support from the perspective of the givers, including the extent of interest in the agenda of teaching for democracy and social justice, what they actually supported, and the effects of the support. It also looks briefly at these funders' current support for the reform of schools and reform of the teaching profession and how it contrasts with what they supported in the 1990s.

The Philip Morris Companies, Inc., Grant

In 1992 the Philip Morris Companies, Inc. (now Altria Group, Inc.) made a grant of $500,000 to establish the Philip Morris Fellowship Program at the Institute for Educational Inquiry. The company's support of teacher education evolved out of two developments within the company. After Philip Morris acquired Kraft Foods in 1988, the CEO of the company called for a strategic review of all its giving programs in order to create a coordinated, integrated approach to grant making and community relations. It decided that there should be two or three sharply defined areas that would receive the bulk of the corporate resources. A second development concerned the company's commitment to education reform. The company saw public schools as vital to the company's interest in having an educated, qualified, and diverse population from which its future workforce would be recruited. Consequently, upon completion of the strategic review, the company decided to encourage its operating companies to support P–12 programs in their communities and to focus its national corporate giving on teacher education.

The company decided to look for "visionaries" in the areas that it was interested in funding and to support their most innovative activities. It made a major grant to the University of Tennessee at Knoxville to enable Richard Wisniewski, then the dean, to design an innovative teacher preparation program, and it made a grant to enable Wendy Kopp to institutionalize Teach for America, an alternative teacher preparation program that did not involve a college. The company knew that Teach for America was controversial among many established teacher educators. The company's support was premised on the view that Wendy Kopp was a visionary, and that she was flexible and able to adapt her program to respond to criticism. The company believed that there could be many roads to improving teacher education. Philip Morris also provided support to the work of James Comer, National Commission on Teaching and America's Future (NCTF) and NBPTS.

The company's research had also identified John Goodlad as a visionary in teacher education. When Anne Dowling, then director of Corporate Contributions at Philip Morris, met Goodlad at a conference, she found him to be intelligent, thoughtful, and practical. She was particularly impressed with his answer to the question," How do we get systemic reform in public education?"

"You can't," he answered, "because there is no system. We have to reform schoolhouse by schoolhouse." Goodlad's belief that school reform required a long-term commitment and a willingness to make hard choices. The emphasis in the Goodlad agenda on the role of education in a democracy was, according to Dowling, an important consideration in the company's support for his work. "It reinforced our belief that public schools were the one place where children of an incredibly diverse population could be invested with the values needed to become active, engaged citizens."

The initial grant to the Institute for Educational Inquiry (IEI) was in support of its Leadership Associates Program. The Leadership Associates Program was intended to "empower a cadre of leaders deeply committed to the agenda who will work to carry out the vision of renewing simultaneously America's schools and the education of educators." Participants would:

Develop a deeper understanding of the moral dimensions of teaching in a democracy.
Collaborate with P–12 educators, education professors, and arts and sciences professors toward the simultaneous renewal of schools and the education of educators.
Become effective agents of change in their institutions and settings.
Conduct inquiry into the nature of simultaneous renewal in the NNER.
Contribute to the work of simultaneous renewal by serving as presenters, advisors, facilitators, and friendly critics to the sixteen settings of the NNER.

The IEI staff decided that participants in the Leadership Associates should consist of teams from the schools, the colleges of arts and sciences, and from teacher education, and that each cohort should have no more than twenty-one participants, in order to facilitate discussion. The program would be intensive—four four-and-a-half-day sessions over the course of a year—and would focus on four themes: enculturating the young in a social and political democracy, providing access to knowledge for all children and youths, engaging in a nurturing pedagogy, and serving as moral stewards of schools. Sessions would focus on shared reading and each participant would conduct an inquiry project—a year-long investigation into an aspect of educational renewal.

The first Leadership Associates Program took place in 1993. Over the next six years, Philip Morris supported the program with an additional $500,000. The company considered its support of the Leadership Associates Program as an investment in the future. It was not looking for short-term measurable gains. It was looking to seed a program that would serve as a model, that could be replicated, that would be an inspiration, a beacon.

Since 1993 more than 300 educators have participated in the program, which continues to welcome new cohorts each year. The NNER has come to depend on the Leadership Associates Program as a means of expanding to new settings. NNER requirements for admission to the network include, among other things, that faculty representing the tripartite have completed leadership preparation through the IEI or comparable preparation. Two regional leadership programs have been offered, one in the northeast and one in the west, to teams from institutions that are seeking to gain membership in the NNER. Many of the settings that are members of the NNER have replicated the Leadership Associates Program on their own campuses, as a way of developing a cadre of people who are committed to the agenda for education in a democracy. The Leadership Associates Programs have become largely institutionalized, with NNER member institutions supporting the participation of teams in the national program. In some years funding is sufficient to allow the program to pick up all costs except for airfare, and in other years settings pay for airfare and lodging costs associated with the program. For the NNER, the Leadership Associates Program has become an essential tool for developing an informed commitment to the work it has undertaken.

The DeWittWallace–Reader's Digest Fund Grant

In 1994 the DeWitt Wallace–Reader's Digest Fund (now the Wallace Foundation) made a grant of $2,935,800 to the Institute for Educational Inquiry. The grant was made under the foundation's category of grants for

"Comprehensive School Restructuring and Reform." The fund's 1994 annual report describes the category this way:

> The Fund supports a select group of organizations that are leading national efforts to reform and restructure schools to make teaching and learning more effective. *The major thrust of these activities is to improve schools so that teaching and learning focus on problem solving, critical analysis and higher order thinking skills* (italics added).

In order to promote this agenda, the DeWitt Wallace–Reader's Digest Fund (DWRD) identified four grant-making strategies under the umbrella of school reform:

1. assisting particular schools and districts in reforming their leadership, improving school climate, supporting student-centered teaching and learning, and revising their expectations for students,
2. promoting reform of the teaching profession,
3. supporting national networks of reforming schools, and
4. disseminating information to and promoting collaboration among school reform practitioners.

Support for the IEI fell under the second strategy. Three grants to the NBPTS, beginning in 1990 and totaling $7.1 million, also came under this category. Under the other strategies, the foundation provided major grants to the Coalition of Essential Schools, and the National Center for Restructuring Education, Schools, and Teaching (NCREST) at Teachers College, headed by Ann Lieberman and Linda Darling-Hammond.

When the IEI approached the DeWitt Wallace–Reader's Digest Fund for support, it asked the foundation to underwrite a program of incentive grants to the institutions participating in the NNER. The incentive grants were to be used to accelerate progress by the institutions in implementing its nineteen conditions for the simultaneous renewal of schools and teacher preparation institutions. Funds awarded would have to be matched by the institution on a two-to-one basis. As the proposal put it, "Needed are the resources that both fuel enthusiasm and provide support for key personnel beginning to grow weary. The financial resources requested of the DeWitt Wallace–Reader's Digest Fund are critical to that extra push required to achieve success envisioned but still some distance down the road. The distance already traveled is substantial; the momentum must be sustained and intensified."

The fund's 1994 annual report describes the grant this way:

> To implement the DeWitt Wallace–Reader's Digest Fund Incentive
> Awards in Teacher Education, an effort to create a core group of
> teacher preparation programs that can serve as models for schools
> of education throughout the United States. The goal is to enable
> teacher training institutions that are members of the National Net-
> work for Educational Renewal to phase out their existing programs
> and replace them with ones that meet the criteria set out in John
> Goodlad's *Teachers for Our Nation's Schools*.

Interestingly, neither the foundation's description nor the IEI's proposal
explicitly mentions education in a democracy or social justice. However,
the IEI refers to the role of an educator in a democratic society in several
of its nineteen conditions, including the seventh, which also mentions critical thinking:

> Programs for the education of educators, whether elementary or
> secondary, must carry the responsibility to ensure that all candi-
> dates progressing through them possess or acquire the literacy and
> critical thinking abilities associated with the concept of an educated
> person.

From the foundation's point of view, the grant fit well with its interest
in supporting reform of the teaching profession, including the preparation
of teachers, and with its interest in promoting improvements to education
that would lead to a greater emphasis on critical thinking in schools and
a move away from rote learning and so-called basic skills. The role of
the teacher in a democratic society was not a particular interest of the
foundation.

Over the years of the DWRD grant, the IEI awarded incentive grants of
up to $75,000 to settings within the NNER. In order to receive one of the
incentive grants, each interested NNER member institution had to submit
an application outlining what it wanted to do with the money, what it
hoped to achieve, and what funds it would use to match the award.

In its 1994 application for an incentive award, one institution, Montclair State University set an ambitious agenda for itself toward meeting the
nineteen conditions for effective teacher preparation. This agenda was
focused on the moral dimensions of teaching, on the teacher's rule in
enculturating the young into a political and social democracy, and on the
teacher's role as steward of best practice.

First, Montclair planned to join all of its faculty who prepared teachers, including those in education, arts and sciences, and in its partner schools into a Center of Pedagogy. But the proposal recognized that this was not simply an administrative task, that it needed to "ground the members of the Center in a common foundation from which the set of beliefs that govern the simultaneous renewal of the education of educators and of the schools can move forward." It requested funds to develop a Center of Pedagogy Associates Program in which 20 center associates would meet in two seminars, each five days in length "to consider issues related to the moral dimensions of teaching, enculturation of the young into a political and social democracy, and stewardship of best practice." This would be modeled after the national Leadership Associates Program funded by Philip Morris.

Second, Montclair aspired to revise its admissions process "to take into account the initial commitment of students to the moral dimensions of teaching, to their enculturating responsibilities, and to their roles as stewards of best practice." Funds were requested to develop promotional materials describing the nature and expectations of Montclair's program so that prospective students would be informed about the program's goals. Montclair also sought to improve its recruitment of students of color and students with disabilities into teacher education and asked for funds to continue and expand Future Teachers of Newark Clubs in four Newark high schools and to support a graduate student to help in this recruitment effort.

Third, Montclair sought to revise its teacher education program, providing students with a general education program that reflected the goals of the teacher preparation program and revising all education coursework "to include appropriate emphasis on the moral dimensions, enculturation, and stewardship, while continuing work in critical thinking." To further these goals, Montclair requested support to involve faculty in revising general education courses and for a retreat and planning sessions to revise education courses and design a new teacher preparation program to begin with the class entering in fall 1997.

Fourth, Montclair sought to expand its recruitment of clinical faculty from the schools and to develop new sites for students' field experiences. It requested funds for materials that would recruit new collaborating schools and to expand its ability to offer workshops for clinical faculty members. It also asked for support for teacher study groups at each interested partner school.

Fifth, and finally, Montclair aimed to change the placement and roles of student teachers, transforming them into "junior faculty" who could help schools with the "ongoing process of renewal." It sought support for planning time for teachers to consider new ways of using student teachers and to have university faculty plan experiences for student teachers in keeping with the junior faculty concept.

Montclair requested a $50,000 DWRD grant to be matched by $50,000 of university funds and $50,000 of other funding it had raised. The one-year incentive grant was made in December 1994. Montclair was required to report back to the IEI (and the fund) on its progress in the summer of 1995.

The report describes significant progress toward its five goals. Asked to answer the questions, "What was the value added to your work? How is your setting different today as a result of this grant?" Montclair responded as follows:

> 1. We have a Center of Pedagogy. Our setting is dramatically differ-
> ent in that all constituents look to the Center for leadership I
> teacher education rather than to one of the traditional academic
> units. Additionally, we have increased the involvement of arts and
> science faculty as a result of our Leadership Associates Program.
> 2. Our admissions process is now one that seeks out and selects
> rather than screens to a much greater extent than before. We have
> become explicit in describing our expectations and goals, allowing
> students to make informed choices and allowing us to be more
> selective. We have sensitized our faculty to the need for recruitment
> of students of color, and it is an increasing part of our work.
> 3. There is no question that the moral and other aspects of the
> [moral] dimensions [of teaching] are part and parcel of our aca-
> demic program at all levels. No course exists without some ground-
> ing in the dimensions. This is a dramatically different situation
> than prior to the grant. Members of a cohort of leaders committed
> to the work on campus are in key positions across the university,
> and more change is expected.
> 4. Our Network [of collaborating schools] is dramatically different.
> Teacher Study Groups have provided cement to bring together
> teachers around the issues of the agenda. We have succeeded in
> expanding the network, including adding districts with many more
> students of color. The Network is more sophisticated, more widely
> supported, and an unmistakable part of the fabric of education in
> New Jersey as a result of the grant.
> 5. First steps were taken to change the relationships between the
> university and the schools, and the way in which junior faculty
> are used. Four schools are on the way to becoming professional

development schools. The grant has permitted this work to begin and to move forward.

The following year, Montclair requested a second incentive award, this time for $75,000. It requested support to consolidate and extend the activities funded by the first incentive award. When Montclair reported on the second award in the summer of 1997, it described considerable progress toward making the changes advocated by the agenda set out in *Teachers for Our Nation's Schools*. Both the Center of Pedagogy and its Leadership Associates Program had been institutionalized and were now "part of the fabric of the University." The teacher education admissions process had been refined even further, and the university had made substantial commitments to the continued recruitment of students of color into the program. Most of the curricular and structural changes Montclair had undertaken had been adopted. Montclair had expanded its network of partner schools and most courses were now taught in those schools by teams of university faculty and school faculty.

In 2004, ten years after the first incentive grant to Montclair University, the changes spurred by the grant have become institutionalized and expanded. Examples of that institutionalization and expansion include:

- The creation and continuation of a position titled "coordinator of the Agenda for Education in a Democracy." The office serves to consider all activities planned to assess their impact on the "vision" embodied in the work of the agenda.
- The university continued the Leadership Associates Program, always seeking membership from education, arts and sciences, and the schools. The number of individuals who completed the program begun with Wallace Funds support is now in excess of 200. Many of these people continue to provide leadership to the work at Montclair.
- The university developed a Teacher Education Advocacy Center designed to support the recruitment and preparation of students from minority groups into teaching. The center grew out of the commitment to diverse, democratic programs and includes academic advising support beyond that given as a matter of course, a freshman cohort program with a support system for the transition from high school to college, and a Minority Teacher Candidate organization to provide networking for minority students.
- The Center of Pedagogy continues to function largely as intended. The third director since its inception recently assumed office. Clearly, the idea of a "hybrid educator," one who spans the cultures of education, arts and science, and the schools, is a difficult position.

The leadership of the Institute for Educational Inquiry has begun to recognize that special preparation for such a position is necessary, probably through a specialized Leadership Associates Program.

While each of these represented significant and institutionalized changes in teacher education, the piece most directly funded by external support is the local Leadership Associates Program. It is seen by faculty and administrators at the University as a key to broadening support for the work and to involving members of the tripartite—faculty in education, arts and science, and the schools—in systematic consideration of very complex issues. Being able to reflect on the grounding of education for democracy and social justice without immediately turning to the practical day-to-day implications may seem to be a luxury, but it is essential in the development of a long-term vision that will be enduring. External funding allowed for that luxury to begin at Montclair and other NNER settings, and the value of the work led to its institutionalization.[1]

In December 2001 Nicholas Michelli, then dean at Montclair State University and chair of the NNER (as of 2004 university dean for teacher education at the City University of New York), wrote to the president of the DeWitt Wallace–Reader's Digest Fund:

> Beginning in 1994 the DeWitt Wallace–Reader's Digest Fund supported grants to NNER settings to engage in a fundamental redesign of teacher education. A condition of this support was a double match—from within the university and from another outside source. Montclair was one of the recipients of those funds, which were used to establish a program for intensive collaboration and leadership development among arts and science faculty, education faculty, and public school faculty to renew schools with an emphasis on high academic standards and learning to live in a democracy. After three years of funding, the entire program was carried forward in the University's base budget, and continues to the present. To date, more than 200 leaders have been prepared through the Leadership Associates Program of Montclair State's Agenda for Education in a Democracy. Montclair's teacher education program is now widely known nationally as a model of excellence.

> But Montclair was only one setting in the NNER to benefit from your funding. In my role as Chair I have seen the effects of your good work across many of our settings. The work is reported in a series of books, including *Leadership for Educational Renewal,* edited by Wilma Smith and Gary Fenstermacher, published by

Jossey Bass in 1999. I have taken what I learned at Montclair with me to the City University of New York where we are engaged in renewal across the 20 campuses of the University.

None of this would have been possible without the support of your foundation, and I thank you on behalf of the National Network for that support.[2]

Conclusion

The grants that were made by the Philip Morris Companies, Inc., and the DeWitt Wallace–Reader's Digest Fund in the 1990s have continued to have an important impact on the NNER and its member institutions. Both grants share certain features. The work that they supported was defined and developed by the NNER and IEI. It was work that the grantees felt would deepen commitment to and implementation of their agenda for teaching in a democracy. It was built around a set of beliefs about the purpose of education in a democracy. Both the IEI, with its Leadership Associates Program, and Montclair State, with its incentive award, focused heavily on building informed support and leadership for the work to which they were committed through an increased understanding of the beliefs underpinning the NNER agenda.

Although both grants were for the purpose of fostering improvements in the preparation of teachers, neither promised predetermined or specific outcomes. The DeWitt Wallace grant was made with the expectation that the settings that received incentive awards would make changes in alignment with the nineteen conditions for the simultaneous renewal of schools and teacher preparation institutions, but it did not require the IEI to specify at the outset what these changes would be. Both donors, in effect, wished to support John Goodlad and the network of teacher preparation institutions that he had formed and allowed the network to tell them what it needed to move the work forward.

The two donors have turned to other work. The Wallace Foundation, still committed to education, now focuses on "strategies to help principals and superintendents be more effective in their work." The foundation believes that "Without strong leaders to run schools and districts, efforts to produce changes that yield quality instruction for all students–especially in America's low-performing public schools—are not likely to succeed or be sustained." Thus, the foundation no longer gives support for efforts to strengthen teaching or teacher education or to reform schools.

In 1998 Altria shifted its focus from education to other areas. Its main giving areas are domestic violence, arts, and hunger relief. Formerly, Philip

Morris had focused its giving to education on teacher education because it allowed the company to have an impact on education in a systemic way and because it could thereby benefit education and youth without giving directly to schools or districts.

The company's chairman encouraged the creation of a grant-making program in combating domestic violence instead. The company is one of very few corporations addressing this issue. The program has met with much success, according to Diane Eidman, and has established Altria as a leader in this field. The company also discovered that modest grants were having an enormous impact, particularly on underserved communities across the United States. Impacts were easier to measure, quantify, and report. Hunger relief, a natural focus for a corporation that included a major food company, fit within a new theme of "serving people in need." The company's support for the arts, begun 45 years ago, has continued.

It is perhaps, inevitable, that private donors change their focus over time. They frequently aspire to be catalysts, funding cutting-edge work that needs a kind of venture capital. However, in the era of No Child Left Behind, the foundation community has moved in directions that make the grants of the 1990s for education reform less likely today. The change in direction of the Wallace Foundation and the Altria Group is mirrored by other foundations that offered support to education reform in the 1990s. Like the Altria Group (and the federal government), many private funders focus increasingly on measurable outcomes. The challenges that the corporate giving staff at Philip Morris faced in the 1990s in explaining the results of its education reform to management would be even greater today. And the Wallace Foundation are not alone in its support for school and district leadership, a focus that has become more popular in the foundation community in recent years.

There are, it seems, two shifts in private funding that make it less likely that foundations would now support the kind of work that Philip Morris and the Wallace Foundation supported in the 1990s. Foundations are driven by the policy context that affects all education in the early Twenty-First Century, a context that now emphasizes high-stakes testing and narrow definitions of student achievement. Both Philip Morris and Wallace, as we have noted, went into the support of the Agenda for Education in a Democracy without explicit outcomes specified. In fact, the explicit focus on democracy and social justice reported in this book was just one among many areas embedded in the work funded, although some settings made it their primary work. It is difficult of course to know for sure, but it is not clear that funding would have been forthcoming if in fact that had been the primary or only focus of the proposal.

Second, and perhaps most notable, is the shift among large private funders in the education field to large initiatives that the funder designs and develops, defining outcomes and criteria, and selecting sites that exemplify the criteria and commit to the outcomes. Perhaps the best example of this trend is the Teachers for a New Era initiative, funded by the Carnegie Corporation of New York, the Ford Foundation, the Annenberg Foundation, and the Rockefeller Foundation for more than $40 million. The foundations chose 11 teacher preparing institutions that it invited to participate, based on criteria that the funders felt would produce model programs. The Carnegie Corporation website (www.carnegie. org) states:

> Given Carnegie's Corporation's history of attention to the problems of the field, the foundation is well positioned to stimulate a major restructuring of teacher education. The Education Division designed a program that will require a substantial reorientation of position for teacher education faculty, other education faculty, arts and sciences faculty and perhaps, especially for academic administrators. What is needed is a thoroughgoing reform that engages institutions of higher education through all the academic programs that contribute to the education of prospective teachers.

Also, Carnegie has taken the lead on funding education to support further development of the civic mission of schools, and the preparation of teachers for such a mission is likely to follow.

And so, what are the implications for teacher education programs and public schools seeking foundation support for work that is squarely focused on education for democracy and social justice? We have several suggestions.

1. Remember that even if we think that education and social justice are the most important or among the most important outcomes we hope for from our schools, they are not the only outcomes.
2. Evaluation designs that will assess outcomes in the area of democracy and social justice are likely to be qualitative and should be combined with quantitative outcomes as well. The CUNY evaluation study reported in this volume takes this approach.
3. Proposals that come from collaborating colleges and P–12 school systems are much more likely to be attractive.
4. Priorities shift, and sometimes they shift because excellent proposals suggest different directions for foundations. Getting to know program officers can help to shape giving and directions.

5. Watch the work of lead foundations like Carnegie, and of major educational associations including AASCU and AAU who are taking the lead in reshaping education.
6. Join with other colleges and universities with similar missions to make support from foundations more cost effective.

It would seem that educators in the early Twenty-First Century are faced with mandates and directives from both the private and public sectors. Whether this defectiveness will lead to improvements in teaching and learning and ultimately in the qualities of education supported in this book remains to be seen. Those committed to the work cannot wait for the priorities of policy makers or foundations to keep pace but instead must demonstrate the impact on students and their lives.

Notes

1. See Wilma F. Smith and Gary D. Fenstermacher, eds., *Leadership for Educational Renewal* (San Francisco: Jossey-Bass Publishers, 1999) for an overview of the Leadership Associates Program, and the chapter by Tina J. Jacobowitz and Nicholas M. Michelli, "Montclair State University and the New Jersey Network for Educational Renewal," for a focus on the local leadership program at Montclair.
2. Letter from Nicholas M. Michelli to M. Christian DeVeta, Dec. 6, 2001.

SECTION **4**

Moving Forward

Conclusion

NICHOLAS M. MICHELLI AND DAVID LEE KEISER

We opened with the view that teacher education for democracy and social justice is an essential direction for public education in the United States of America in order to attain and sustain the hopes engendered by four enduring purposes for education:

1. preparing students to be critical, active, involved participants in our democracy
2. providing students with access to knowledge and critical thinking within the disciplines
3. preparing students to lead rich and rewarding personal lives, and to be responsible and responsive community members
4. preparing students to assume the highest possible place in the economy

We further asked: How can educators who believe in the historic purposes of public education related to the promotion of democracy and social justice continue our work when those purposes are being eroded by national and state policy?

After reading the aforementioned chapters, the answer seems clearer. In the following pages, we will not summarize each chapter or section as they speak so well for themselves. Instead we will extract a few of the key points that can guide and promote our work. Our examination of education for democracy leads us to the need to be clear about what we mean by democracy and preparation for it. Although this task can be approached in a simplistic and mechanistic way, reflective of the "Problems of American Democracy" courses prevalent in the 1950s and early 1960s, there are wider meanings of democracy that go beyond learning about government and citizenship, meanings that can and should be embedded in every classroom. We argue, for example, that education which encourages civility and the ability to argue well is essential to democratic society. We also need to listen to the position of scholars such as Benjamin Barber, who remind us of the fragility and rarity of successful democracy.

Teacher educators need support for this work, because teaching for democracy is a contested concept, faced with barriers erected by some powerful organizations and individuals in government and public policy. Joining with organizations that support our work—whether higher education associations or networks of colleges and schools—helps enormously. Funding can be found to support this work, but can also be a temporary solution. While we can't ignore the mandates of policy makers to assess our work—in part because assessment itself is not problematic—contributors to this work, however, have pointed to the effects of unreasonable testing. Programs that focus on preparing students to live in a democratic and socially just society must also prioritize academic outcomes central to the eventual civic participation of students.

As with democracy, we need to define what we mean by social justice, as it, too, is a contested concept. One contributor was told by his university's press office to never use the word social justice with the press. Democracy was okay, equity was okay, equal access to education was okay, but not social justice. Why? Our contributor was told that the Board of Governors of the university thought "social justice" meant taking their money and giving it to others. As Keiser suggests, there is a need to define what we mean by social justice and what it entails. He cites Darling-Hammond's view that it involves understanding self in relation to others as well as understanding the societal construction of privilege and inequality. Greene and Rawls caution that we must go beyond moral frameworks and address the issue of material arrangements for all people. Maybe the aforementioned Board of Governors was right; we do want to redistribute resources toward a more holistic understanding and implementation of teacher education.

Lucas believes that one starts understanding social justice by understanding injustice. But how do we do this? In our early chapters we suggested some principles to govern our work, including:

- Teacher education programs and programs in public schools must be renewed simultaneously.
- Teacher education must be carried out by faculty in education, the arts and sciences, and the public schools as equal partners in the preparation of future educators and the renewal of current educators.

- Structures and policies to allow deep collaboration must be present, and appropriate connections with the communities must be nurtured.
- Programs for preparing teachers and public school educators must have a clear, unambiguous shared vision that addresses the four enduring purposes of public education. The vision must be the basis for all-important decisions, and the program must be assessed based on the vision.
- We must be clear about the meaning of terms we use and the challenges we face.
- We must reinforce the potential of schools to promote both social justice and democracy.
- We must promote and emulate successful programs.
- We need to organize and join advocates for teaching for democracy and social justice at the federal, state, and local levels to support and defend public schools, teachers, and teacher education programs that take a strong position in this area.

All of these require that we become policy activists to support the ends we need.

Earley's analysis shows us that the achievement of our goals is not helped by current policy. The competitive orientation of No Child Left Behind (NCLB) follows the theory of the Higher Education Act as amended in 1998. The presumption, as Earley cogently points out, is that children taught by a teacher graduating from a college with a high pass rate is somehow better than a candidate from a college with a lower pass rate, even if they had the same score on the same test. Further, the assumption that there is some link between the institution's pass rate and the performance of P–12 students is untested, yet it is the focal point for evaluation. How do we promote democratic practice when the private purpose of social mobility seems to be the exclusive guiding vision? NCLB seems to work directly against these ends in Earley's analysis. There is, however, some hope in the efforts to achieve fiscal equity that focus on the responsibility of schools to prepare students for the full responsibility of democratic participation, and the subsequent acceptance by courts of this argument. By giving us specific changes that would enhance both NCLB and the Higher Education Act, Earley reminds us not to fall into the trap of thinking that the issue is only inadequate funding. She presents the case that the problems are systemic and not solely about funding.

Three powerful suggestions can guide us in pursuing our work as policy advocates toward the changes she outlines:

- Be aware of which level of government has enacted a troublesome policy.
- Study the problem and decide what could be done to resolve it.
- Take the opportunity to forward positive information about what is happening in education to policy makers.

Earley explores each of these suggestions and gives sound advice for moving forward; moreover, she cites the need to include language about developing inquiry communities so students can learn the skills to inform their personal judgments. Her conclusions are consistent with our arguments for infusing critical thinking into the curriculum.

So what does it all mean programmatically? Four of our chapters focus specifically on what this work means in teacher education programs and schools—Rubin-Justice, Maulucci-Barton, Holzer, and Keiser's second chapter. Lucas and Keiser both provide examples of service learning for promoting social justice. Clearly teacher educators need to think about what it means to involve students in communities. Unguided efforts and the absence of reflection after experiences do not define good service learning. The struggles of individual teacher educators remind us how important it is that we reflect on our own work, and that we do so in dialogue with others.

The four curricular areas included here—special education, social studies, science, and aesthetic education—provide further cause for optimism, as each embraces the possibility of education for democracy and social justice across a broad spectrum. Certainly, we could have included other areas—literacy and mathematics, for example—and there is ample evidence of the attention to democracy and social justice in these areas, but we specifically chose important curricular areas not within the high-stakes testing core. Among the areas described, social studies is the place most look to for teaching about both democracy and social justice; and conversely, aesthetic education is among the areas most likely to be cut in pursuit of high-stakes testing. Both have very important places within the consideration of teacher education for democracy and social justice.

Rubin and Justice argue that the history of social studies education for social justice has been mixed. They cite elementary teachers who have had negative past experiences with, and uncertainty about, the meaning of the social studies, and they describe inconsistencies between field experiences and college-based courses. They present examples of secondary teachers who know their "content" but are unfamiliar with their students and the sociocultural aspects of learning. Even within what seems to be the most likely field, we need to focus on recentering social studies education on the goals of education for democracy and social justice. We are concerned about the lack of social studies content knowledge in future elementary education teachers, who still carry the brunt of responsibility for preparing our children for democratic society. Rubin and Justice use the terms evangelism and boot camp—two seemingly incongruous metaphors—to succeed in breaking through passive resistance to the importance of social studies education. Students who seek to use the social studies to teach critical inquiry and understand the connection of such inquiry to democracy and social justice face some of the same challenges many educators face: Will we be allowed to? Can we get in trouble? One of the themes of the National Network for Educational Renewal is the issue of preparing all teachers for stewardship for best practice. Clearly Rubin and Justice understand that they needed to talk about their concerns and face them head on.

Future teachers worry too about limited time—with social studies and science being compromised for the focus on literacy and numeracy, which are more likely to be tested. Of course teacher worries about the outcomes of testing dominate as well, but in facing these issues directly Rubin and Justice's students get a lesson in the realities and politics of education. We believe they will be better teachers for the consideration of these issues, even if they cannot immediately capitalize on their knowledge of the importance of high-level social studies education in elementary school.

The same can be said of secondary teachers as well, but the deficits are reversed; the content knowledge is there, but lacking is the ability to think holistically about children and to conceptualize how to take into account adolescents' needs. Justice and Rubin teach to extend the ability of students to theorize about classroom life—especially contrasting life in different classrooms across socioeconomic levels. They put into practice the notion of turning critical thinking onto their practice, and they use it to generate positions and theories about what they see and experience. The students leaving Rubin and Justice's classes have engaged in a consideration of critical social and educational issues, but the concern of these future teachers about whether they will be allowed to act upon their knowledge in their future classrooms remains a critical challenge. One way to begin to meet this challenge is through the simultaneous renewal of the education of educators and the schools.

In terms of science, we understand the social justice issues involved in denying students, especially urban and rural students, access to doing science in excellent laboratories. Maulucci and Barton take us beyond that issue, however, to show the ethical and moral imperative in providing excellent and equitable science education for all students. They reenvision science to be transformative with social justice as the frame. Understanding the moral and political aspects of science, as well as the place of science in the lives of teachers and learners, and encouraging critical understandings and doing so within learning communities represent a democratic and socially just science education. It is in keeping with our view that we must consider the potential of schools to teach within all disciplines for social justice and democracy.

Anyone who doubts the possibility of this approach to the teaching of science need only follow "Randi" through the eyes of Maulucci and Barton. Randi has learned how to practice what Maulucci and Barton call "the freedom to teach" by connecting literacy and science, learning to be flexible with her teaching schedule, and using her knowledge of the system. But is Randi exceptional? Is it her deep knowledge of the different subject that allows her to see "how different subjects intersected in support of curricular decisions that countered official school policy"? This sense of healthy subversiveness brings one right back to Postman and Weingartner's conception of teaching as a subversive activity. But 36 years after Postman and Weingartner, we are reminded that in many settings a teacher must be willing to take risks in order to act on a belief about the moral obligations that good teaching requires.[1] We see in Randi's class exactly what we would hope to see in students engaged in "doing" science: students discovering their own agency toward the ability to produce scientific knowledge. We would expect that these students would do well in their academic performance as well.

Two City University of New York (CUNY) faculty members, William Sweeney and Pamela Mills, both professors of chemistry at Hunter College, have demonstrated that students who fail the standardized Regents Examination can, in an environment characterized by questioning and the promotion of democratic and socially just practices, turn around their academic performance in a relatively short period of time. We must continue to demonstrate that education for democracy and social justice is consistent with high academic achievement for students.

We were careful not to leave out the arts. The Lincoln Center Institute (LCI), now working collaboratively with similar arts organizations around the country, has taken the lead in recognizing that teacher education is critical if we are to prepare literate students who know the place of aesthetics within education for democracy and social justice. The LCI focus is well positioned for such an endeavor. As Holzer points out, it isn't art for art's sake, or art for the sake of learning some other subject, but rather for developing perception, cognition, affect, and imagination, done through transacting with works of art. The pedagogies employed by the LCI, for example, having teaching artists work with teachers, future teachers, and P–12 students to examine different works of art and to raise appropriate questions, create a perfect opportunity for exploring ideas in communities of inquiry central to democratic practice. Groups working with the LCI experience the same works of art, but the internalization is different in every case; in the LCI experience, participants learn interdependence and connection, they relate their own lives to the works of art, and they learn to share multiple perspectives and to build on each other's views. The work is done with a clear eye to what it means to live in a democratic and socially just society, and how important aesthetics and the protection of the freedom needed to enjoy the arts are in such a society.

Implementation

Four of our chapters, Lucas, Wilson-Davidson, Martin and Asher-Eidman, along with parts of Michelli's, explored what are largely broad implementation issues and advice. We have already examined Earley's insightful analysis of the politics at the federal level that impact schools through both No Child Left Behind and the Higher Education Act Amendments of 1998. If we truly believe in democratic action, then we need to take her advice and become active. Policy makers can be persuaded, and the more local they are the more likely it is that we can reach them. Our local congressional delegations, our state assemblies and senates, our trustees, our state policy makers, and our communities are all places where we need to work.

Lucas believes that teachers who are supervised by qualified, culturally sensitive adults can, through service learning, enhance their development as socially aware and culturally responsive teachers. She also concludes that such a focus with service learning is rare.

We struggled in one of our opening chapters with the question of whether we should admit students based on their current dispositions or seek to develop them. Lucas's work suggests that they can be cultivated because "[t]hrough service learning, prospective teachers can get to know flesh-and-blood teachers who experience inequity and can then be guided to reflect on and discuss those inequities." This certainly brings us back to Darling-Hammond and Greene's hope that we will understand the structural inequities and not see individuals who suffer inequities as somehow responsible for their own situations. Service learning is a very promising practice, supported by such organizations as the American Democracy Project. By focusing on a specific case, Lucas gives us good guidance to avoid the potential pitfalls and achieve the promise that is possible.

Both Michelli and Martin see critical thinking as central to education for democracy. By providing examples of both teacher behaviors to promote critical thinking and models for teacher education programs they give us bases for action. Like social justice and democracy, critical thinking can mean different things to different individuals. Teacher education programs need to make clear the meaning of critical thinking in the context of their particular setting, but the ideas of promoting questioning, suspending judgment, engaging in dialogue about important issues, and learning how to argue well are central if we are to use critical thinking for the purposes we suggest. We expect that critics will continue to argue against questioning basic values and beliefs as unpatriotic, or against "the American way," but we believe critical thinking is the very essence of democracy.

Asher's chapter, written with Eidman, explores the current scene of foundation support for teacher education and democratic practice. The examples used are funding to the Institute for Educational Inquiry (IEI) and one of the settings of the National Network for Educational Renewal to track how the support was used and to promote democracy and social justice through teacher education. When they were program officers at the Philip Morris Companies and the DeWitt Wallace–Reader's Digest Fund, they oversaw the grants they describe. The models that emerged from this series of grants for the needed professional development of educators in arts and science and the schools to focus on teacher education for democracy and social justice have made an enormous difference. The IEI programs, and the leadership programs that emerged at settings of the National Network for Educational Renewal, continue to have broad impact.

The lesson, however, is that neither Philip Morris (now the Altria Group) nor DeWitt Wallace set out to support teacher education for democracy. In fact the original application from the IEI and the description that DeWitt Wallace provides of the proposal are not explicit about the focus on democracy and social justice. And even though these two foundations have moved away from a focus on teacher education, we must continue to seek out and develop support in the foundation communities. Perhaps we need to be more political. If we believe that our programs support both education for democracy and social justice and high academic achievement, why not lead with academic achievement? We do not suggest shying away from the importance of democracy and social justice, but rather moving forward in ways that take into account the context in which we work.

Finally, Wilson and Davidson share the evolution and impact of a statewide network of colleges and public schools in Colorado. The strategy we have come back to time and again is the building of networks—local networks of schools and colleges and national networks of partnerships with a clear and unambiguous vision of the public purposes of education that includes democracy and social justice. The Colorado Partnership for Educational Renewal (CoPER) has many of the hallmarks of successful partnerships. There is equity among the partners, now including sixteen school districts, eight senior colleges and universities, and the state's community college system. That equity extends to sharing costs and sharing management of the network, with superintendents, deans of education and arts and science, and others serving on the board. CoPER, because of its broad inclusiveness and clear position on education for democracy, has been able to influence policy. Wilson and Davidson report that schools have come forth in support of colleges and the colleges in support of schools when onerous policy or undue scrutiny has surfaced.

CoPER has broad credibility in Colorado because of its inclusive nature, so that when Colorado created its first Professional Standards Board the CoPER executive director and a CoPER dean co-chaired the board. When Colorado entered a conservative period, CoPER fought to include democracy and democratic practice as part of the expectations for teacher education program and supported institutions fighting to overcome prohibitions on the use of the concept of "diversity," which became explicit in actions of state government.

Interestingly, the authors believe that part of their success was never becoming a "vocal extreme advocacy group" which would put at risk their bridging capability. Instead, citing Chrislip, they focus on collaboration and engagement, dialogue instead of debate, inclusion instead of exclusion, shared power instead of domination and control, and mutual learning instead of rigid adherence to mutually exclusive positions. That is good advice. Of course we must know well the positions to which we adhere, which means not joining with others whose positions make a moral agenda promoting democracy and social justice impossible.

What have we found? We know that many of the readers of this volume seek, as we do, to be certain that children in our schools are prepared to be critical, caring members of our emerging democracy. We maintain that social justice is an intrinsic element of democracy and future teachers, and that future students need to reflect a commitment to social justice in their work. We believe none of this inhibits academic excellence and very high expectations for students. If we were to develop programs that promote socially just democratic practice but that do not provide equity in academic knowledge, we would be doomed to fail to achieve either democratic or academic goals. We must, as we have said, demonstrate the connections between democratic programs with social justice themes and high academic achievement.

These positions are the moral bedrock of our work based on respect for children, for public education, for democracy, and for social justice. All of those who contributed to this volume believe that we must go on in this direction no matter how difficult the times may seem. In fact, the future of our society depends more in the long run on the quality of the education we provide than on anything else.

Note

1. Neil Postman and Charles Weingartner, *Teaching as a Subversive* (New York: Bantam, 1968).

Afterword

RICHARD W. CLARK

There are many words for push, take, shove, carry, load, and no words for love, or happiness, or the sounds which birds make in the morning.[1]

Sometimes a little light summer reading can be a source from which deep truths spring. While reading the first book in a series about a lady detective in Botswana, the delightful and insightful *The No. 1 Ladies' Detective Agency*, I discovered the preceding description of Funagalo (also spelled Fanagalo), a language used primarily for giving orders underground to conscripted mine workers in South African.

After reading the preceding chapters, I have concluded that there is a considerable correspondence between Funagalo and the language being spoken by many who are enunciating educational policy as the United States begins the Twenty-First Century. Whether speaking of the specific requirements of No Child Left Behind or the general expectations for pushing and shoving students toward economic productivity, the preceding chapters recognize the limited, soulless nature of the education that children are receiving. Maybe the language of those shaping our current educational enterprise should be labeled as "polieduspeak" and recognized for the dangers inherent in it.

Polieduspeak produces schooling that focuses primarily on a narrow range of literacy and numeracy skills and factoids. Economic utility dominates as the end purpose for the schooling those who speak this language advocate. When I hear it spoken, I am reminded of a speech I heard from an owner of a number of small, Southern steel mills. He told a group assembled in Little Rock that his company supported education for the children of all their workers—but they were careful to make sure the children did not get too much education for fear they might become dissatisfied with the working conditions and opportunities provided to those who worked in his mills.

In contrast to the steel mill owner's remarks, the authors in this book have offered an array of thoughts about preparing teachers so that schools will support the development of children ready for full participation in a socially just, joyous, democratic society.

Using the four historic purposes of education as organizers, in this afterword I reflect on the themes set forth by the authors in this book, contrasting their views with the present dominant approach to schooling. I close with a discussion of three future considerations regarding what needs to be emphasized as we educate teachers for their role in preparing students to participate in a democratic society.

Reflection on Themes in the Book

What if teacher education (preservice, induction, and continuing professional growth) proceeded as polieduspeakers suggest it should? Would teachers simply be educated so they were unhappy in their workplace as the steel mill owner was afraid the youth in his communities would be? Would teachers expect more or less from their students?

Careful reading of the preceding chapters provides unambiguous answers to such questions. Teachers who understand the centrality of their work to the establishment and maintenance of a fair and just society take justifiable pride in their profession. Teachers who think critically about their work and who help their students develop as critical thinkers have the capacity to work with colleagues to renew schools. They are productive participants in school-university partnerships such as the Colorado Partnership for Educational Renewal and others described in the text. Teachers with an understanding of the joys of learning science, the insights and pleasures provided by engaging with the arts, and the excitement of pursuing ideas in well-taught social studies classes demand and get more from their students than any whose role has been reduced to satisfying the protocols of scripted lessons intended to raise student performance on high-stakes tests.

In the opening chapter, Michelli identifies four purposes for public education that he describes as historically enduring:

1. preparing students to be critical, active, involved participants in our democracy
2. providing students with access to knowledge and critical thinking within the disciplines

3. reparing students to lead rich and rewarding personal lives, and to be responsible and responsive community members

4. preparing students to assume the highest possible place in the economy.

Those who use polieduspeak have their own version of the purposes of public education which I take to be:

1. developing in students the ability to read, write, and perform basic arithmetic functions to the extent such abilities can be easily and quickly measured by high-stakes tests

2. preparing students to assume a role as a cog in the nation's economic system.

On the surface these two purposes seem to be similar to purposes two and four identified by Michelli. In reality, they are much narrower. The scope of knowledge and what the students are expected to be able to do with what they learn have been reduced by current policy makers. Furthermore, educating teachers to work in a system that has the broader vision requires a much different approach from that required to train people to accomplish the narrower aims.

Consider with me some of the implications for education and the preparation of teachers that grow out of thinking about each of the four historic purposes.

Preparing Students to be Critical, Active, Involved Participants in Our Democracy

On a recent long flight I engaged in a conversation with the man seated next to me. For our purposes here, I will call him Chester. He was a school board member who was frustrated because the students in his community were not performing as well as he thought they should be on the state-mandated reading and arithmetic tests. Chester blamed the community saying that the people did not care whether children learned or not.

I said it was unfortunate that the test scores were low but that I believe schools should be doing more than just getting students to pass these tests.

"Like what?" he asked.

I replied that perhaps the lack of concern about schooling in the community and some of the other failings he suggested were present in his community reflected the lack of success of schools in developing the capacity of students to participate actively and knowledgeably in the affairs of their community, in other words, that they were not prepared by their schools to function as effective members of a democratic society.

Chester said that sounded like something they have in their school district mission statement—something about that "democracy stuff." However, he observed, "it always seems sort of vague, sort of 'apple pieish.'" "What," he asked, "could they do that would make any difference?"

Many of my answers to him would sound familiar to those of you who have read thus far in this book. First, I suggested the schools should help students understand what a democratic society is. They should know that it is much more than one in which the majority vote determines what actions are taken. They should have an understanding of a democratic society that is populated by people who value equally individual freedom and the welfare of the entire community. I suggested that there are a number of very specific skills one needs the ability to engage in critical thinking, to advocate for a position, and to discern what is fair and just from that which may favor a select few at the expense of others.

As the conversation continued throughout the five and a half hours of the flight, Chester began to nod and to recognize the significance of such aims for schooling—would that we could get all policy makers on such a flight and have the opportunity to engage them in consideration of such questions.

In chapter 2, Michelli offers several answers regarding what would be meant by teaching democracy that I wish I had had handy when talking to my traveling companion. Michelli summarizes his comments as follows:

> Our contention is that all of these elements come together in defining what teaching for democracy can be—teaching for the civic responsibility of students, teaching for the civil responsibility of students, teaching for the understanding of what it means to be free and to engage in the "apprenticeship of liberty," becoming aesthetically literate, and learning to make excellent judgments and to argue well for one's beliefs. But focusing on democracy in this way…is incomplete unless we consider what it means to be civically engaged and how we can promote such engagement.

Michelli continues by suggesting that for education for a democracy to become central, public education "must embrace this as a purpose in practice, and not only in rhetoric…. and simultaneously, we must examine our teacher education programs to be certain that teachers are indeed prepared to teach for these purposes."

The latter point would certainly ring true for Chester. He believed that the teachers in his system were not prepared to fulfill the broader mission I was suggesting they should take on. Moreover, he doubted that they were adequately prepared to teach the content of the various disciplines.

Providing Students with Access to Knowledge and Critical Thinking Within the Disciplines.

Most of those who practice polieduspeak advocate learning the content of the disciplines. In practice they have narrowed the scope of those disciplines in the public schools to a set of understandings regarding literacy and numeracy at the same time they have complained of inferior performance of American students in comparison with those of other parts of the world. I share their desire for the students to become informed about the essential knowledge, skills, and dispositions that can be derived from the academic disciplines—so do the others writing in this book. However, there are some differences in our views regarding what knowledge is, the breadth of knowledge that should be acquired, the way in which students derive meaning (acquire knowledge), and what one does with acquired information. The authors here recognize that *knowing* is different from accumulating a mass of decontextualized information. Maulucci and Calabrese-Barton address this as they describe how science students make meaning. They emphasize that students need to have an active role in the process of producing scientific knowledge, and not simply be passive recipients of the previous work of scientists. In their chapter they share the view of learning in this discipline that Goodlad and others refer to as they observe that

> We would do well to remember that if scientists were certain about their understanding of the world around them, there would be no scientific advancement, and hence no science. Science is based on *uncertainty*, not certainty. Most of what scientists have ever thought to be true has, in time, proven not to be. It makes much more sense for youngsters to learn how to ask questions and search for more answers than it does to "teach" them what science "knows."[2]

Chester started our conversation convinced that if he could just get the kids to master some basic math skills he would have accomplished all that was needed—but as we talked he acknowledged that his concern was that they also did not know how to apply those skills. He also acknowledged that he was not sure whether, as they moved into more complex mathematics, having developed speed in adding, subtracting, multiplying, and dividing would be all they would need to know. In other words, he acknowledged that he had not thought deeply about what it meant to "know" something. It was also apparent to me that he had not thought about the importance of developing critical thinking skills, of being able to analyze information as a part of truly knowing something.

For years John Goodlad has spoken of the purpose of "access to knowledge" as being that of enabling students to "enter the human conversation." By that, he means that the well-educated person is sufficiently knowledgeable in the various fields of study; that he or she can engage with ideas from these fields in an intelligent and productive manner. As Goodlad, Mantle-Bromley, and Goodlad put it at the close of their chapter on "Democracy, Education and the Human Conversation,"

> Schools alone cannot create or guarantee a wise and thoughtful public that is conscious of being part of the human conversation and thus prepared to create, sustain, and effectively participate in a democracy. Many elements must come together to do such work. But schools can provide the soil of democracy with a large portion of the nutrients it needs. Schools are where, with the right care and nurturing, the habits of democracy take root and begin to grow, where the young become aware of the human conversation in all of its glorious diversity and begin to participate in it.[3]

Schools can prepare students with the knowledge that enables them to enter the "human conversation" only if their teachers are educated well enough to enter the conversation themselves and are educated to understand that preparing students in this manner is one of the key responsibilities of schools. The authors in this text would extend the argument to include the importance of being able to think critically about the disciplines as they enter this conversation.

Preparing Students to Lead Rich and Rewarding Personal Lives, and to be Responsible and Responsive Community Members

In her chapter, Earley makes it clear that the justification for federal involvement in public education derives from the constitutional mandate that government is responsible for providing for the general welfare of its citizens. She cites the "general welfare clause" (Article I, Section 8) as the source of federal authority to make an increasingly broader range of interventions into the nation's schools. As several of the authors note, the extent to which state and federal governments are responsible for "the general welfare," as opposed to a narrow interpretation of education as the building of minimal skills has been disputed in our courts and legislative bodies. In Congress as it considered legislation such as the No Child Left Behind Act or the revision of the Higher Education Act, the question should have been whether the government is responsible for education that helps students lead rich and rewarding personal lives or for the general welfare of its citizens only to the extent they provide for minimal skills and knowledge.

The authors in this book leave little doubt that they believe the schools' responsibilities are broad. They say in various ways that schools are responsible for a broad range of individual development and for preparing students to create stronger communities.

Chester, at least at the outset of our conversation, was more inclined to agree with those who see schools as responsible for developing a limited set of academic skills and knowledge. On the flight, one of his sons joined us from time to time to demonstrate how fast he was getting in completing a series of timed arithmetic operations. Chester was so convinced that such operations were important that he had set a goal with students in his sons' school that when all could complete these addition and subtraction tasks in less than two minutes, he would take them all across the state to a major league baseball game. The question for him that the authors in this text (and I) raise is what will they do with these skills when they have mastered them. Will they know when they need to apply them? Will they be able to use them as a tool as they think about problems that face their community? As they acquire the equally important, to Chester, ability to spell all the words on the weekly spelling list, will they apply their spelling skill in writing that persuades, informs, and entertains with style and grace?

The answers to these questions depend very much on the extent teachers are educated to address them. If, for example, teachers believe that the weekly spelling list is an end unto itself as opposed to the sharpening of a skill that could be helpful in writing, the writing their students do is not likely to be of high quality.

The answers to the questions regarding the breadth of education schools should be responsible for lie also in the importance of developing knowledge of history, science, and the fine arts—all subjects that are deemphasized by the polieduspeakers but stressed by various authors in this book.

Bartlett and von Zastrow speak directly to this narrowing of the curriculum as they report on the results of a survey of around 1,000 principals conducted by the Washington based Council for Basic Education. Among the findings they report are the following:

The most troubling evidence of curricular erosion occurred in schools with large minority populations, the very populations whose access to a full liberal arts curriculum has been historically most limited. Nearly half (47 percent) of principals in high-minority schools reported decreases in elementary school social studies.

More than four in 10 (42 percent) anticipated decreases in instructional time for the arts, and nearly three in 10 (29 percent) foresaw decreases in instructional time for foreign language.[4]

Conveying a message to which the the authors in this book would concur, Bartlett and von Zastrow go on to warn that "we have substituted one form of educational inequity for another, denying our most vulnerable students the kind of curriculum available routinely to the wealthy."[5]

Service learning is one way authors in this book broaden the concept of education. As Lucas points out, "service learning, which involves organizing the content and pedagogy of a course so that community service is integrated into academic content, can lay the foundation for a commitment to social justice among prospective teachers." Teachers who understand the potential of service learning and are able to integrate it into their own teaching are well positioned to develop students as responsive members of their communities. When service learning deliberately seeks to engage teachers and students in racially, ethnically, and socioeconomically diverse experiences, it is more likely that they will be responsive to their entire community and not just a segment of it with which they are familiar.

Preparing students to assume the highest possible place in the economy

In their narrow view of the purposes of education, the polieduspeakers have reduced the required contributions of education to the economic system to the development of someone with basic skills who can fit into a job slot as opposed to someone who can contribute to a healthy economy. Before proceeding, it is important that I make it clear that I do not reject the role of schooling in preparing people for employment. As Goodlad, Mantle-Bromley, and Goodlad observe, "there is nothing wrong with having a competent workforce or with students getting higher scores on standardized tests, even though the latter accomplishment correlates with little other than further test performance."[6] What is wrong, as the authors in this book make clear, is the failure to pay attention to other highly significant educational purposes.

Ironically, by narrowing the scope of schooling to literacy and numeracy skills that can be measured on high-stakes tests, polieduspeakers contribute to schooling that ignores many of the basic skills and dispositions that employers repeatedly say they want in workers. As schools ignore higher order thinking skills, they produce workers who are limited in their ability to solve problems. As schools concentrate on a narrow set of academic skills, they fail to develop their students' ability to collaborate, to be the team members that employers consistently say they want.

But the problem with the dominant policy approaches to education is more than a failure to provide for the kind of education that would really help people be successful in the workplace. It is also more than a slight overemphasis on one of several purposes for education. Neil Postman stated it well when he said it is the absolute focus of these policy makers on the God of Economic Utility as the "preeminent reason for schooling." As Postman described it, this focus makes a covenant of sorts with students saying:

> If you will pay attention in school, and do your homework, and score well on tests, and behave yourself, you will be rewarded with a well-paying job when you are done. Its driving idea is that the purpose of schooling is to prepare children for competent entry into the economic life of a community. It follows from this that any school activity not designed to further this end is seen as a frill or an ornament—which is to say, a waste of valuable time.[7]

Preparing students to fill the highest possible place in the economy, as one of the four purposes of schooling, is far different from this single-minded allegiance to the economic utility. Chester rejected such narrow mindedness as he spoke of the kinds of employees he needed in his business and the qualities he hoped the schools would help develop in his sons.

Future Considerations

As we educate teachers, we need to help them understand the importance of (1) the local context in which they will teach, (2) knowing their students well, and (3) ensuring school is a place for joy and for the student's voice to be heard.

Consideration Must Be Given to the Local Context

Chester comes from a small, rural community with concerns about unemployment produced by the declining logging industry and about the number of young people dropping out of school, or, if they complete high school, leaving for urban areas where they perceive life is better. He expressed concerns about the problems in the community that stem from a seeming inability to attract able leaders to positions in local government. At the same time, it is a beautiful area with a low crime rate and many other amenities that attract people to it as an alternative to the stress of city living.

The destination for our flight, like Chester's community, has high drop-out rates and issues related to community leadership. Also like his community it has an economic base built on the backs of many minimum-wage workers and a high percentage of students enrolled in private schools out of dissatisfaction with the local public system. In spite of such similarities, there are many differences. For instance, unlike Chester's home town, our destination is a large, racially and culturally diverse city. Each of the cultures has its own views regarding how important education is and how it should be shaped.

Even the polieduspeakers who take time to make a cursory examination of the two communities would instantly recognize that the educational needs of the two communities differ. Some of the many variables that help define a community are:

- racial and ethnic makeup of the people
- the culture of the community, and of the subcommunities within a given locale, including language and communication patterns
- the value the people of a community place on education—and what they mean by education
- the size of the community and its attendant impact on communications among people within the community
- the extent to which the dominant groups within the community value democracy, and how they define that which they value
- economic conditions within the community such as the kinds of jobs people perform, the health of the local economy, the distribution of wealth within the community
- geographic/climate conditions that affect lifestyles
- housing patterns
- governance, including the extent to which people are actively engaged, the quality of leadership, and the effectiveness of various mechanisms.

Teachers who do not understand these and other characteristics of the communities that shape their students inevitably fail to construct the kinds of learning experiences that youth most need. Curriculum that may make sense in Chester's Northwest woods, may seem odd and confusing to children of the Pacific beach city we were traveling to or to the young people of an East Coast city. Teachers need to understand the context for the students in order to help them grow to understand that context and the world beyond it.

Teachers can help students address what is fair and just in a society only if, as adults, they understand the society that is most immediately affecting the lives of their students. Likewise, those making education policy should not mandate a one-size-fits-all program that ignores the defining characteristics of the various communities. Yet, that is what the polieduspeakers do.

Educators Must Know Their Students

After I had been talking with Chester for four hours of the five-and-a-half-hour flight I must admit I had him pretty well stereotyped. He appeared to be fairly representative of those who view high-stakes testing as important, think schools should emphasize "basic" skills—in general someone with a narrow view of education. I had him labeled as one of the polieduspeakers, even if he did appear to be somewhat more open to alternative views than most of the people I think of as falling into that group.

It was at this point that he disclosed a little more about himself. With one of his two elementary-school-age sons sitting nearby, he looked me directly in the eye and said, "The reason I think knowledge is so important is that I was kept locked in a closet until I was 11 years old." He went on to explain that he had escaped and lived on the streets until he lied about his age and enlisted in the military. He was booted out of the service and rapidly heading for a dead-end life when on a bet with a friend he sought out enrollment in a local college. Although he had not graduated from high school, he talked his way into a semester scholarship at the college. Three years, another college, and several scholarships later he had a degree and admission to dental school. In addition to being a dentist he now runs his own business and volunteers to teach math at the school his boys attend.

With these revelations, I could no longer classify him in the somewhat simplistic way I had. It was clear that his experiences with what was fair and just in our society far exceeded mine. Now, I had to take into account that his interest in schooling was passionate, deeply rooted, not something arrived at casually or through the unexamined lens of political followership. I needed to rethink what I was going to say as I continued my conversation with him regarding the need for schools to emphasize the preparation of students for their role in a democratic society. I began to consider how I could get him to reflect about his own personal experiences as a means of understanding what the schools need to accomplish.

I tell this story because for me it mirrors closely the situation teachers often face. Just as I needed to better understand Chester, teachers need to know their students and to frame instruction properly in light of what they know about their students. Teacher educators must help their students understand this truth and help teachers develop the skills, understandings, and dispositions required to help students build on what they already know. If the students are to learn to be fair and just, to contribute to a fair and just democratic society, they will need to be helped to do so by teachers who understand what students already know and believe about human relationships.

The authors in this book share some ideas on how teachers can be helped to work with students regarding matters such as social justice, critical thinking, and development of democratic character. In addition educators should be helped to learn of the advantages of small learning communities and how to use such communities to get to know each student well enough to teach him or her well.

There Must Be a Place for Joy and for the Student's Voice

There is a message in the excerpt from *The No. 1 Ladies' Detective Agency* with which I began these remarks that is present in several of the chapters but which I believe deserves more emphasis. The authors of this volume rightly focus on the significance of preparing teachers so students will be educated as participants in a social and political democracy. Beyond that several of the chapters address the additional educational goals of helping students create a full, joyous life. If attention to requirements for participating in a democracy are lacking in the schools produced by polieduspeak, the notion that children should find joy and beauty in the educational experience is totally absent. There is no room to listen to "the sounds which the birds make in the morning." School districts are eliminating experiences in the fine arts and other areas that do not lead directly, in their views, to the correct responses on high-stakes tests. Too seldom do teachers have the opportunities to engage in the kinds of creative and imaginative teaching of science Calabrese-Barton and Maulucci describe, or the exploration and the arts that Holzer provides in her discussion of aesthetic education.

A slight young girl served as my guide during a visit I made to a large urban high school. As she took me through the halls, in and out of classrooms, and up and down the four stories of stairs, she had little to say. What she said tended to be in one- or two-word phrases. She knew her way around the school, but there was little evidence that the places we were seeing had much interest to her. Completely unsuccessful in drawing her into a conversation, I wondered why she had been chosen by the principal to serve as a host. The tour complete, she returned me to the office, then, looking mainly at the floor as she had throughout much of the visit, excused herself to get to her next class. At this point the principal took over as tour guide and escorted me to a third-floor classroom we had not stopped in earlier. There I found my guide and learned a lesson. The class was orchestra. The girl was playing a violin. The music was unbelievably clear and sweet. The instrument was her voice—through it she could express all the feeling, the joys, and the sorrows that were missing when she was speaking to me earlier. Of twenty-one nonmagnet high schools of its kind in the city, this was the only one where there was an orchestra. In all the other schools, there would have been no place for this splendid voice to be heard. Unfortunately, throughout the country there are too many schools that deny children the opportunity to express themselves.

David Keiser begins his chapter in this book with reference to Maxine Greene's observations about "present demands and prescriptions." At least since her comments in 1988, the dominant approach to schooling by those who control state and federal policies has been to treat learners as widgets—to assume that all children are the same and that it is desirable to have as an end the producing of a standard product. As Keiser notes, states have been using "static measures to test dynamic processes of learning." This approach is the only one that has guided schooling for an entire generation of students—most students now in grades P–12 know no other approach. Invariably, this approach erases the individual voices and talents of the students and demeans the teachers who seek to help students develop these talents. We cannot afford to continue the present policies at the cost of another generation being treated as widgets in the marketplace.

As we look to the future of schooling in the United States, we must find a way for all children to have their voices heard. We must recognize the diversity of talents and interests that prevail in our young. We must create schools that value all children and prepare them to live the varied and interesting lives that a fair and just society permits. We will do these things, only if we prepare teachers, and provide the continuing education for teachers that will allow them to recognize the critical importance of such goals in our schools. We will create such schools only if the teachers have the knowledge, skills, and dispositions required of all who live in a fair and just, social and political democracy.

Notes

1. Alexander McCall Smith, *The No. 1 Ladies' Detective Agency* (New York: Anchor Books, 2002), 23.
2. John I. Goodlad, Corinne Mantle-Bromley, and Stephen John Goodlad, *Education for Everyone: Agenda for Education in a Democracy* (San Francisco: Jossey-Bass, 2004), 58.
3. Goodlad et al., 100.
4. Raymond "Buzz" Bartlett and Claus von Zastrow, "Academic Atrophy: The Condition of Liberal Arts in America's Public Schools," *Education Week* (April 7, 2004): 48.
5. Ibid.,
6. Goodlad et al., 88.
7. Neil Postman, *The End of Education: Redefining the Value of School* (New York: Vintage Books, 1995), 27–28.

Contributors

Carla Asher is University Director of Teacher Education Initiatives at The City University of New York. Previously she was Director for Teaching Quality at the National Commission on Teaching and America's Future, a program officer at the DeWitt Wallace–Reader's Digest Fund, a faculty member at Lehman College of the City University of New York, and a New York City high school teacher.

Angela Calabrese Barton is an Associate Professor of Science Education at Teachers College Columbia University in NYC. Her teaching and research experiences have been in urban centers, and have focused keenly on the needs of high poverty urban youth and their teachers. Her research addresses issues of social justice, feminism, and science education, and she is author of Teaching Science for Social Justice, and Feminist Science Education and co-author (with W. Michael Roth) of Re/thinking Scientific Literacy.

Richard W. Clark is a senior associate at the Institute for Educational Inquiry in Seattle. He has been a teacher, principal, assistant and deputy superintendent, and university lecturer and instructor. He has worked with the National Network for Educational Renewal since its creation and served as its first Executive Director. He is the author of *Effective Professional Development Schools*, and a co-author of *Kids and School Reform*. In addition he has authored secondary school textbooks for speech and English classes and written numerous chapters and articles on a wide-range of educational topics.

Roscoe Davidson is currently the Deputy Commissioner for the Colorado Department of Education. His previous experience includes that of superintendent for the Englewood Public Schools, as well as associate superintendent, principal, and teacher in the Denver Public Schools. He served as the initial chair of the Colorado Partnership for Educational Renewal and remained in that role for subsequent terms at the request of the board. Davidson has taught in leadership programs at the University of Denver and the University of Colorado. He has written and spoken on a topics ranging from leadership, schools as living democracies, the importance of school renewal to school improvement.

Penelope M. Earley is Director of the Center for Education Policy and a professor in the Graduate School of Education at George Mason University. Before joining the GMU faculty, Earley was a vice president with the American Association of Colleges for Teacher Education. At AACTE she directed federal and state governmental relations, issue analysis, and policy studies. Dr. Earley has served as a member of a number of educational advisory boards including the NCES Consultative Committee on Title II Accountability; AASCU Commission on Teacher Preparation, Accountability, and Evaluation; Teacher Mentor Project; and Coalition for Women's Appointments in Government. She has authored book chapters for the *Politics of Education Yearbook, Handbook of Research on Teacher Education* and *Developing Language Teachers for a Changing World* as well as various issue briefs and journal articles. In 2001 she received the Martha J. Fields Award for Excellence in Education from the National Association of State Directors of Special Education.

Diane Eidman is Director, Contributions Programs at Altria Group, Inc. in New York City. Ms. Eidman directs the overall strategic direction of the company's worldwide philanthropy, with a focus on domestic violence, hunger relief, and arts and culture. Ms. Eidman was responsible for initiating, developing, and supervising the company's grantmaking strategies and programs in the area of domestic violence prevention and awareness, and has been honored by numerous organizations for her work on this critical issue. Prior to joining Altria, Ms. Eidman was a publications associate in educational marketing, merchandising, and development with the Metropolitan Museum of Art.

Madeleine F. Holzer is the Program Development Director at Lincoln Center Institute for the Arts in Education where her major responsibility is the Teacher Education Collaborative. She is the primary author of *Aesthetic*

Education, Practice and Traditions: Education Traditions, one in a series of White Papers published by the Institute. Prior to working at LCI, she was the Director of Arts in Education at the New York State Council on the Arts and formerly directed programs at New York University and Cornell University. Her poetry and essays have appeared in publications such as the literary journals *Pearl* and *Footwork: The Paterson Literary Review,* as well as *Education Week.*

Benjamin Justice is an Assistant Professor of Education and (by courtesy) History at Rutgers University. Along with Beth Rubin, he is Co-Director of the Social Studies Education Program at the Graduate School of Education. Dr. Justice teaches courses in elementary and secondary social studies, history of education, and school reform. His publications include the book, *The War That Wasn't: Religious Conflict and Compromise in the Common Schools of New York State, 1865–1900* (Albany: SUNY Press, 2004) and articles in *Social Education, New York History,* and *History of Education Quarterly.* In addition, he has written book chapters on a variety of topics within the fields of civic education, social studies education, and history.

David Lee Keiser is a teacher educator in the College of Education and Human Services at Montclair State University. His teaching and research activities include school-university partnerships, culturally responsive teaching, and mindfulness in teacher education. An active participant in the National Network for Educational Renewal, he is now Coordinator for the Agenda for Education in a Democracy at Montclair State University. Recent publications have included contributions in *Critical Voices in School Reform: Students Living through Change,* and *Invisible Children in the Society and Its Schools.*

Tamara Lucas, professor at Montclair State University, has devoted her career to research, teaching, and work with schools addressing issues of equity and social justice in the education of culturally and linguistically diverse students. Most of her work has focused on the education of English language learners and on the preparation of culturally responsive teachers. Her publications include the book *Educating Culturally Responsive Teachers: A Coherent Approach,* with Ana María Villegas (2002), and "Promoting the Success of Latino Language Minority Students: An Exploratory Study of Six High Schools," co-authored with R. Hence and R. Donator (1990, *Harvard Educational Review*).

David S. Martin, Ph.D., is Professor/Dean Emeritus of Education at Gallardo University in Washington, D.C. He has elsewhere been a teacher, school principal, curriculum developer, and director of curriculum and instruction. He is a graduate of Yale, Harvard, and Boston College. His published works include research in social studies education, cognitive education, deaf education, and teacher education. He resides in Massachusetts and is currently Adjunct Professor at the University of Massachusetts at Boston, Lesley University, and Suffolk University, and is an educational consultant for schools and universities.

Maria S. Rivera Maulucci is a doctoral student in science education at Teachers College, Columbia University and science staff developer for Region One in the Bronx. Her research interests are exploring social justice in science education through qualitative methods.

Nicholas M. Michelli is University Dean for Teacher Education for the City University of New York and Professor in the University's Ph.D. program in urban education. He is responsible for overseeing teacher education at the nation's largest public urban university in programs located at the eleven senior colleges and six community colleges of the University. He is also liaison for teacher education between the University, the New York City Public Schools, and the cultural institutions of New York City. Prior to this appointment, he served as Dean of the College of Education and Human Services at Montclair State University for twenty years, where he is professor and dean emeritus. His primary academic interests include urban education, teacher education, school-university partnerships, public policy for teacher education, education for democracy and social justice, and teaching for critical thinking. He is the co-author of *Centers of Pedagogy: New Structures for Educational Renewal*, published in 1999 by Jossey-Bass. He is the author of more than thirty articles and book chapters dealing with his academic interests. Michelli is a member of the New York State Professional Standards and Practices Board for Teaching, the Regents policy board on teaching. For eight years he chaired the American Association of Colleges for Teacher Education's (AACTE) Committee on Governmental Relations. He served for five years as first Chair the Governing Council of the National Network for Educational Renewal.

Beth C. Rubin is an assistant professor of education at Rutgers, The State University of New Jersey. She uses a sociocultural lens and an interpretive research methodology to examine issues relating to educational equity in U.S. high schools. Her current research explores detracking in the classrooms of racially and socioeconomically diverse schools, and students' constructions of civic identity across a variety of settings. Her recently published work includes "Unpacking Detracking: When Progressive Pedagogy Meets Students' Social Worlds" in the *American Educational Research Journal,* and *Critical Voices in School Reform: Students Living Through Change* (with E. Silva), RoutledgeFalmer.

Carol A. Wilson has worked in education for more than 30 years, as teacher, high school principal, assistant superintendent, university instructor, and consultant. For the past 16 years, she has served as executive director of the Colorado Partnership for Educational renewal, a collaborative including 16 school districts with approximately 600 schools, eight universities and colleges, and the Colorado Community Colleges system. One of 23 settings in the National Network for Educational Renewal, CoPER's work promotes continuous and simultaneous renewal of schools and programs that prepare educators so that *all* students will be educated well. It is grounded in understandings of what it means to teach and learn in our democracy. Wilson currently serves as chair of NNER's governing council.

Index